DEI
deconstructed

DEI
deconstructed

YOUR NO-NONSENSE GUIDE TO DOING
THE WORK AND DOING IT RIGHT

LILY ZHENG

Berrett–Koehler Publishers, Inc.

Berrett-Koehler Publishers, Inc.
1333 Broadway, Suite P100
Oakland, CA 94612-1921
Tel: (510) 817-2277
Fax: (510) 817-2278
bkconnection.com

ORDERING INFORMATION

QUANTITY SALES. Special discounts are available on quantity purchases by corporations, associations, and others. For details, please go to bkconnection.com to see our bulk discounts or contact bookorders@bkpub.com for more information.
INDIVIDUAL SALES. Berrett-Koehler publications are available through most bookstores. They can also be ordered directly from Berrett-Koehler: Tel: (800) 929-2929; Fax: (802) 864-7626; bkconnection.com.
ORDERS FOR COLLEGE TEXTBOOK / COURSE ADOPTION USE. Please contact Berrett-Koehler: Tel: (800) 929-2929; Fax: (802) 864-7626.

Distributed to the US trade and internationally by Penguin Random House Publisher Services.
Berrett-Koehler and the BK logo are registered trademarks of Berrett-Koehler Publishers, Inc.

Printed in Canada

Berrett-Koehler books are printed on long-lasting acid-free paper. When it is available, we choose paper that has been manufactured by environmentally responsible processes. These may include using trees grown in sustainable forests, incorporating recycled paper, minimizing chlorine in bleaching, or recycling the energy produced at the paper mill.

Library of Congress Cataloging-in-Publication Data

Names: Zheng, Lily, author.
Title: DEI deconstructed : your no-nonsense guide to doing the work and doing it right / Lily Zheng.
Description: First paperback edition. | Oakland, CA : Berrett-Koehler Publishers, [2024] | Includes bibliographical references and index.
Identifiers: LCCN 2024933969 (print) | LCCN 2022019790 (ebook) | ISBN 9798890570505 (paperback) | ISBN 9781523002771 (hardcover ; alk. paper) | ISBN 9781523002788 (pdf) | ISBN 9781523002795 (epub) | ISBN 9781523002801 (audio)
Subjects: LCSH: Diversity in the workplace. | Racism in the workplace. | Discrimination in employment. | Multiculturalism. | Equality.
Classification: LCC HF5549.5.M5 Z459 2023 (print) | LCC HF5549.5.M5 (ebook) | DDC 658.3008—dc23/eng/20220422
LC record available at https://lccn.loc.gov/2024933969
LC ebook record available at https://lccn.loc.gov/2022019790

First Paperback Edition

32 31 30 29 28 27 26 25 24 | 10 9 8 7 6 5 4 3 2 1

Book production: David Peattie / BookMatters
Cover design: Frances Baca

*To everyone striving toward a better,
more inclusive, more equitable world.*

*You are powerful. You are enough.
You are your ancestors' dreams made real.*

CONTENTS

Conclusion   271

PREFACE

"$15,000 for a talk, huh?"

The corporate vice president I was speaking to nodded. "If that works for you."

I studied his slightly pixelated face in the Zoom window and then spoke again. "You know, as much as I believe in the talks I give, there's only so much I can do in sixty minutes…even if the audience for this conference is as big as you say."

"Are you saying you're not interested in the opportunity?"

"Not exactly—just that $15,000 of work gets you quite a bit if we put it toward other things. We could run a survey, for starters, and several interviews. We could analyze that data to get at least a basic sense of the state of DEI in your company and the things you and your leadership team could address to make progress. I can tell you that doing this would make far more impact than a single talk could. It'd create more lasting value, too."

His demeanor shifted. "Well, ah—I'm not sure we have the budget for…it's not exactly in the, ah, scope of what I was planning to talk to you about today. I'm sure, I'm sure I could connect you to a colleague of mine that might be interested in talking about other ways to partner afterward. For now, let's focus on this talk. Does the offer work for you?"

I hesitated for a moment, but only a moment. "Sure. $15,000 for the sixty-minute talk. How could I say no?"

A month later, I delivered the talk over Zoom, and a month after that, I received my check. I never heard from the VP or his colleague again. I didn't follow up.

In the summer of 2020, as protests erupted across the United States and around the world following George Floyd's murder, my website contact form was flooded by inquiries. The subject lines were all uncannily similar. "Help us process our emotions in a workshop." "Help us discuss this tough issue in a listening session." "Help us say the right thing on social media." "Help us do something about diversity in our own organization with an unconscious bias training."

The magnitude of the demand was on a scale larger than anything I had seen in my career as a diversity, equity, and inclusion (DEI) consultant, but at the same time, something was off. Maybe it was the panicked surprise evident in many of the messages. Maybe it was the blatant desire to solve enormous problems in a single session. Maybe it was the laughably meager budgets that decision-makers were allocating to address their employees' racial justice concerns (one lead, who for their own sake I won't name, offered $200).

I sent most contacts the same question in response. "Before I meet with you, what exactly are you hoping happens after I provide these services?"

While I waited for responses, the news cycle moved swiftly. One day, the hashtag #BlackoutTuesday went viral on social media. Millions of users, large companies among them, began to post black squares on social media "in solidarity" with the Black Lives Matter movement— only to take them down that same afternoon as frustration and disapproval mounted from Black community members and organizers who opposed the tactic. Companies posted #BlackLivesMatter hashtags on their social media accounts and made showy pledges[1] to donate vast sums of money toward supplier diversity, diversifying their work-force, and NGOs like the American Civil Liberties Union. But few provided means to ensure any accountable follow-through of these commitments.

And, of course, companies frantically searched far and wide for DEI consultants and facilitators to deliver unconscious bias training to their workforce,[2] at times reaching back out to the consultants and facilita-tors they had laid off at the beginning of the COVID-19 pandemic.[3] It was like a tsunami—the tide went out from under our feet, only to surge back with such ferocity that we were left drowning in the demand for DEI work.

Each time I retell this story, I get the same eager questions. Was there a happy ending? Did companies finally recognize the value of diversity, equity, and inclusion work and enable the many experts, practitioners, educators, and consultants to work their magic? Did a new cohort of companies triumphantly emerge from 2020, having turned over a new leaf, as a new vanguard of the diverse, equitable, and inclusion organi-zations of the future?

Well, no. Unfortunately, none of that happened. What happened is that an industry whose sole job it was to make a difference, that had fought for years for a seat at the table, was catapulted into the spotlight more suddenly than anyone could have predicted. After a year of our efforts, what we have to show for it is…inconclusive, at best. Systemic inequity is still alive and well. Organizations worldwide still struggle with representation on multiple dimensions, from race and gender to age, class, sexuality, religion, and more. As societies, we still face the same enormous challenges we faced in 2019 and have faced for decades and centuries.

Diversity, equity, and inclusion, however, are undeniably in vogue. More companies than ever have turned to the industry, asking for professional help. More new and aspiring practitioners have jumped into the industry seeking experience, knowledge, or even just a piece of the very lucrative pie. Yet, despite this scramble, I've noticed an increasing undercurrent of concern coming from the people whose job it is to lead or even just exist in the workplaces DEI practitioners sell to and opine on.

"How can I be sure that any of this stuff will work?" "How can I make sure my company does this right?" "What am I supposed to know if I want to engage with this?" and "What is my role in this work?"

My clients ask me these questions frequently. Hell, *I* ask myself these questions frequently and then find myself hours later digging through research papers and corporate reports looking for promising leads, putting what looks most promising into practice, and refining it all into cohesive answers. With any luck, you're reading this book because you want to hear what those are and take something concrete and impactful to your organizations to start making a difference.

I'll say this up front: this book is not a deep dive into critical race theory, organizational sociology, or change management, though all these and more will inform the content you'll be reading. This is on purpose—I've aimed to provide a well-rounded, interdisciplinary, and comprehensive foundation that can enable any thoughtful newcomer to do effective DEI work. In my experience, you don't need to be a subject matter expert to be an effective change-maker. You just need to have enough of a knowledge base to begin gaining experience and refining your impact.

To that end, this book is distinctly focused on the actionable above all else. It is not a compilation of discrimination or trauma porn;[4] I am assuming that if you do not already have some measure of empathy, you wouldn't be reading this book. It is not a collection of inspirational stories of real-life success; learning about the minority of people who succeed *despite* systems not built for them is not enough to build better systems yourself, and inspiration without efficacy results in little. This book will not dedicate much time to convince you that inequity is real; that preparatory work is important but done better elsewhere. This book is also not about me or my life, though undoubtedly, my own identities and experiences have informed my work, and undoubtedly you'll learn something about me through reading this.

So what *is* this book, then? It is my attempt to take apart DEI—the industry and the work alike—and formulate this work so that anyone can do it and do it effectively. I'll share the heaviest, thorniest, and most complex challenges that, left unsolved, cause the best intentions to fizzle and fail. I've been asked many times before writing this book to write a guide and a handbook for DEI professionals. Something with enough "hard" practice to be pragmatic without being dogmatic and with enough "soft" framing to be nuanced. This is that book, and I wrote it to democratize access to the tools of change for everyone. It doesn't matter if you're an executive who's never thought about DEI before opening this book. It doesn't matter if you're an ERG (employee resource group) lead who would never think about going into the industry full-time. If you're involved or interested in making genuine, measurable change, turning your good intentions into real impact, you're at the exact place many practitioners begin. My goal is straightforward: to ensure that the influence you can and will make through your diversity, equity, and inclusion work is far greater after reading this book than it was before.

Introduction

Who I Am

I'm a diversity, equity, and inclusion practitioner. That much is obvious, I hope. But the job title itself doesn't tell you much about what I think is the most important aspect of this work: how it gets done and what it achieves. So once more, from the top: I'm a DEI practitioner, and I help companies get it right. My approach is laser-focused on outcomes and sees tactics and interventions as items in an ever-growing toolbox leveraged to turn homogenous, exclusive, and inequitable organizations into the opposite.

Over the last five years, I've worked with dozens of organizations, from small nonprofits to multinational Fortune 500 corporations, government agencies, higher education, small B2Cs, large B2Bs, and everything in between, on DEI challenges that run the gamut from "hiring more Black and brown people" to "reworking our company culture from the ground up." I'm a DEI practitioner, but I'm also a vocal critic of my industry and the outdated, ineffective, and sometimes even harmful practices that keep the inequitable status quo frozen in place. I have strong opinions about this work, the people doing it, and the world we are all creating through our actions—or inactions—each and every day.

As a queer, Chinese American, neurodivergent, nonbinary trans person, I have personal reasons to be involved: I want organizations to build environments where people with many marginalized identities and from disadvantaged backgrounds, including those I share, can thrive. Pretty words and good intentions can't do that on their own. As a practitioner who works closely with all manner of workers and other stakeholders, I am constantly aware of the fact that I often have more in common with the people I interview and survey than I do with the people who hire me, and yet I am seen by members of marginalized communities as a tool wielded by the same status quo that disadvantages them. These communities rarely have kind words for the status quo. They scoff at their HR leaders, who put far too much faith in formal policies alone to make change and write off continuing complaints of inequity as the grumblings of "discontented individuals." They scorn executive coaches and trainers who extend the benefit of the doubt repeatedly to leaders whose failure to change causes enormous harm to their organizations and workforces. They lament grassroots organizing efforts that devolve into factions, posturing, and a toxic mix of purity[1] and disposability politics.[2] They blast the ludicrously unbalanced incentives in the DEI industry that would see speakers paid tens of thousands of dollars to share an inspiring story of their journey but scrape the bottom of the barrel to compensate and resource those doing genuinely effective change work. And they question me—despite, or perhaps especially, because I look like them. They ask me whether I'm just another paid "token minority"[3] consulted to make their company look good but leave it just as much of a mess as I found it.

In the past, I didn't always have the answer to these questions, and that just wasn't acceptable. It wasn't okay to finish a six-month engagement and only have "positive feelings of progress" from a few leaders as my indicators for success. I needed answers, both for my conscience and to hold myself accountable to those I worked for. Finding those answers shaped who I am today and this book.

So who am I? I'm someone who deeply and personally feels the imperative of making better organizations and a better world. I'm someone who wants to use their understanding of the world, of organizations, systems, and people, to fix things that have been broken for a long time—perhaps even within our lifetimes. I am radically impatient and uncompromising when centering those negatively impacted by systems. I work to understand the structures, cultures, people, and processes that constitute systems to help people make better ones. I rely on data of all kinds to understand, justify, process, and enable change. I believe that people can change and grow, that systems can adapt to undo inequity rather than perpetuate it, and that we can both build *and* fight our way to a better world.

I've spent much time thinking about this work, and obviously, I have a lot of opinions. To the extent those opinions show up in this book, especially if they feel surprising, unfamiliar, or even radical, I share them to introduce what I believe to be some of the most effective and evidence-based ways to achieve the outcomes that matter. You don't need to share or like all of my opinions, or even any of them for that matter. But understanding where I'm coming from and what I'm trying to do will help you interpret and use the resources I'll be sharing throughout this book.

Who You Are

You are someone who wants to do DEI right. Maybe you're a full-time practitioner looking for a solid companion guide to inform the messy work you do as part of your day-to-day. Maybe you're an internal employee advocate or volunteer looking to beef up your passion and interest in this topic with a crash course of know-how and actionable advice. Maybe you're a mid-level manager or leader who wants a more comprehensive understanding of what DEI looks like as a real organizational commitment in action rather than a collection of inspirational speeches. Maybe you're an HR leader, chief diversity officer, or another executive tasked to "lead on DEI" and want to know what that actually means.

You're not someone just looking for inspiration, and if you are, I hope you won't take this too harshly: this isn't a book for you. DEI work isn't always inspirational. Sometimes it's terrifying, depressing, or overwhelming. Many times, it can be quite dry. You are unlikely to find many stories in this book that will bring a tear to your eye, make you jump for joy, or single-handedly renew your faith in humanity. It's not my thing (and look, "no-nonsense" was in the title—you've been warned).

I make it a point not to talk down to the folks in my practice, and readers of this book are no different: you are grown adults with the ability to think and engage critically with content, and I'll treat you like that. Whatever experience and expectations you bring to the table, keep in mind that practicing these skills as you read the book will enhance your experience:

Open-Mindedness

I'm going to have hard words for something, at some point, that you care deeply about. Maybe it's a practice practitioners long considered inclusive that new research suggests just isn't. Maybe it's an everyday behavior that you've deeply integrated with your organizational practices or even your identity, and evidence increasingly shows it is more likely than not to harm. I'm not telling you to take my words as gospel or do whatever I say without asking. Just consider that there is nothing I would share with you that I do not believe would be good for you or your organization, and take a moment to consider that seriously.

Emotional Regulation

You might feel strong emotions while reading this book. Some of those emotions might be inspired by the text. Some you might bring in from the outside: I've certainly had my fair share of experiences furiously looking up research to "prove" an obstinate client wrong; you might at some point find yourself reading this text with similar feelings. When you feel these things, remember to breathe deep—four counts—and exhale slowly—six counts. Sometimes, to process what you read, you might want to put this book down, talk it over with a friend, or even debate a point in it with a colleague before coming back. Be mindful of the emotions you bring into that process, and take your time.

Criticality

DEI isn't just an art but a science. Even if you believe that what I am saying is right, you should consider it for its own merits in the context of what you know. I am not, and will never be, a subject matter expert in every subject that DEI touches—no matter how much research I've done to write this work or will do in the future. That's where you come in. I want you to use your knowledge to engage critically with mine. Hell, tear pages out and scribble in the margins if you would like! In the future, someone will write a book that definitively improves on this one, and that won't happen unless you go beyond simply consuming my opinions to engaging with them as peers.

Graciousness

Despite my best efforts, I bet you'll find something wrong in this book. Perhaps I'll have a perspective that ages poorly, that ends up in the context of when you read this to be a bad take. More likely than not, I'll

overlook something important. An idea of mine might not be fully inclusive for every marginalized social group, or I've decided to use language that history decides isn't right. When (and not if) this happens,
I invite you to be critical *and* extend grace and understanding that this
work is messy, ever-changing, and imperfect. Proceed thoughtfully
with that in mind—and when you can, use my mistakes to expand and
build upon your nuanced understanding of this work. That's how we
grow.

A Brief Note about Language

You may have already noticed that I use one particular acronym, "DEI,"
to refer to "diversity, equity, and inclusion." I've chosen this acronym
not because I think it's the "best" (attempting to declare a "best" acronym in the sea of DEI acronyms would fill the pages of this book),
but because I think it's a start. There is no shortage of acronyms in this
space, from "EDI" to "D&I" to "DEIB," "IDEA," and "JEDI" (the "B"
is for "belonging"; the "A" is for "accessibility"; the "J" is for "justice").
The most popular one? That varies by industry, region, and generation.
I have lost count of the number of earnest advocates and practitioners
who have told me that their acronym of choice is best and all others are
outdated or insufficient.

I don't know if "DEI" is the best acronym, but it's more than enough
to start with. If other terms resonate better with you, I invite you to
replace "DEI" with them instead as you read. The same goes for other
words I may use in this book, whether identity-related terminology or
social science concepts.[4] It may very well be the case that by the time
you pick up the book, some of the wording I've used is no longer "best
practice." If you see something like that, note that down—but please,
don't let terminology stop you from engaging with the text. Whatever
your thoughts on language, so long as you get something valuable out
of this text, I'll be satisfied as an author.

How to Use This Book

This book is laid out into ten chapters, organized into three parts, each discussing a critical facet of effective DEI work. *Part 1, Foundation*, establishes the scope and magnitude of the challenge ahead of us and ensures we're aligned on what we're solving. *Part 2, Pillars*, focuses on the tactical and solutions-oriented side of DEI work. These chapters will introduce the most impassable roadblocks that have stymied DEI practitioners past and present and feature evidence-based, effective, and surprising ways to overcome them. *Part 3, Toolbox*, takes a final look at the concrete practices at the forefront of the DEI space and the considerations practitioners must make as they problem solve. It is the culmination of my answer to "what works?" The *Conclusion* closes out the book with parting thoughts on what it takes for us to achieve DEI as outcomes in our organizations together.

Chapter 1: Intentions Aren't Enough lays out the case for why common approaches that intend to make organizations more diverse, equitable, and inclusive fail—and what we all need to learn if we are to understand and deploy effective alternatives. You'll get a lay of the DEI ecosystem, become familiar with the challenges we set out to solve and learn about the DEI-Industrial Complex—the informal relationship between DEI and organizations that perpetuates an inequitable status quo.

Chapter 2: DEI Building Blocks is my take on an actually useful DEI 101. I reformulate the key terms and concepts of the DEI space away from their feel-good buzzword roots and toward operationalized and tangible outcomes. This chapter goes against the grain of most "terms and definitions" chapters out there. It turns DEI 101 from an amorphous body of conceptual and abstract information into a concrete set of objectives and approaches that can be consistently deployed and achieved in practice.

Chapter 3: To What End? will help you understand the evolution of DEI as an industry and how the goalposts of this work leading up to the present day have shifted over time. You'll learn how DEI became what it is today, the origin of modern-day staples like the "business case for diversity," and how accountability, the holy grail of DEI work, has remained conspicuously watered-down, weakened, or absent over time. You'll learn just what it takes to stop history from repeating itself and the challenges that practitioners at the forefront of this work are laboring to solve.

Chapter 4: Real Change looks at modern discontent when organizations promise to change, summed up by the popular phrase "performative allyship." You'll learn why the era we find ourselves in post-2020 represents a turning point for accountability, stakeholder trust, and organizational change, and the new, higher standards that consumers, communities, employees, and investors have for organizations when it comes to their role in an uncertain and inequitable world.

Chapter 5: Knowing, Using, Ceding Power is where we get into the details of making change. This chapter will be an overview of how organizational structure, culture, and strategy affect individuals and systems alike. You'll learn how those with formal and informal power—which every stakeholder in every organization has to some degree—can use that power to achieve DEI outcomes. A common phrase in the industry is, "everyone can make a difference no matter who they are." This chapter puts some teeth to that platitude.

Chapter 6: Identity and Difference wades into the often controversial bog of addressing race, gender, ability, sexuality, age, class, and other social dimensions of difference in the workplace. One part an identity primer and two parts tactics and advice, this chapter will give you the knowledge and the language you need to start engaging effectively with identity—both yours and others'—in the context of power and change, striking a middle path between identity-as-dogma and identity denial. Read this if you or your organization are navigating a highly salient identity-based conflict situation.

Chapter 7: Change-Maker: Everyone lays out the various roles needed to actually create diversity, equity, and inclusion as outcomes of an initiative or campaign and focuses on the far-easier-said-than-done work of coalition-building as a means to make change. This is where to go if you're looking for help wrangling the various stakeholders and constituents in your organization to engage them most effectively in change-making. This is where to go if you're looking to find a role for yourself to make a difference in your organization without being overwhelmed.

Chapter 8: Achieving DEI is the strategy chapter, where you'll learn how to use and gain trust as the currency of change. I'll be honest about what happens when the work gets messy and what to do when the neatness of theory meets the complexity of practice. You'll learn how to carve out a path for yourself and your organization toward diversity, equity, and inclusion that gets things done, whether your stakeholders trust their leadership to lead DEI step-by-step or have so little trust that even good-faith consideration of DEI sounds like wishful thinking.

Chapter 9: Expanding Your Repertoire summarizes and lays out the practices that I think collectively best serve organizations seeking to achieve DEI, drawing from the leading edge of DEI research and understanding in the early 2020s. This chapter is a resource best contextualized by the rest of the book and spans effective practices that achieve an organization's DEI foundation, internal DEI processes, and external DEI outcomes. Chapter 9 is intended as a reference chapter to be read and referred back to multiple times by any practitioner, advocate, or change-maker—and added to by future practitioners as our field's knowledge progresses.

The **Conclusion** caps it all off. You'll look at the past and future of DEI through a pragmatic lens, review the challenges to solve in the present and receive a final primer on how we collectively dismantle the DEI-Industrial Complex and achieve the outcomes we want to see in our lifetimes. You might get a few inspirational words from me. Maybe.

At the end of every chapter, you'll find **Takeaways** summarizing the major themes and ideas. Use these to check your learning and refresh your understanding upon rereading. Following them, the **Exercise** and **Reflection** sections help bridge the conceptual with the practical, with prompts that directly make use of learnings from each chapter.

At the end of the book lives many of the **Resources** mentioned in the book, including a **Reading List** curated to introduce you to important DEI-related topics. You'll also find **Notes**, all 450+ of the citations and resources referenced in the book, ordered by chapter. These resources will be an easy way to refresh yourself on the content you found useful, reference interventions to apply in your own practice, and dive deeper into interesting material.

This book is intended to be read front-to-back, as each chapter builds on the last, but the content is flexible enough that chapters can stand on their own. If identity-related issues are top of mind for you, you may want to revisit Chapter 6 immediately after your first read through. If you're hoping to learn more tactics and interventions to apply, maybe Chapters 7 and 8 will be your focus. If your working group wants to establish a common language, perhaps linger a little longer on Chapter 2.

Your learning is your own. What I'll provide are the frameworks, knowledge base, and tools I've built on, adapted, and developed from researching, trying, and testing dozens of strategies, tactics, and interventions to achieve DEI as outcomes, not just intentions.

Please use this book as a resource to help you do the same.

PART 1

FOUNDATION

━ ONE ━

Intentions Aren't Enough

"So then I told him, 'intent isn't impact,' and it totally blew his mind! I bet he had never thought before that the effort he was putting in trying to do the right thing might be causing harm." The DEI practitioner grinned as she shared the story with me, and I nodded along. I had heard and told some version of this story many times, but there was always a nagging question following it. So I asked it.

"What about your own work, then?"

She looked at me, slightly put off. "My own work? I facilitate hard conversations to help people recognize their unconscious biases and become allies to marginalized communities. Are you suggesting that it doesn't work?"

"I guess I am, yeah," I said hesitantly. "How do you know that people actually change? How do you know that they even recognize their own biases at all…or that even if they do, that they then follow-up with changed behavior?"

She looked at me, and neither of us said anything.

There was more I wanted to ask.

How do we know that, when people tell us they "enjoyed the session," this means our interventions did what we wanted them to do? Even if they say we changed their mind, how would we know if that were true?

How do we decide which interventions to apply during the session, and how do we know if they work? If they do, how do we know if positive impact sticks around after even a day?

Do we track the impact of our work over time? Do we even have a way to measure impact? Do we have a way to reach the marginalized communities we interact with for accountability? Do we ever see them again after the single session we do?

The other practitioner flashed a conciliatory smile. "I know in my heart that what I do works. And other people do, too. Isn't that enough?"

I forced a smile in return and nodded. I didn't agree.

Everything about how I approached diversity, equity, and inclusion changed in 2016 when I first read an article in the *Harvard Business Review* (it's not every day I mark a period of my life with a business article but still, bear with me). The article? "Why Diversity Programs Fail," by Frank Dobbin and Alexandra Kalev. Both sociologists argue that companies' command-and-control deployment of diversity programs, hiring tests, and grievance processes have failed to move the needle on the representation of women and non-White racial groups in the US. Their data are hard to argue with.

"Among all US companies with 100 or more employees," Dobbin and Kalev write, "the proportion of black men in management increased just slightly—from 3% to 3.3%—from 1985 to 2014. White women saw bigger gains from 1985 to 2000—rising from 22% to 29% of managers— but their numbers haven't budged since then."[1]

And the real kicker: when DEI programs were implemented, at least in the five years of data the authors collected, the representation of most groups outside of White men *decreased* afterward.

Why? Dobbin and Kalev identify a few interesting mechanisms: backlash effects, where individuals told to act a certain way respond

Change over Five Years in Representation among Managers (%)

Type of program	White		Black		Hispanic		Asian	
	Men	Women	Men	Women	Men	Women	Men	Women
Mandatory diversity training	—	—	—	-9.2	—	—	-4.5	-5.4
Job tests	—	-3.8	-10.2	-9.1	-6.7	-8.8	—	-9.3
Grievance systems	—	-2.7	-7.3	-4.8		-4.7	-11.3	-4.1

Note: — indicates no statistical certainty of a program's effect.

FIGURE 1. Representation for Black, Hispanic, and Asian managers drops in the five years following the implementation of some of the most popular DEI initiatives.

Source: "Why Diversity Programs Fail," by Frank Dobbin and Alexandra Kalev, July–August 2016. Authors' study of 829 midsize and large US firms.

by decisively doing the opposite, and selective standards, where raters ignore quantitative scores on job tests for friends and those they like while strictly applying score cutoffs for all other candidates. The general point that Dobbin and Kalev make is that when DEI interventions attempt to compel or control the behavior of people in power, these people often respond with counterproductive behavior that jeopardizes the outcomes the interventions are trying to create, resulting in the unintended effects shown in Figure 1.

When I first read this article, it felt like the floor had fallen from under me. *I offered diversity training*—and had up until that point been a big advocate for making them mandatory. I was similarly an advocate for mandating job tests, grievance systems, scrubbing identifying information from resumes, and other DEI interventions that seemed uncontroversial and widely popular "best practices."

For the first time, I had to ask myself: *How can I be sure that the work I'm doing is achieving what I think it is?* And then, the inevitable follow-ups: *How many practitioners are doing work that might be ineffective or even do more harm than good?" "How many don't know and don't care enough to find out?*

For years, I sought out answers to these questions, and what I saw indicated that dubiously effective or even blatantly harmful practices were entrenched into widespread understandings of what "the work" looked like—including my own. As I'll explore shortly, the "gold standard" of DEI work and interventions was too often just fool's gold: shiny, exciting, but ultimately disappointing and of little value. I'll share why this is the case and how to identify these "fool's gold standards" so we can build an understanding of how those of us intent on effective work can do better.

(Fool's) Gold Standards

When people think of "DEI work," a few different focus areas consistently appear. These include DEI policies, training/workshops, surveys, talks, and volunteerism. This is because these arenas of DEI work are some of the most common ones defined by DEI professionals and are often lifted as "gold standards" or examples of "successful work" by advocates. Here's the thing: DEI work poorly executed in any of these focus areas can turn even a substantial investment of time, resources, and effort into a zero-impact or even negative-impact outcome.

DEI Policies

Diversity policies are typically high-visibility statements that establish an organization's intentions on DEI. They span a wide range of forms, from generic policies embodying an organization's commitment to DEI[2] to more specific policies governing hiring, training, or diversity goals. DEI policies are typically trumpeted as relatively low-effort best practices for organizations, but they aren't perceived the same way by different demographic groups within organizations, and even the same policy framed in different ways can garner more or less support from different groups.[3] For example, when considering a generic diversity policy, the gap between levels of Black employee versus White employee support can be as large as 30%. Regardless of support, how effective are the policies once implemented? Here's the kicker—in organizations with diversity policies, members of advantaged groups are far less likely to perceive discrimination against disadvantaged groups, *regardless of the actual level of discrimination.*[4] When these policies are deployed in isolation as uncomplicated "fix-alls" with no additional accountability mechanisms, especially if they are perceived as passive HR policies rather than commitments that require active effort from leadership to achieve, they have the potential to simply obscure the inequity of the status quo rather than improve it. It's quite possible (and even common) for even the most well-written DEI policy created by expert DEI practitioners to do more harm than good when deployed on its own.

DEI Training

The bread and butter of the DEI industry, "DEI training," varies enormously in content and approach. "Courageous Conversations" (also known as "Brave Spaces" or "dialogues on [topic]") aim to engage people in conversation about tough issues of identity and inequity. "Sensitivity Training" aims to introduce participants to inclusive language and behaviors and prescribe "do's and don'ts" for various marginalized social groups like women, Black people, disabled people, older people, LGBTQ+ people, and more. "Allyship Training" aims to activate individuals with socially advantaged identities to play an active role in supporting their colleagues with socially disadvantaged identities. "Unconscious Bias Training" aims to help participants unpack their biases about social groups, especially biases that they aren't aware they have (hence, unconscious), and use that awareness to act more inclusively toward others.

All of these varieties of training have their challenges, if not in their

fundamental assumptions about creating impact, then in their haphaz-
ard and inconsistent deployment. Many kinds of DEI training promise
lasting attitude and behavioral changes from relatively simplistic exercises and reflections, for example, but pull their exercises from sources
ranging from social psychology research and grassroots organizing
work to self-help guides or simply a practitioner's own imagination.

Content aside, the logistical deployment of DEI training is often
one-time and too short in length to create any sort of lasting impact: for
example, many iterations of allyship training aim to increase bystander
intervention,[5] but effective bystander intervention training often takes
five hours or more,[6] while allyship training can often be even as short
as an hour.

Done wrong, training can do more harm than good. Poorly executed
training can reduce complex issues spanning centuries of conflict
into reductive lists of "good" and "bad" behaviors; foster resentment
among participants who are blamed for causing harm they don't understand; lack safeguards to prevent conversations from becoming
emotionally distressing, verbally abusive, or highly triggering for one
or more parties; force individuals to self-disclose personal identities
they aren't ready to share; or push them to take on educator roles, and
create an inflated sense of efficacy in participants to create organizational change.

I've seen these outcomes myself, whether from the perspective of
a workshop participant or in helping organizations do damage control
after another practitioner's clumsily executed training.

One participant of a training that focused on inclusive language for
LGBTQ+ communities later told a colleague that "transsexual" was
outdated and un-inclusive language. Their colleague, who had happily
identified as transsexual for years, was less than thrilled to hear that
her own identity was somehow "un-inclusive" from someone who
wasn't trans themself.

One training devolved into name-calling and profoundly unproductive conflict when one workshop participant called another a "White supremacist bigot" to his face, that participant told the first participant that they would "burn in hell" for being LGBTQ+, and the facilitator did nothing as the session erupted into chaos.

One training found itself only attended by employees with no power to actually put into action anything they learned, who later reported in a follow-up survey that since the fundamental systemic barrier preventing them from using the skills they learned hadn't budged, neither had their inaction.

Is every kind of DEI training likely to create these unintended outcomes? No, but at present, there are few safeguards in the industry to prevent them. Few practitioners collect impact metrics on the outcomes of their training, and few organizations do so on their side, either. Longitudinal impacts are virtually never tracked. Practitioners come into the field with experience ranging from full-on PhDs in intergroup conflict resolution to having read one or two books about race or gender in their spare time. Organizations that don't recognize this might bring someone in to deliver an unconscious bias training expecting a professional familiar with the research and its nuances in execution, only to get someone reading out instructions on an exercise that attendees could look up online and participate in on their own. Unless the lack of quality control and consistency within the field changes soon, hastily deploying a DEI practitioner to deliver training, even a practitioner with a "good reputation," will continue to mean taking a gamble with organizational outcomes and employee well-being on the line.

DEI Surveys

DEI surveys collect employee self-reported data on metrics like fairness, belonging, engagement, and well-being, then disaggregate it by demographics like race, gender, sexuality, age, and more to uncover disparities and inequities in outcomes. The promise of DEI surveying is that armed with good data, organizations can direct their efforts toward programs and interventions that are most likely to succeed. The challenge with DEI surveys is that "good data" is much easier said than gathered. International variation on the legal collection of sensitive demographic data notwithstanding,[7] DEI surveys often involve a large degree of vulnerability from respondents and sensitivity on the part of employers and/or third parties engaging in data collection. There are numerous failure modes that arise when the respondent vulnerability is lacking or survey administrators lack the appropriate sensitivity: low response rates caused by a low level of respondent trust can jeopardize quantitative data; high levels of hostility and distrust among employees can lead to survey reporting being used as a vehicle for organizational politics or interpersonal agendas; mishandling of sensitive employee data can fuel illegal retaliation and discrimination; failure to handle small-n problems[8] when only a small number of employees of a certain disadvantaged identity (e.g., "gay") exist can compromise anonymity. In addition to challenges ensuring that identified disparities reflect real disparities and not simply a researcher's own predispositions,[9] DEI surveys create the expectation that collected data will be used to address identified issues as expeditiously as possible. If data transparency is lacking or company leadership is unwilling to act on all the findings from the data, this can substantially erode trust and demoralize a workforce.

Even when designed with all of these concerns in mind, DEI surveys have fundamental weaknesses: a single survey only measures reality at one point in time and cannot be used to prove causation, that one action *causes* another. Even if two outcomes appear to be linked—for example, a department with more diversity has greater productivity than a department with less diversity—there can be any number of other explanations for the correlation and substantial risk associated with hastily concluding that adding diversity to another department will thus increase its productivity.

DEI surveys are only as good as the practitioner or expert administering them and the organizational leaders following up (or not) on their findings. Ineffective deployments of DEI surveys can result in unintended consequences, including retaliation, decreased employee trust in leadership, and unhelpful interventions informed by inaccurate survey conclusions.

DEI Talks

One of the most commonly used ways to bring DEI-related content into an organization, DEI-related talks, lectures, keynotes, and other speaking engagements typically involve one or more speakers and advocates addressing an internal audience of employees on any number of DEI topics. Pick any DEI concept you can think of and look it up—there's likely a DEI talk about it somewhere on the internet. As an intervention, DEI talks are typically used as organizations' go-to way to demonstrate their commitment to DEI through a high-visibility engagement and introduce attendees to "new" DEI-related content and ideas. While they are indeed effective for raising the visibility of issues or topics and increasing momentum for new or existing initiatives, DEI talks themselves have little ability to create long-term behavior or organizational changes. For example, while a DEI talk exhorting the value of flexible working arrangements on mental health may be inspirational, unless employers actively follow up by enabling greater flexibility, through policy and practice, mental health won't actually change. Unfortunately, employers rarely follow up on DEI talks—and recycling talk footage for external-facing marketing doesn't count.

This doesn't stop employers from requesting DEI talks, however, and investing sizable budgets into getting celebrity speakers onto their stages. But when budgets for genuinely impactful DEI work are a tenth or hundredth of speaker budgets, this can often result in frustration, growing impatience among a workforce, and a perception that DEI efforts are "performative" and intended only for show rather than impact.

DEI Volunteerism

The final category of common DEI work is volunteerism, where DEI work is undertaken by passionate employee volunteers, typically organized into informal or formal workplace groups. The structure of these groups can vary: employee resource groups (ERGs) are usually organized around one particular identity or affinity (e.g., Black, woman, LGBTQ+, disability), while councils, working groups, and committees are formed to address DEI issues more broadly. DEI volunteer groups, specifically ERGs, have a long and storied history: the first was founded in 1970 by Black employees at Xerox as a forum to discuss shared experiences and advocate for racial equity and became the template for ERGs to this day.[10] In the fifty years since their inception, however, ERGs were slowly repurposed to increasingly center organizational goals rather than community ones. Today's ERGs and other volunteer groups are often proudly described by organizations as helping solve key business challenges, develop DEI strategy, and consult on complex topics of identity and inequity at work.

This is a problem because employee-led groups often lack the authority to make real decisions and the resources to act effectively. They may be able to advocate for changes like creating hiring rubrics or conducting a DEI survey but must rely on the goodwill of actual decision-makers to act on their recommendations. In other cases, these groups can be tasked with not only advocating for DEI, but carrying out the organization's DEI work in its entirety. They might be asked to gauge employee sentiment, analyze survey data, develop a DEI strategy, and coordinate organizational change themselves. This is an enormous risk for several reasons. One, the magnitude of this work almost always burns out employees who engage in it but receive no additional support, resources, or recognition for doing so. Two, the lack of experience or expertise among these employee volunteers often results in poor DEI decision-making with the high potential to do more harm than good—if your corporate office had a sitewide plumbing issue, would you solicit passionate employee volunteers who had fixed an occasional plumbing issue in their houses to fix it? Third, the lack of resources these groups are allocated cheapens DEI work for everyone. I've been approached by more apologetic ERGs than I can count, asking me to perform an organization-wide assessment and analysis for scraps because no other department in the organization was willing to take that work on. In one case, an ERG desperately offered me $600 to do at least fifty hours of work—a generous use of 75% of their entire yearly operating budget.

There's nothing wrong with DEI volunteerism as a way to augment effective efforts. But when scope-crept DEI volunteerism is used as a *replacement* for well-resourced DEI work undertaken by trained professionals, it can become a way to exploit passionate employees for their labor, avoid accountability, and perpetuate a glacial pace of change.

Am I trying to say with all this that "DEI doesn't work"? No—something quite different. I'm saying that DEI done wrong doesn't work, and DEI that doesn't work is often the case because it was done wrong.

DEI policies aren't inherently bad. Neither are trainings, surveys, talks, or volunteer efforts. But they aren't inherently effective just by virtue of existing, and this is where many well-intentioned practitioners and advocates trip up. Every practitioner I know has a heartfelt story about a workshop participant whose mind was changed on an important issue or who tearfully shared a reflection about how they had never realized their own privilege or committed publicly to be a better ally. But we don't just evaluate salespeople on how compelling their stories about eager customers are. We don't just assess web designers on how inspired we feel hearing them talk about coding.

Diversity, equity, and inclusion work in organizations is about achieving diversity, equity, and inclusion as tangible outcomes at a scale beyond the individual. This is true whether we are consultants, practitioners, workplace leaders, employee volunteers, or anyone else who wants to do DEI. Given the state of the working world, we don't have the luxury of centering our own feel-good narratives about change over actual results. Either we know that our work is effective and can prove it, or we don't and need to find out.

Inequitable, Exclusive, Homogenous

In Silicon Valley, following widespread calls for tech companies to release data on the diversity of their workforce in the mid-2010s, the number of Black and Latine (pronounced "lah-ti-neh") workers actually dropped.[11] Meta-analyses show that, in US labor markets, hiring discrimination against Black workers hasn't changed since 1989 and declined only slightly[12] for Latine workers. Employment discrimination charges filed under the Americans with Disabilities Act (ADA) have held constant over time;[13] a good 70% of physicians don't even know how to meet their legal requirements to treat people with disabilities.[14] While American women's educational attainment has surpassed that of men, their labor force representation, pay, and leadership representation in businesses and government remain lower than that of men, with gains having stagnated for decades.[15] This list is endless: discrimination is alive and well in the US against Native Americans,[16] the LGBTQ+ community,[17] pregnant people,[18] people experiencing poverty,[19] and many more social groups and dimensions than just these.

While the exact dimensions of identity and social status affected by discrimination and inequity differ across the world, discrimination in the workplace is a global phenomenon.

A meta-analysis identified racial discrimination in Belgium, Canada, France, the UK, Germany, the Netherlands, Norway, and Sweden—with the worst racial discrimination documented in Sweden and France.[20] While data is sparser in some regions,[21] workplace discrimination and inequity are also documented across east Asia[22,23] southeast Asia,[24] sub-Saharan Africa,[25] and West Asia and North Africa (WANA),[26] with far more data existing than makes sense to share here.

More tangible examples closer to home? Take the #MeToo movement started in 2006 by activist Tarana Burke, which went viral in 2017 following widespread sexual abuse allegations against former film producer Harvey Weinstein.[27] A movement driven by social media on every continent, spanning tens of millions of tweets and thousands of articles, #MeToo prominently brought issues of sexual assault, harassment, and discrimination to the forefront.[28]

Now, five years later, the effects of the movement are starting to materialize. The #MeToo movement undeniably increased reporting of sexual assault and harassment by empowering victims to share their stories—with a smaller but notable increase in arrests, as well.[29] But belief in the benefits of the movement is polarizing, with only 25% of men in a US study believing that recent attention to sexual misconduct had a positive impact, versus 61% of women.[30] This split is far from the only concerning effect. Within workplaces, following the #MeToo movement, a 2019 study found that 60% of managers who are men felt uncomfortable mentoring, working alone with, or socializing with women—a 32% jump in discomfort from just the year prior, with 36% reporting that this discomfort stems from worries that engaging in any way would be seen poorly.[31] This trend is exacerbated in senior-level men, who are now *12 times more likely* to hesitate to have 1-on-1 meetings with junior-level women than before.

At the same time, while more blatant sexual harassment like sexual coercion and unwanted sexual attention decreased in the period between 2016 and 2018, at the height of the movement, gender-related harassment *increased*.[32] The #MeToo backlash, as this trend became known, continued to worsen in 2019—men's fears around unfair accusations and women's concerns that men would simply continue harassing more discreetly only increased, with disastrous impacts on men's desire to interact with women in hiring, mentoring, or traveling.[33] As the movement spread outside the US, its impact diverged in ways we continue to study. China's fledgling movement is facing a crackdown;[34] France's movement faced enormous backlash in the late 2010s but may be gaining greater support now;[35] Latin American movements across Mexico, Chile, Brazil, and Argentina focused on femicide, or the murder of women;[36] Japan's movement never quite took off.[37] And the #MeToo movement is only one facet of the ongoing work to achieve gender parity and gender equity worldwide—an end state that, according to the World Economic Forum, was nearly 100 years away from becoming a reality after 2020 and 135.6 years away after 2021 when the impacts of the COVID-19 pandemic were taken into account.[38]

This is just one example, but the lessons we should take away from it should be sobering. As societies and as a world, we are far from where we need to be, and our efforts to do good may result in unpredictable consequences—and harm—we are unprepared to handle.

Even if we do DEI work each and every day, it's wishful thinking to believe that the trajectory of the world will take us automatically toward equity and that all we have to do is ride the current to get there eventually. There is no such thing. If we achieve DEI, it is because all of us have put in the thoughtful, intentional effort to do our best and do things *right*. Dr. Beverly Daniel Tatum says it well when she uses the metaphor of a moving airport walkway, or a conveyor belt, to describe racism; I believe the metaphor applies effectively to other systemic inequities, too.

"Active racist behavior is equivalent to walking fast on the conveyor belt. The person engaged in active racist behavior has identified with the ideology of White supremacy and is moving with it. Passive racist behavior is equivalent to standing still on the walkway. No overt effort is being made, but the conveyor belt moves the bystanders along to the same destination as those who are actively walking. Some of the bystanders may feel the motion of the conveyor belt, see the active racists ahead of them, and choose to turn around, unwilling to go in the same destination as the White supremacists. **But unless they are walking actively in the opposite direction faster than the conveyor belt—unless they are actively antiracist—they will find themselves carried along with the others.**"[39]

Every time I think of this analogy, I'm struck by the final line. One part of it, in particular: "a speed faster than the conveyor belt." Too many of us assume that simply turning around to move against the flow of injustice already makes us effective antiracists, effective advocates for women, LGBTQ+ people, disabled people, and so on. But as this metaphor powerfully illustrates, regardless of your intentions, there is a certain—perhaps even objective—amount of progress you must achieve to say that you are making and have made a difference.

Move too slowly? You'll be facing the right direction, but an onlooker will still see you going the wrong way. You'll be earnestly, vigorously, and even haughtily moonwalking toward inequity.

An uncomfortable percentage of modern DEI work amounts to moonwalking toward inequity, from poorly designed training to irresponsibly deployed policy to earnest but unskilled volunteer initiatives.

"But Lily, our leaders have their hearts in the right place"—it's their actions and impacts that matter more.

"But Lily, our company has a racial justice commitment"—racial justice outcomes are more important than statements of commitment.

"But Lily, at least our company is an industry leader on issues of disability"—being the least inaccessible or inequitable isn't the same as achieving accessibility and equity.

I want you, myself, and everyone else to read this and sit with the discomfort:

Our organizations, and certainly our world, continue to be unacceptably inequitable, exclusive, and homogenous. And despite the best of intentions, we as leaders, advocates, activists, and practitioners don't yet have a collective handle on how to meaningfully change that at scale.

The DEI-Industrial Complex

It's one thing to say that, as a collective, the DEI industry doesn't have a handle on how to ensure effectiveness and quality control as a standard. That's not a problem on its own—many emerging industries and fields experience similar challenges. The problem is that if you look up "DEI" or "diversity equity and inclusion" on any internet search, that's the last impression you would get of what you'd find.

Endless articles on terms and definitions. Think pieces, webinars, and infographics galore. Then, the sponsored ads—for consulting firms, executive coaching, online courses, training and workshops, and every other DEI service under the sun. If I didn't know better, I'd say that far from a fledgling industry figuring itself out, DEI was a well-oiled machine that brought profits to the people driving it without being accountable for the lofty goals it preaches.

This critique of the industry is increasingly common. More and more, critics are asking if the DEI industry does more harm than good[40] and going so far as to call the relationship between DEI and the corporate world the "DEI-Industrial Complex"[41]—arguing that the nearly $10 billion-dollar[42] and growing DEI industry enables the inequitable status quo and corporate misconduct to continue existing.[43] They make the case that the DEI industry is in the process of being (if it hasn't been already) co-opted by corporate leaders who want the reputational benefits of having "engaged in diversity, equity, and inclusion work" without needing to fundamentally make any real change. And DEI professionals are either intentionally or unwittingly enabling those intentions by doing work that doesn't work, dressed up in inspiring language like "antiracism" and "social justice."

This critique frames DEI practitioners and corporate leaders in a mutually beneficial, symbiotic relationship. Companies get their inspirational talk or training or initiative, reputational boost, and a few more months of their employees' patience. DEI practitioners get money in their pockets. But employees dealing with microaggressions find the source of their problems unchanged when the good feelings from the DEI talk wear off. Employees being retaliated against by their managers don't see any lasting changes in behavior after the mandatory workshop. Employees seeing no future for themselves in the all-White, all-male senior leadership at their company are no more hopeful than they were following the expensive "antiracist exercise" at the leadership retreat. Candidates facing hiring discrimination are no closer to getting jobs after the shiny nondiscrimination statement was lauded on social media.

To be clear, some organizations take their DEI budgets seriously and rigorously screen the practitioners they bring in. But even then, these efforts can miss the mark. I've seen some organizations request that the workshop practitioners who will train a small fraction of their workforce have ten years of experience delivering training that was only developed five years ago while booking a speaker to address their entire workforce on the sole basis that the head of HR liked hearing that speaker five years earlier. I've seen some organizations request "data-driven" DEI practitioners able to put bleeding-edge research never applied in the field into practice but who somehow already have a "measurable track record" of using those same practices.

And the vast majority of organizations don't even do this. They hire the cheapest practitioner they can find, pay to record one 90-minute training, and subject their entire workforce to the recording as a one-size-fits-all mandatory "training." They hire inspirational speakers who lack skills in interpersonal facilitation and conflict resolution to facilitate their "hard conversations" that predictably go wildly off the rails, then conclude from the experience that "DEI isn't worth engaging in." It's infuriating.

In the face of this, I don't blame many people, including even former DEI advocates, for becoming skeptical of DEI work. Real progress is stagnating while the industry's profile skyrockets, with the intended beneficiaries of this work being exposed all the while to DEI interventions that are lackluster, ineffective, outdated, or just plain offensive.

Recently, for example, a colleague with no previous exposure to corporate DEI shared with me a story of sitting through a mandatory DEI training, led by a person who was not White, in which the facilitator referred to different racial groups as "Negroids, Caucasoids, and Mongoloids" before listing a long list of racial stereotypes to the unwitting audience. I couldn't believe what I was hearing—a racial classification system developed in the 1780s still deployed in 2021. The training deeply confused and upset the audience. "What is wrong with DEI practitioners?" demanded my colleague afterward, and all I could do was shake my head and apologize on behalf of a person I had never met. What *is* wrong with DEI practitioners?

Maybe it's the complete lack of standardization or quality control in our industry. Maybe it's the fact that there are zero qualifications required to enter the industry and that while some practitioners enter with industrial-organizational psychology, education, human resources, learning & development, grassroots organizing, or organizational development backgrounds, others enter with nothing but "passion and lived experience as a minority social group." Maybe it's the fact that there are no ways to distinguish effective certification programs from the ones peddling fluff and that even the best programs lack a unified approach to what it requires or even what it means to do the work.

Critics point to these factors as reasons why the DEI industry does more harm than good, and some go so far as to claim it is past saving, suggesting that those who care would be better off disengaging from it completely. The most idealistic advocates brush off these factors as slight complications alongside an otherwise unproblematic and hopeful upward trajectory. Both have a point, but both mischaracterize the path ahead of us.

Hope for a better future is important. We need to see the DEI industry and DEI work in general as an endlessly improving discipline with room to grow that *has* meaningfully achieved change. Much of this progress was not achieved in isolation but instead in collaboration with and supporting social movements, activists, and advocates who unapologetically work toward a better world. At the same time, our actions have consequences, and we bear an enormous responsibility toward all marginalized groups to ensure our work moves the needle in the right direction and mitigates unforeseen negative consequences.

Accountability is important. We need to see the development of mechanisms and means for people anywhere and everywhere to hold DEI work accountable in the same way DEI work aims to hold organizations accountable. For accountability, the industry needs transparency, structure, and community so that anyone can understand the work being done, how and why leaders and practitioners know what they do, and to what extent any of it is creating changed outcomes—with consequences for work that consistently solicits the trust and patience of marginalized communities without delivering meaningful change in return. At the same time, transforming the current state of DEI work won't happen immediately, and we need to stay focused on the end goal without demanding perfection from every step required to get there.

This, in my opinion, is the next evolution of DEI work beyond simply "good intentions." It is DEI without the bells and whistles, boiled down to what is pragmatic, rigorous, and effective for solving challenges, changing outcomes, and achieving the impacts we need to.

I won't dress it up any more than that—I have no intention of selling "pragmatic DEI" as an exciting new thing to spice up your DEI work. To me, the explosive and growing interest in this industry and this work is nothing less than an existential threat. Either we all figure out how to do DEI and do it right, or this work implodes under the weight of its popularity and everyone doing it becomes irrevocably complicit in the inequitable status quo.

We DEI practitioners like to say that "intentions do not equal impact." It's time for us to face the music—that saying applies to us, as well. I have no interest in reading an article in a few years titled, "Your Company Started Talking About DEI. Here's How to Quit." If you don't either, then we have to collectively get our act together and do this work *right*.

TAKEAWAYS

- **DEI at present doesn't create the impact it promises**. Despite the long history of what many now call diversity, equity, and inclusion (DEI) (and many other related acronyms), much of this work has been demonstrated to have only a limited impact, not commensurate with the enormous financial investment in the industry.

- **DEI work is unaccountable and inconsistent**. While a wide range of work exists under the DEI umbrella, a lack of quality control, support, and accountability among the practitioners and advocates who undertake that work means that impacts can be inconsistent or nonexistent at best and actively harmful at worst.

- **Good intentions haven't moved the needle at scale.** Many change-making efforts in society are driven by positive intentions and result in high-visibility movements aimed at creating lasting change. However, inequity continues to be the status quo across the world, and important outcomes like rates of workplace discrimination have stayed persistently constant even as awareness and efforts to make change have increased.

- **Trust in DEI is tenuous as skepticism grows.** As change fails to materialize while the DEI industry becomes ever-more lucrative and high profile, critics increasingly speak of a DEI-Industrial Complex: an informal partnership between the DEI industry and organizations in which money flows but the status quo remains unchanged or even strengthened.

- **We can do better.** Pragmatically doing DEI work requires tempering hope for a better future with the accountability to take ownership for impacts in the present. By centering outcomes and focusing on gaining greater understanding and efficacy to make a change, we can collectively challenge the DEI-Industrial Complex by doing DEI right.

EXERCISES AND REFLECTIONS

1. How does your organization address DEI? Name as many initiatives, interventions, or commitments as you can (you can look them up if needed). How effective have these been in achieving what they were intended for? How do you know?

2. Write down a list of three DEI practices you've heard of before— any three. Then, imagine hearing that a DEI practitioner has been hired to implement each practice. Next to each practice on your

list, write a number from one to five to describe your reaction to
this news, with five being "extremely hopeful" and one being "not
hopeful at all." Reflect on your responses. Why did you answer the
way you did?

3. Name a DEI practice or intervention that you trust highly—you
believe that it's likely to result in positive outcomes when deployed.
Then, name a DEI practice or intervention that you *distrust*
highly—you're skeptical that it's likely to result in positive outcomes
when deployed. Why did you categorize those two practices or
interventions the way you did?

◾ TWO ◾

DEI Building Blocks

It didn't matter whether I was delivering a diversity 101 training or designing a new hiring process; inevitably, I'd get the same question in the engagement: "So what *is* DEI?" Easy answers ("DEI means diversity, equity, and inclusion") beget far more complicated questions.

"What counts as diversity?"

"Our titles are inherently different and 'unequal.' Does 'equity' mean demolishing our structure?"

"Is there anyone we *should* exclude, and how do we decide that?"

And on and on. Working with organizations eager to jump into DEI interventions is like this: no matter what angle you take, you always need to start from the same beginning or risk doing harm. I compare it to working with someone who wants to renovate their house by knocking down several load-bearing walls. You can tell them it's not the best idea, but you can't be certain they won't do it anyway unless they fully understand why. In Chapter 1, I wasted no time in laying out my thoughts on the urgency to do DEI work pragmatically and effectively and the many problems inherent in our industry. It was my hope that, even if you didn't have a firm understanding of what I meant every time I slung around the acronym or talked about "the work," you understood the point I was trying to make.

So thanks for your patience—I'll be explaining it from the top. A pragmatic approach to DEI is centered on achieving outcomes. With that grounding, we can start spelling out and deconstructing in plain language concepts that can often feel needlessly complex and contradictory and relating them to the outcomes that matter.

Equity

We're starting with the hardest term first. What is equity? To pick an existing definition, the University of Washington College of the Environment defines "equity" as:

> The fair treatment, access, opportunity, and advancement for all people, while at the same time striving to identify and eliminate barriers that prevent the full participation of some groups. The principle of equity acknowledges that there are historically underserved and underrepresented populations and that fairness regarding these unbalanced conditions is necessary to provide equal opportunities to all groups.[1]

Let's play with this definition for a little bit. Immediately, the word "fair" jumps out at me. What is "fair"? How do we determine "fairness"? Clearly, it's easy to determine examples that are *not* fair: getting prioritized for a promotion because you're friends with a manager isn't fair. Getting a larger raise than your colleague just because your boss likes you more isn't fair. It'd be easy to conclude that fairness is simply about treating everyone the same.

But take another few scenarios. You're taking a hiring test alongside another candidate, but they're red-green colorblind and can't parse the (inaccessible) illustration-dense instructions document. They request a new document using contrasting patterns rather than colors or additional black and white text explaining the charts. The proctor extends the candidate's test for an hour while they procure an updated document version. Was that fair, even though you didn't get the same extension? What if the other candidate showed up a few minutes late to the hiring test because their child felt ill and needed to be taken to the hospital? The candidate is clearly distressed and anxious, so the proctor decides to reschedule their hiring test for another day. Was that fair, even though the other candidate wasn't being treated in the same way as you?

Most people would say "yes" to these examples. Why? Because many people acknowledge that it is "fair" to give people the accommodations they need to succeed and that those accommodations may look different for different people in different circumstances.

What if the company had a policy that hiring test documents couldn't be reprinted or that hiring tests couldn't be rescheduled? Wouldn't those policies punish people for things out of their control? Even if they resulted in everyone being treated the same, would they be "fair"? Most people would say "no." This means that there's something more to fairness than simply equal treatment.

Let's return to the definition we're playing with. The next part is "striving to identify and eliminate barriers that prevent the full participation of some groups." This is very much an example of a "feel-good" definition that centers on intentions ("striving to identify and eliminate") rather than impacts ("eliminate"). The outcome, however, is a little odd—"full participation." Is this suggesting that participating in every meeting on a team while still facing enormous wage discrimination is "equity"? We can improve on this wording, which we'll do in a bit.

"The principle of equity acknowledges that there are historically underserved and underrepresented populations and that fairness regarding these unbalanced conditions is necessary to provide equal opportunities to all groups." This is a big mouthful. It seems like the definition itself is acknowledging that the "starting line" for different populations is different due to historic conditions. This is true: for example, the median wealth of Black families in the US in 2019 was $24,100, while for White families, it was $189,100—a direct and indirect consequence of slavery, segregation, and Jim Crow laws, and well-documented institutional racism continuing into the present day.[2]

But beyond acknowledging that people start at different places, the definition doesn't give much to work with. "Fairness regarding these unbalanced conditions is necessary." Vague, much? Is the definition suggesting that fairness can only be created if conditions are rebalanced in the present? Is it suggesting that fairness can look like treating different groups differently, and if so, how?

I have nothing against this particular definition—it may surprise you to know, however, that this is one of the better ones I could find. Many "good" definitions of equity do a few things: they acknowledge the presence of structural or systemic inequity in the present day, identify the long historical roots of these inequities, and set an intention to do their utmost to dismantle present-day barriers to achieve some standard of "fairness."

But lacking among all this is a clear understanding of what specific outcomes their good intentions are trying to create, and that lack of clarity means that most definitions out there boil down to "equity means trying to make things better." That's not good enough for our needs. Let's try to do one better.

Building on our earlier discussion of fairness, we've identified that it is "fair" to give people what they need, and that needs differ. Building on the precedent set by the sample definition, it also seems "fair" to dismantle historical and present-day barriers to success like discrimination and policies, processes, and practices that punish people for having different needs.

The result of meeting people's needs? At least when it comes to organizations and individuals, equity is achieved when everyone in an environment is thriving and set up for success.

Let's try and put this all together.

> **Equity** is the measured experience of individual, interpersonal, and organizational success and well-being across all stakeholder populations and the *absence* of discrimination, mistreatment, or abuse for all. Equity is achieved by eliminating structural barriers resulting from historical and present-day inequities and meeting individuals', groups', and organizations' unique needs.

So now we have two sets of outcomes: "the measured experience of individual, interpersonal, and organizational success and well-being across all stakeholder populations," and "the *absence* of discrimination, mistreatment, or abuse for all." In a workplace, it's relatively easy to know whether these outcomes have been achieved, too (though the bar for that is high), through employer-side metrics like retention, advancement, pay, hiring pass-through rate, and discrimination complaints; consumer-side metrics like trust, reputation, engagement, usage rates, and complaints; and other stakeholder metrics like social and environmental impacts.

And what's a stakeholder? Anyone who has a stake in what an organization does and how it operates. That includes employees, shareholders, executive boards, institutions and institutional investors, local communities, customers, and more. While we can interpret stakeholders to include virtually everyone in every society, different organizations will have different stakeholders most impacted by the organizations' actions—the key stakeholders of a nonprofit serving low-income urban communities will be dramatically different compared to the key stakeholders of a corporation whose services target other corporations with deep pockets.

Under this definition, equity is achieved through a particular strategy: "eliminating structural barriers resulting from historical and present-day inequities and meeting individuals', groups', and organizations' unique needs." This twofold acknowledgment thus encapsulates many existing definitions in the space while integrating a clear and unyielding focus on outcomes. Is this definition perfect? Far from it, but it's undoubtedly more functional and useful than others we've explored. It meets the minimum standard of knowing when we're getting it right.

Historical Barriers; Unique Needs

Thought I would get to "inclusion" or "diversity" next, did you? Before we get to those important terms, we need to unpack one of the phrases we used in our definition of "equity": "historical and present-day barriers and...unique needs." I could spend an entire book simply expanding on what this means. I'll give you the short version.

Some folks are satisfied when they hear a simple definition of DEI terms and sagely nod when they hear terms like "historical inequities." They may not know what is being referred to exactly, but they get the sense that it's something worth fixing. Others furrow their brows at the term and immediately start asking questions.

"Which inequities? What are they? For whom? Which still exist, and which have been resolved?"

All good questions. To answer these questions, we can draw on expertise spanning fields, including anthropology, history, sociology, public policy, political science, and race, gender, disability, and LGBTQ+ studies. And while the answers vary substantially in style by field of study, their substance is remarkably consistent. Turns out, in most societies around the world, there's pretty substantial overlap in which populations have been historically underserved, underrepresented, marginalized, and mistreated.

Women. Racial and ethnic minorities. Gender and sexual minorities. Religious minorities. Disabled people. Poor, old, and/or sick people.

People who are members of these groups and others, in more socie-ties than I can list, routinely experience persecution, marginalization, and discrimination, with few exceptions. They enjoy fewer legal rights; in some cases, their mistreatment is sanctioned or even encouraged by the law. They have less access to some or all areas of society. They are more frequently ostracized, targeted, looked down upon, or simply widely seen as inferior and treated accordingly, even by "benevolent" members of their societies. Importantly, their marginalization is built into core institutions in society, from healthcare to education, from law to policing, from business to social safety, from finance to housing, and everything in between. What this means is that, even as attitudes shift, systemic inequities with historical origins are unlikely to all resolve at the same pace. And thus, historical barriers predictably become present-day barriers along the same lines of marginalization—whether or not present-day people are even aware of them.

In general, the many common dimensions of inequity remain broadly constant across different societies. Don't let this trick you into thinking every society's issues are comparable, or that unique issues don't exist within individual societies. While gender-related disparities may exist in two different countries, they are likely to emerge from dif-ferent expectations, norms, and prescriptions for women and feminine people in those societies. While race-related disparities may exist in two different countries, different races may have different associations or stereotypes applied to them and face discrimination in differing ways depending on the history of racial and ethnic minorities in those countries. In the US, for example, understanding race-related systemic inequity requires an understanding of anti-Blackness, xenophobia, col-orism, Islamophobia, settler colonialism, imperialism, anti-Semitism, White supremacy, and many other complex concepts.

This book will not focus deeply on the many details associated with teasing apart every dimension of difference and inequity, and it's not from a lack of interest on my part. There's a part of me that wants to spend this entire book talking about the one-drop rule and blood quantum, reproductive justice, the social model of disability, cisnormativity, institutional ageism, and much more, but luckily, many authors other than myself do so effectively elsewhere. I highly recommend that you seek out learning on these many topics, as the more you know about marginalization and its history, the better equipped you are to achieve DEI outcomes. A short Reading List included in the resources section at the end of the book contains many of my personal recommendations for English-language resources to start with. Reading this list is *not* required to benefit from this book, but I would argue that the kind of deep content knowledge that lists like these scratch the surface of *is* required to do excellent, and not just good, DEI work. I strongly recommend engaging with it and other resources to supplement your efficacy as a practitioner and add valuable context when reading and rereading *DEI Deconstructed*.

Diversity

As far as basic definitions go, this term is relatively short and, at first, deceptively simple. Globaldiversitypractice.com defines it as:

> Any dimension that can be used to differentiate groups and people from one another.[3]

"Diversity" encompasses social identities like race, gender, ability, nationality, sexuality, religion, and age, as well as statuses including immigrant status, veteran status, parental status, income level, and many more. It includes other dimensions like introversion/extroversion, which region of your country you grew up in, your educational level, the shade of your skin, and many more characteristics. Essentially, "diversity" is everything that makes us different from each other.

But let's keep it real. You and I know that few people use this definition of diversity in practice. Think of the following sentences:

"Our company seeks to create a diverse workplace."

"This senior leadership team lacks diversity."

"We're hoping to diversify our workforce."

We both know that people aren't trying to say that "this senior leadership team lacks dimensions that can be used to differentiate people from one another." In many ways, that's impossible. Unless everyone went to the same school, has all the same social identities, same family backgrounds, same income levels, same way of problem-solving, and so on and so forth, there's virtually no way that a group can truly lack diversity in every way. But that's not what people are trying to say when they ask for more "diversity," is it?

If you're thinking what I'm thinking, then we'll say it on the count of three. One...two...

"WE NEED MORE PEOPLE WHO AREN'T (WHITE)[4] MEN."

This sentiment is all over social media. It's expressed over productivity platforms and emails; it's said in meeting rooms and at restaurants and bars after work. When many people say "diversity," in practice, they're often referring specifically to race, gender, and at times sexuality, disability, religion, and class. Why?

Well, this is why I made that aside about equity.

> Many people's de facto understanding of diversity rests on at least a surface-level understanding that "diversity" must aim to correct historical and present-day inequities.

In that sense, if an organization has only recently begun employing women and is still largely dominated by men, when stakeholders of that organization say "diversity," they will reference that inequity.

If an organization's enduring racial discrimination and anti-Asian attitudes drive Asian employees to quit, when stakeholders of that organization say "diversity," they will reference that inequity.

And in a society, if issues of race or gender, caste, class, religion, and disability are more salient or visible or widely understood? Then when people in that society say "diversity," they will reference those inequities.

We must work with this emergent, situational, and complex definition of diversity rather than the simplified version of "any dimension of difference" as we're creating our new outcome-oriented definitions. If we don't, we risk coming up with something that only *appears* useful— something like, "Diversity is measured by the presence of dimensions of difference."

Can you imagine that? Employees calling for more diversity, and corporate leaders responding with, "Well, Jim worked in Germany for a year, and I haven't, so that's diversity?" Yeah, well, get your chuckles out. I've been told that once.

If we're trying to make "diversity" outcome oriented and reflective of how many people understand and use the term, we have to ensure that we find some way to integrate the fact that what "diversity" requires necessarily varies by society, according to historical and present-day inequities.

We also need to grapple with the fact that people calling for greater diversity in an environment often want better representation not for its own sake but out of a belief that this will change the outcomes experienced by underrepresented groups on a wider scale. Is this true? This is a question that, thankfully, has a clear answer well-supported by social science research: *yes*, at least when it comes to race and gender.[5] Homogenous groups are more prone to make mistakes and converge in their thinking—a process called groupthink[6]—while more diverse groups are more rigorous in their decision-making and make decisions that are more effective for more groups of people. And when organizations gain more diversity, especially among their senior leadership, biased language elsewhere in the organization decreases.[7] Now, can most people calling for greater diversity directly cite social science research supporting their claims? Probably not. They're often advocating from a more proximal desire: the frustrating feeling of looking up and not seeing someone like them in a leadership position and suffering from decisions that were clearly made with other people in mind.

There's an interesting flipside to this fact, however: *it's quite possible to have representation in the form of demographic diversity that even people with the same social identities don't feel represented by.* Not just possible, by the way. Common. It's called "tokenism," or when an organization puts people with the same surface-level attributes as an aggrieved group in leadership positions to give the appearance that they care about this group's needs, with no intention of actually doing anything differently after the fact.[8] Said another way by Black author Zora Neale Hurston, "skinfolk ain't kinfolk"[9]—simply sharing an identity doesn't make someone accountable to the needs of your community.

Many of us can speak to the feeling of seeing someone who might be like us in a leadership position but struggling to articulate why we don't feel glad to see their face. Maybe it's a single woman leader whose sole talking point around gender is to "lean in," with no regard for the many systemic and structural barriers to gender parity. Maybe it's one LGBTQ+ person who believes that queer and trans people should be "respectable" and hide their identities and has little sympathy for those who don't, won't, or can't. Maybe it's a disabled person who frequently puts the burden of well-being on disabled people themselves to "try harder" rather than on the organization to make itself accessible.

In all these senses, diversity is about not the simple "presence" of difference in a given environment but rather the felt experience of being "seen" or "represented" by those in the environment for their

difference, especially when it comes to historical and present-day dimensions of inequality.

Putting these ideas together?

> **Diversity** is the workforce composition that all stakeholders,
> especially underserved and marginalized populations, trust
> to be representative and accountable. Diversity is achieved
> through actions that explicitly counter present-day and histor-
> ical inequities and meet the unique needs of all populations.

This definition is a little controversial—not least because it's on its
face more complex than what we started with, but primarily because
it suggests that achieving diversity under this definition requires more
than simply upping an organization's hiring numbers, perhaps *the* most
widely deployed "diversity strategy" in the DEI space. It also takes the
step of acknowledging the presence of "underserved and marginalized
populations" as key stakeholders whose seal of approval is required to
achieve diversity as a goal. Even if these stakeholders are a numerical
minority, the increasing power and authority their voice holds in the
DEI conversation make attaining their trust critical.

The trust of many stakeholder groups, not just one or two, is required
for an organization to genuinely consider itself "diverse." If a board of
directors of seven people adds two seats to bring on two women, and
those two women trust that the group will help them feel heard and
enabled, is that board of directors "diverse" by gender? Not until employees think so. Not until institutional investors think so. Not until the
general public thinks so. In most parts of the world, they are unlikely to
think so until representation more or less reaches parity: 50–50 gender
representation, or close to it.

Why didn't I just say that diversity equals representational parity—where the demographics of a group are proportional to the

demographics of broader stakeholder communities? Honestly, I thought about it. It's not a bad proxy, and we'd be better off if every company aimed for representation that paralleled exactly the demographic makeup of its region or country. But if companies achieved representational parity somehow by hiring only people who weren't accountable to their communities, calls for "true diversity" would simply continue. And if a team of three people aimed for representational racial parity, it would be quite literally impossible to achieve; yet, many small teams are able to earn the label of "diverse" or "representative" without literally representing every social group imaginable. Why is it that a leadership team of two White people and two non-White people, two of them men and two of them women, with one of them LGBTQ+, might still be accused of needing "more diversity," while a leadership team with nominally less representational parity might not?

It's *trust*, **often achieved through representational parity but not always requiring it, that dictates whether we consider a given entity "diverse."** If a diverse and varied group of stakeholders trust the organization and its leaders to represent and advocate for them, the actual minutia of demographic representation percentages doesn't matter as much as we might think.

I find this idea intriguing because it completely overturns traditional narratives and the "rules of the game" in the DEI industry related to achieving diversity. Everything you read when you search "How do I diversify my company?" online is about putting butts in seats. You'll find a plethora of advice talking about hiring pipelines, visibility campaigns, and, frankly, how to engage in a somewhat cynical effort to make "diversity hires" out of unwitting candidates with underserved or marginalized identities to appease the critics.[10] Aside from it being a generally terrible strategy for making the candidates you hire feel valued, this framing utterly abandons small companies, shrinking companies, and companies that don't hire often. "If your status quo isn't diverse and you don't completely replace your workforce," says this narrative, "you will never achieve diversity."

I don't know about you, but I prefer to think that success is always possible.

"I'm trying to make my first hire, and I don't know what to do," one founder told me. Like many founders of start-ups in the US, he was a White man—but unlike many founders, he was thinking proactively about DEI from the start. "I know I should hire a woman, but I don't know if she should be Black. Or Asian American?" He threw his hands up in the air. "How do I find the nearest LGBTQ, non–Ivy League graduate, disabled, non-White immigrant woman with the skills I'm looking for by this time next month?!" he asked incredulously, half-joking. I gave him a disapproving look, but chuckled along with him. We both knew that this wasn't the right way to think about it.

"Think about it differently," I said. "It's not about identities to check off on a list. Instead, ask yourself the following: 'What communities am I able to build trust with that are important for the success of my start-up? Which of these communities am I less able to reach, and what kind of person might reach them?' Add those as additional critéria to the technical ones in your head—that will help guide your decisions."

"What if the person I bring on doesn't reach every community that I can't at once?"

"Then you have some clue about how to consider your second and third hires. You're not trying to hire the 'perfect diverse person'—you're trying to create a diverse organization."

So let's say you're trying to follow this advice. In some ways, the new goal post of "a demographic composition that all populations trust as representative and accountable" is both easier and harder to reach than the old goal of representative parity. Achieving representational parity often requires that organizations fully solve problems far larger than themselves, from the talent pipeline and its roots in education, access, and industry to the last-mile problem of getting a 55–45 gender split to a 50–50 one. If "trust" becomes the new indicator, then a 55–45 gender split would be good enough if stakeholders believed it so.

On the flip side, if "trust" becomes the new indicator, then there's a chance that even with a 50–50 gender mix, stakeholders aren't happy.

It's not as rare as you might think. A senior executive team brings in a number of women and non-White people to fill new roles, but they're people with existing strong ties to the current leadership team and satisfied with enabling, not changing, the status quo. Conditions don't change—and these new members have no problem being used as shields against accusations of homogeneity. If we're only defining diversity as representational parity, then has the leadership team in this example achieved diversity? Yes, technically. And this exact failure mode is the problem with defining diversity solely in terms of representational parity. We over-focus on the identities that people bring to the table as boxes to check rather than focusing on the actions these people take and the outcomes they're able to achieve. In my experience, it's possible for a team that is majority White to create a workplace in which non-White people feel seen and heard by their leadership. In my experience, it's possible for a team that is entirely made of women to create a workplace in which women still *don't* feel seen and heard by their leadership.

This is what's happening when people ask for "more diversity" in environments that, at least on their surface, already "look diverse." They're not asking for more boxes to be checked. They're asking for a team that, partially by dint of its diversity but not only because of it, successfully earns and maintains their trust. Their possessing a diverse demographic composition is one part of the answer, but not all of it. The rest?

Inclusion

I'll be honest, out of all the terms in the DEI acronym used colloquially in the industry, "inclusion" is by far my least favorite.

Ideal.com's definition:

Inclusion is the extent to which various team members, employees, and other people feel a sense of belonging and value within a given organizational setting.[11]

Okay, well. What's "belonging?"

Cornell University's definition:

Belonging is the feeling of security and support when there is a sense of acceptance, inclusion, and identity for a member of a certain group.[12]

This isn't getting us anywhere. How about definitions from research?

Turns out, nothing conclusive. Most efforts to define "inclusion" simply ask survey participants what the nebulous term means to them and generalize their responses into something snappy.[13] This means, however, that there are as many different definitions of "inclusion" as there are efforts to define it. Some of these definitions, compiled by a K4D helpdesk report in the following unwieldy paragraph (line breaks added for clarity), follow:

Inclusion involves utilizing difference to benefit the organization.

Inclusion embraces the concepts of awareness, acceptance, respect, and understanding. Inclusion is defined by equal opportunity for participation. Each individual must be valued for his or her distinctive skills, experiences, and perspectives. Inclusion is also about creating a global community.

Inclusion within organizations involves fostering an environment that allows people with different backgrounds, characteristics, and ways of thinking, to work effectively together and fulfill their potential. To achieve an inclusive culture, people must feel valued, listened to and respected.

Inclusiveness is an environment that maximizes the diversity of all employees.

Inclusion involves organizational practices that ensure that the backgrounds of different groups or individuals are culturally and socially accepted, welcomed, and equally treated. For individuals within an organization, inclusion is a sense of belonging based on respect and being valued.

Inclusion for organizations is driven from grassroots, but steered from the top.

Inclusive leaders must challenge biases whilst being aware of their own unconscious biases. They must take responsibility for inclusion and hold all employees accountable for inclusion in the workplace.

For inclusion to work, organizations must create an atmosphere that espouses supportive energy and commitment. Individuals must be engaged and valued.[14]

This is, to put it lightly, a complete dumpster fire of definitions.

Some of these definitions define inclusion as what seems like a strategy of "utilizing difference," "embracing concepts," "creating a global community," and "driven from grassroots but steered from the top." But does that mean that simply trying to achieve these goals is enough for an organization to be considered inclusive, whether or not it succeeds? And, for that matter, is success in these definitions even possible if it's never defined?

Some of these definitions seem centered on a tangible outcome but disagree wildly on what that outcome is. "An environment that maximizes the diversity of all employees"? Sounds wildly illegal and not necessarily useful. "An atmosphere that espouses supportive energy and commitment"? Espouse all the supportive energy you want, but it's naive to think that alone creates inclusion.

The most believable outcome present among these definitions can be distilled to roughly the following: "an environment in which a demographically diverse workforce can work effectively together and fulfill their potential." Essentially, when demographic diversity is able to exist in a space free of mistreatment and connected through intentional efforts to create mutual respect, engagement, empowerment, and feelings of value, people and the organization all benefit.

This is enough to build on and connect to our first definition of diversity:

> **Diversity** is the workforce composition that all stakeholders, especially underserved and marginalized populations, trust to be representative and accountable. Diversity is achieved through actions that explicitly counter present-day and historical inequities and meet the unique needs of all populations.

The trust of demographically diverse populations, as we've explored, isn't just achieved through the presence of people with certain social identities. From the "inclusion" definitions, it seems like there's something about the environment of the workplace itself that creates positive outcomes and, through these outcomes, fosters trust. We can then establish "inclusion" as having a related definition to "diversity":

> **Inclusion** is the achievement of an environment that all stakeholders, especially underserved and marginalized populations, trust to be respectful and accountable. Inclusion is achieved through actions that explicitly counter present-day and historical inequities and meet the unique needs of all populations.

This definition of inclusion centers on the relationship between people and their environment. To achieve inclusion at work, all groups must feel like the workplace is one in which they are valued and respected—an outcome measured through metrics like engagement, well-being, access to decision-making, net promoter score, and more. To create these outcomes for a diverse range of groups, organizations need to counter inequities and meet a wide range of unique needs.

By integrating the idea of trust into this definition, we make space for the overwhelming plurality of definitions and strategies for achieving inclusion in the DEI space: any strategy for achieving inclusion is valid if it results in the outcome of stakeholders trusting that an environment is respectful and accountable. This is where achieving inclusion is in many ways harder than achieving diversity or equity. Equity is about enabling individual and organizational success, often through policy, structure, and process that eliminate barriers. Diversity is about enabling trust through having the right mix of people present. Inclusion is about enabling trust through everything else—the intangibles of modern organizations like organizational culture, interpersonal norms, employee well-being, and so much more.

Everything Else

Okay, okay, I'm being a little tongue-in-cheek here. There are many other terms that are important, as well. But, if you've made it this far, you've parsed some of the most complex and complicated challenges in understanding and conceptualizing DEI. Together, we've deconstructed three terms that are arguably far more complicated than they need to be and reformulated them as outcome-oriented definitions that are deeply interrelated.

Equity is the achievement of structural success, well-being, and enablement for stakeholder populations, including employees, customers, institutional investors, leaders, and local communities.

Diversity is the achievement of a workforce composition that stakeholder populations trust and feel represented by on all levels.

Inclusion is the achievement of a felt environment that stakeholder populations trust as respectful and accountable.

Achieving any of these requires a strategy that dismantles historical inequities and meets people's unique needs.

From this point onward, because these terms serve as such a strong foundation, we can easily slot in and relate other DEI terms to what we already know—because every other term is a way to conceptualize some aspect of diversity, equity, or inclusion work, a strategy for achieving them as outcomes, or a metric to further contextualize their outcomes. See for yourself:

Allyship. A strategy to achieve any DEI outcome whereby people possessing socially advantaged identities utilize those advantaged identities to create change.

Belonging. The extent to which people feel part of a larger whole in a group setting.[15] It's a metric by which we measure inclusion.

Bias. A tendency (intentional or not) toward certain people, groups, ideas, or outcomes.

- **Unconscious/Implicit Bias:** Bias in individual thinking. Unconscious bias is a proxy metric[16] to measure diversity, equity, or inclusion.

- **Structural Bias:** Bias in processes, policies, or practices. Structural bias is a metric by which we measure equity.

Intersectionality. An analytical perspective in which different dimensions of identity, difference, and inequity (e.g., race, class, gender, ability, sexuality, etc.) are considered concurrently. A key goal of intersectional analyses is understanding how different combinations—or intersections—of dimensions yield different experiences that expose nuances in larger patterns of inequity and inform future action.[17] It's often used in strategies to achieve diversity, equity, and inclusion.

Marginalized / Minoritized / Disadvantaged / Underserved Population. A group sharing an identity, experience, or attribute that has lesser power and endures greater hardship in an environment as a result of those identities, experiences, or attributes. Individuals may be a part of multiple such groups, as well as privileged groups, simultaneously. The concept is often used as a way to conceptualize key constituents.

Microaggression. "Small," often interpersonal or subtle act of exclusion[18] or discrimination. It's a metric by which we measure inclusion, often reversed, so the relative presence of microaggressions indicates the relative lack of inclusion.

Organizational Culture. The underlying beliefs, assumptions, values, expectations, and ways of thinking and doing that drive the behavior of people within an organization. The concept is often used as a way to conceptualize and describe teams, groups, and organizations, as well as inform strategy.

Power. The ability to decide, define, influence, or change outcomes of any kind on individual, interpersonal, or organizational levels. The concept is often used as a way to strategize with key constituents.

Privileged / Majoritized / Advantaged / Overserved Population. A group sharing an identity, experience, or attribute that has greater power and endures lesser hardship in an environment as a result of those identities, experiences, or attributes. Individuals may be a part of multiple such groups, as well as marginalized groups, simultaneously. The concept is often used as a way to conceptualize key constituents.

Psychological Safety. The individual, team, or organization-level belief that a given environment is safe for interpersonal risk-taking, vulnerability, and failure.[19] It's a metric by which we measure inclusion.

If there's a word or a term that I didn't cover here that you're familiar with, try placing it in the context of these new definitions of diversity, equity, and inclusion as outcomes. That we have these concepts as a compass to return to makes it possible to dispense with the long list of definitions (and the tiresome process of constantly learning new definitions for their own sake) so endemic to this work and focus instead on how we can contextualize and operationalize new definitions to get to the "doing" part faster.

It's About What You Don't Do

There's a reason why I didn't begin this book with a list of descriptions, and it's not because I enjoy making things hard for myself. Most people who are eager to begin learning about DEI fixate on definitions, and I mean *fixate*. Tell them that "diversity" has anything to do with hiring, and they'll run off to tell their hiring managers to find the nearest Black candidate. Tell them that "equity" has anything to do with pay, and they'll immediately turn to the nearest woman and ask her if she's disappointed with her salary. Tell them that "inclusion" has anything to do with respect, and they'll rush to promise the gay employee they know that during Pride Month this year, they'll be *extra nice*.

Ugh. I'm getting stressed thinking about it.

The point I'm trying to make is that incomplete knowledge can be far more dangerous than no knowledge at all, and when DEI work involves such high stakes as people's employment, wellness, and survival, it's imperative that we act carefully around knowledge acquisition.

I did my best, at least. I pushed the terms and definitions all the way to Chapter 2.

It should be clear to you, even just from looking at how much of the book there is left to read, that we are far from done talking about DEI. But surely, the rest of this book can't be more definitions? It's not. How about some actionable advice for putting these definitions into practice? There will be some, but we'll be doing much more than that. No, the rest of this book is dedicated to the sort of deep knowledge that sets effective practitioners apart from DEI hobbyists: the knowledge of not just what DEI work *is* but also just what it *isn't*.

This is what researchers call **negative expertise**: knowledge and awareness of what to avoid that typically comes from direct experience but can be learned from the experiences of others.[20] As children, we may learn that hot items are not for touching, for example, precisely from having touched hot objects and learned. If we drive cars, we may discover that it is just as important to know what to *not* do on a rainy day when the car hydroplanes as it is to know what *to* do. It's the accumulation of this kind of knowledge that makes experts true experts, not because they know everything there is to know about a topic, but because they know how to avoid major mistakes, the areas where their own expertise is lacking, the value of failure in revealing new possibilities, and how to "unlearn," or compartmentalize, existing knowledge to make space for new ways of thinking and doing.[21]

Without the jargon?

In a situation where a leader is trying to diversify their team, an enthusiastic but inexperienced advocate might start looking up professional organizations serving disadvantaged communities, for which their team lacks representation.

If they had more negative expertise, they might know that these organizations aren't likely to want to build relationships with companies without a good track record on DEI. Investing money into recruiting in this way is a waste of time and resources. They might know that even in the unlikely event of success, hastily hired candidates are unlikely to remain with a team that doesn't look or act like them without significant changes to the team's culture, process, and practice. They might know these things and decide that the first step to changing team demographics isn't hiring but addressing culture, structure, and strategy.

If you want to become a pragmatic and effective DEI practitioner or advocate, you *must* gain negative expertise and understand how to apply it in practice. In other words, you need to know how things most frequently go wrong before you can meaningfully know how to get them right. In my experience, the most common failure modes can be summed up by the failure to answer or align on just five key questions:

1. **"What are we trying to achieve through DEI work?"** When those doing the work don't share the same understanding of the objective they're trying to create, the work fails. Is the goal a new coat of paint over the same house or a different structure altogether?

2. **"What ought we do for our employees, customers, and the world?"** When perceptions of responsibility differ between those doing the work, the work fails. DEI undertaken in service of shareholder profit only is a different beast than DEI undertaken to meet customers' needs or DEI undertaken to be a responsible steward of the world.

3. **"What is the role of power and the powerful in making a change?"** When strategies regarding the role of powerful people clash between those doing the work, the work fails. If some people believe that the role of leaders is to sit back and let grassroots

movements take the lead and others believe that leaders should be at the forefront of the work, that conflict can undermine efforts entirely.

4. **"How should we approach identity and difference?"** When people's beliefs about the role of identity in DEI and change work differ, the work fails. Identity-denying DEI work ("I don't see race") rarely coexists with identity-centric DEI work ("race is my primary lens to analyze problems and formulate change").

5. **"What does the work look like when it's done effectively?"** When people's expectations about the practice and process of DEI work misalign, the work fails. If some people believe that DEI is a linear path of organizational change; others believe that DEI is an antagonistic battle between opposing camps; others believe that DEI is a political process of negotiations, coalitions, and bargaining; and still others believe that DEI is an emergent or an "organic" process that should be left on its own, the focus and momentum required to do the work disintegrates.

I've found that these are the questions that every engagement with DEI eventually boils down to, regardless of the challenge being addressed. They reflect the deepest anxieties people have about DEI work, fundamental philosophies regarding the work and its delivery, and some of the longstanding unsolved challenges in our field. I've seen folks try to ignore these questions and focus on "easier" questions of tactics and interventions. I think it should be the other way around. We figure these five things out, and everything else falls into place. Let me show you.

TAKEAWAYS

- **DEI definitions should be centered on outcomes, not intentions.** Aspirational outcomes rooted in intentions are too abstract and vague for shared interpretation or, more importantly, consistent execution to achieve outcomes.

- **DEI, defined in terms of outcomes, refers to an organization's demographic composition, structural success, and built environment.** Achieving DEI in any form requires a strategy that dismantles historical inequities and meets people's unique needs, building, leveraging, and maintaining stakeholder trust.

- **All DEI concepts can be contextualized in relation to these core definitions.** If the broader objective is to achieve diversity, equity, and inclusion, other concepts outline challenges to doing so, detail specifics concerning these objectives, and describe stakeholders involved in achieving them.

- **Knowing what *not* to do is key.** To become an effective DEI practitioner, the most valuable piece of learning is not just what works but also what *doesn't* work and why. This negative expertise is gained by experience, especially firsthand experience.

- **Five questions encompass many of the common failure modes that impede effective DEI work.** These questions are: "What are we trying to achieve through DEI work?" "What ought we do for our employees, customers, and the world?" "What is the role of power and the powerful in making a change?" "How should we approach identity and difference?" and "What does the work look like when it's done effectively?"

EXERCISES AND REFLECTIONS

1. How does your organization, or an organization you're familiar with, define diversity, equity, and inclusion? Which aspects of these definitions feel most clear and straightforward to you, and which raise more questions or feel confusing to interpret?

2. If asked to teach or explain "the most important DEI definitions" to someone else, what definitions would you choose, and how would you sum them up? Which definitions would be most challenging for you to explain?

3. Recall (some of) the many dimensions of difference: race, gender identity and expression, sexuality, age, (dis)ability, religion, nationality, class, and size. Everyone has a more comprehensive or intimate knowledge of some of these dimensions than others. If you were to name one or two dimensions you know relatively more about and one or two you know relatively less about, which would these be? Why?

4. Recall the common failure modes of DEI:

   · Misalignment around the objective of the work

   · Differing perceptions of organizational responsibility to stakeholders

   · Differing strategies for the role of leaders with formal power

   · Competing beliefs about the role of social identity

   · Diverging expectations for the trajectory of the work itself

   Which of these conflicts and failure modes have you seen before?

◼ THREE ◼

To What End?

My first foray into corporate DEI work was a humiliating culture shock experience. Having gained much of my DEI experience up until that point in higher education, I hadn't realized that something as funda- mental as "why we do DEI work" was a contentious topic. In my mind, the "why" was as simple as "it's the right thing to do," and from that starting point, we could then focus on the challenges of actually mak- ing change.

But the executive I spoke to, a sales leader in the organization I was doing DEI stakeholder research in, was unimpressed by that rationale.

"I'm a numbers person," he said. "So help me understand this with numbers. You're saying I should be going out of my way to make sure my organization is an 'inclusive environment,' which, by the way, it already is. No one has a problem with things—I can tell you that. All to do what, hire a few more women or minorities?"

He looked at me like he was expecting an answer, then continued regardless. "Tell me what I can expect to get for that investment."

I wish I could say I had a comeback ready and waiting, but I didn't. I froze and could feel my face start to redden. Eventually, I stammered out something about research on greater productivity and innovation for diverse teams and promised to send him a few papers.

"Do that," he said and looked at his smartwatch for his next meeting—because he had already mentally clocked out of ours.

This story still frustrates me today when I recall it. Not simply because I now have the "numbers" to retort—both collections of research[1] and prominent McKinsey reports[2]—but also because the fact that such a conversation could have happened, and is so immediately recognizable by many DEI practitioners, is proof that we've lost our grip on the core rationale of this work, a rationale we can trace all the way back to the US Civil Rights Movement.

Tell me, how could we have gotten from this:

> We are confronted primarily with a moral issue. It is as old as the scriptures, and it is as clear as the American Constitution. The heart of the question is whether all Americans are afforded equal rights and equal opportunities, whether we are going to treat our fellow Americans as we want to be treated. [O]ne hundred years of delay have passed since President Lincoln freed the slaves, yet their heirs, their grandsons, are not fully free. They are not yet free from the bonds of injustice. And this nation, for all its hopes and all its boasts, will not be fully free until all of its citizens are free.
> —President John F. Kennedy, Civil Rights Address, 1963[3]

To this:

> Diversity and inclusion are key business outcomes that will enable innovation, increase productivity, and ultimately support our bottom line. When we can all bring our authentic selves to the workplace, each and every one of us, that itself is a return on investment, and an indication that we've truly built a culture of inclusion and belonging on top of a solid foundation of equity.
> —Adapted from a large organization, 2021

I see these statements, read them again to make sure I understand the jargon, and sigh. My inner cynic rolls their eyes. Sometimes, I start wondering what advocates and activists fighting for and building a better world twenty-five, fifty, and a hundred years ago would think about these kinds of messages.

I imagine that they'd be unimpressed—that they'd shake their heads and ask piercing questions that all the fancy PR in the world can't dodge. "Are any of your workers being discriminated against? Are all your workers being paid what they're worth? Are all your workers supported, satisfied, and safe? Do they go to sleep at night feeling relaxed about their financial well-being and stability?"

I use these questions as a litmus test and try to dig past the inspirational language to find answers. More often than not, I find myself disappointed by what I find, the fact that actions so infrequently align with words, and that the outcomes I'm looking for are so often missing. *It's almost as if the people "doing this work" have forgotten what we're fighting for,* I think.

Well, it's time for a reminder. I've taken you through an exploration of the major terms we should use in this work, but not the legacy behind them. There's a reason why the DEI industry today is a hodgepodge of practitioners and methodologies more different than alike; this is called **path dependence**: we are what we are today because of what we were before.[4] If you want to be able to look out into the vast sea of DEI work in the present with a discerning eye and do better, you need to understand how it all got there, what it's trying to achieve, and why those intentions, after so long, still haven't materialized into outcomes.

In this chapter, I'll walk you through a brief history, with commentary, of what we now call DEI work in the US and talk you through some of the many branching paths that led to the fractured state of present-day practitioners. I focus on the US in this history because, for better or worse, much of the approach to "global" DEI work is informed by the US DEI industry, and variations of DEI work around the world nevertheless import or are inspired by interventions and tactics from the US.

There's a point I want to make with this history: what we now call the "DEI industry" is precisely the result of decades' worth of push and pull between the forces of accountability and avoidance, morals and profits, transparency and opacity, and hope and cynicism. I'll show how every major effort to make DEI and its predecessors accountable, centered on the people experiencing injustice and genuinely impactful, has been countered by efforts to prevent and undo that progress, and modern DEI is no exception. Unless we explicitly protect against these counter-efforts, our present-day DEI work will be sucked into the same false promises of intentions without accountability, flashy performance over nuance and effectiveness, and polarizing, demoralizing, and unproductive conflict. We don't have the luxury of repeating the worst parts of our industry's history this time around. That means it's on us to avoid making our predecessors' mistakes.

Early Encounters

The first instance of proto-DEI work emerged from the work of Kurt Lewin, a German American psychologist, in the form of a small-group workshop called an **encounter group** or t-group (the "t" stood for "training").[5] Employing minimally facilitated conversations intended to use interpersonal conflict to elicit reflection among participants, the encounter group model made its way into the mainstream in the 1960s when it landed in the hands of George Leonard, a White psychologist from the South, and Price Cobbs, a Black psychiatrist, who hoped to use the model to address racial tension.[6] Leonard and Cobbs organized many workshops between White and Black participants using encounter groups hoping to use the tool to pursue racial awareness and reconciliation—including an infamous one in 1967 lasting an astonishing twenty-four hours, in which witnesses reported a chaotic environment where interracial friendships dissolved and all parties experienced heightened levels of distress.[7] Leonard and Cobbs, however, saw the potential for racial reconciliation in this experience and began galvanizing many others to adopt encounter groups as a primary tool in what would be called "racial sensitivity training."

Recall the period. That year in the US, the anti-war movement was raging, the Civil Rights Movement was in full swing, and Dr. Martin Luther King Jr. had announced the Poor People's Campaign in the hopes of uniting poor and disenfranchised Americans of all colors, creeds, and religions. Racial encounter groups, with their ethos of vulnerability and shared growth, were largely seen as embodying the spirit of the times.[8]

Ironically, or perhaps for cynics, unsurprisingly, the assassination of Dr. King only a year later coincided with the widespread adoption of encounter groups throughout corporate America, government, and institutions. Why? One theory is that, in the context of widespread riots, fury, and discontent following Dr. King's murder, racial encounter groups stood out as "safe" ways to help majority-White organizations process the feelings of Black America.[9] Another postulates that encounter groups were simply the trendy fad of the time, and organizations needed a convenient way to proactively fulfill the new affirmative action executive orders pushed by Presidents Kennedy, Johnson, and Nixon—or reactively comply with Equal Employment Opportunity Commission (EEOC) mandates to address racial discrimination.[10] Regardless of the reasons for their popularity following the Civil Rights Movement, racial encounter groups starred prominently in efforts to change race/intergroup relations during the 1970s, most notably in an ambitious effort undertaken by the US Department of Defense to create a race relations training program for more than a million personnel.[11]

The Rise and Fall of Racial Sensitivity Training

Like most American institutions, the US military had been tasked with formally desegregating and integrating their organizations since the 1940s. However, the Civil Rights Movement brought persistent inequities to the forefront of American consciousness, with interracial tensions and conflict remaining high after the close of the 1960s. This was the case within the US military, as it was in many organizations during this time, due to a widespread understanding that the so-called equal opportunities in military provisions did not translate to equity in practice. After a destructive riot at the Travis Air Force Base, the military moved to enact the most comprehensive race relations program any US institution had ever seen.[12]

The race relations training program at the US military, developed by the Defense Race Relations Institute (DRRI), was nothing to scoff at when it came to size. It was intended to train military personnel to become race relations instructors (later called equal opportunity officers) and thus invested a sizable amount of time and resources in their education. The first iteration of the program involved a combined 235 hours of planned activities spread across seven weeks, covering instruction on the history and sociocultural factors related to interracial relations, community interaction activities, guest speakers, group leadership and dynamics training, and practice using critical analysis. It was later modified to append another six-week "Phase 2" program focused on problem-solving, communication, and taking action to deal with the issues participants might face in their new roles, and then later modified again to incorporate new material on organizational development, sexism, anti-Semitism, and cross-cultural subjects.

The program created extraordinarily well-informed advocates for racial equity. But almost immediately, graduates of this program faced enormous challenges trying to implement what they learned. White participants they worked with, whether within encounter groups or through other discussion- and instruction-related techniques, widely resented what they felt were attempts to label them as "racists" and heavy-handed confrontational techniques. One such technique used by some trainers, called Racial Awareness Training, interrogated White participants in "hot seats" about their beliefs to help them more quickly realize (and ideally, cast off) their own prejudices.[13] Unsurprisingly, these tactics generated significant conflict—but surprisingly, trainers were wholly unprepared for it. Workshops that spiraled out of control, with participants feeling threatened and attacking the training and its trainers, frequently failed to resolve on a positive note—perhaps foreshadowing responses to modern DEI initiatives that readers may be familiar with. As H. R. Day notes, "in the field, with less well-trained instructors and with considerably less time to work through any hostilities generated, the approach bordered on disaster."[14]

This backlash to not only the Racial Awareness Training tool but also the graduates of the race relations training program who used these techniques forced significant changes to the program.[15] Following this tumultuous start, decision-makers began reigning back the reach of the program, claiming that DRRI trainers and their training were undermining the authority of unit commanders. The military thus pushed hard for race relations, or as it was later reframed "equal opportunity training," to be swiftly integrated into the chain of command. Training began to be led by unit commanders, none of whom were trained by the DRRI, with graduates of the program serving only as advisors to these commanders. The controversial techniques were pruned back—along with the useful techniques, too. Over time, equal opportunity training shrank and eventually was assimilated into other programs regarding "social problems" like drug and alcohol abuse.[16]

Did the original goals of this program, to create an environment in which differences were treated respectfully, with group cohesion emerging stronger for it, ever materialize? It's hard to answer this question, not least because the training institute that developed the program was *explicitly prohibited from assessing training effectiveness.* We can only speculate as to why. Perhaps leaders couldn't decide on what "success" looked like and were scared of those conversations getting out of hand. Perhaps the program, like its many modern-day descendants, was always meant to be more about the effort than the outcome. Regardless, the few post hoc analyses conducted on these training programs over the following eleven years are the only window we have into these programs' real effectiveness, and their findings are valuable:

1. The involvement of leadership, which in the military's case was commanders at all levels, *did* directly increase the attendance and involvement of participants.[17]

2. When DRRI-trained instructors felt that their mission was being compromised after being put on the sidelines, they were more likely to feel a lower sense of self-efficacy, burn out, and experience high levels of occupational stress.

3. Looking at changes occurring after two years of the program, Black participants saw few differences in their experience of discrimination, but White participants' perception of discrimination decreased. *In other words, the intervention's largest effect was to make White participants more oblivious to continuing inequity without reducing the inequity itself.*[18]

4. As increasing numbers of people perceived the race relations training as a "paper program" and a bureaucratic formality, the racial climate steadily declined while race-related tensions persisted or rose.

In other words, involving leadership increased participation, but greater participation didn't result in greater program effectiveness. Trainer burnout was common. And at the end of the day, the watering-down of the program due to backlash completely negated any positive impact the program could have had.

I want to make sure you understand the sobering implications of this. One of the largest, most well-resourced DEI efforts ever undertaken, utilizing trainers with hundreds of hours of experience, failing to create the outcomes it was built for—or perhaps even making them worse? With such a disappointing show, surely these efforts were taken back to the drawing board to be reevaluated and redesigned, right?

Not at all. What did happen was that the Racial Awareness Training model was exported wholesale to the UK, where it became the starting basis of DEI efforts there.[19] The US military would not significantly change and remains to this day a powerful example of racial inequity's tenaciousness against efforts to erase it—and the enormous challenge facing well-meaning DEI practitioners looking to do good.[20]

With this story as the backdrop, the 1970s nevertheless saw the birth of the proto-DEI industry. As the newly commissioned EEOC began accepting discrimination claims and finding organizations culpable for racial, and later gender, discrimination, it would often prescribe mandatory sensitivity training as a remedy. Overnight, the need for trainers, facilitators, educators, and experts skyrocketed, and the parameters for the "typical" sensitivity training—a one- to four-hour-long training focusing on do's, don'ts, and legal compliance, began emerging.[21]

White workers across the country, like those in the US military, resented it enormously. They resented it as a mandatory interruption of their workday. They resented being told or even hearing it implied that they had done something wrong and that they had problems that needed fixing—that they *were* the problems that needed fixing. And more importantly, because they resented it, they emerged from these training sessions no more interested in or able to create better workplaces or prevent the discrimination that had necessitated the sessions to begin with.

We know that last part with the benefit of hindsight and the wealth of research that's taken place between the '70s and the present. But the trainers at that time certainly didn't know that. Workforces were making rapid gains in the representation of women and non-White groups thanks to affirmative action initiatives.[22] Resistance among participants was seen as simply more indication that the training needed to happen. And perhaps more importantly, feelings of appreciation and gratitude from non-White participants and women participants convinced facilitators that they were truly doing the work that mattered.

Accountability in Retreat

More developments were on the horizon that would shake the fledgling industry. In 1978, the US Supreme Court heard the case of Allan Bakke, a 35-year-old White man who alleged that the University of California, Davis Medical School had denied him admission due to the school's quota system, which reserved sixteen seats out of a 100-person class for minority students. The court's decision? That race could be considered as a factor in admissions, but only in the service of achieving diversity, and that the quota system as a tool of affirmative action was illegal. As Justice Powell, the deciding opinion in an otherwise split court, put it, "There is a measure of inequity in forcing innocent persons in [Bakke's] position to bear the burden of redressing grievances, not of their making.[23]"

This would be the death knell for affirmative action as an outcome-oriented practice centered on meaningfully changing representational numbers for underserved communities and the birth of a new way of talking about and understanding these issues: as a nebulous outcome dependent on the intentions and consideration of an individual, and only in the service of a banal "increase in diversity" of a group.

Justice Powell was a believer in an increasingly popular idea that it was the acknowledgment of race and identity that contributed to inequity and that true equity was achieved by decreasing our acknowledgment of race: race denial, also known then as "color blindness."[24] This shift in thinking promoted by the *Bakke* decision appeared on its surface to protect a key driver of racial equity won by the Civil Rights Movement but laid the groundwork that would dilute and diminish it.

Two years later, when President Ronald Reagan was elected on a platform of government deregulation, race denial became a core principle in his administration's approach to race. Reagan's Department of Justice almost immediately began targeting affirmative action programs, building on a new narrative of "reverse discrimination."[25] (If you've heard the phrase in the modern day, thank Reagan.) For the corporate world, Reaganomics would put his belief in government deregulation into practice by slashing funding for the Environmental Protection Agency,[26] dramatically weakening labor unions,[27] encouraging laxer expectations for corporate compliance with nondiscrimination legislation, and appointing Clarence Thomas, a Black lawyer with similar political beliefs, to chair the EEOC. All of these actions worked to shift the balance of corporate power firmly toward the side of employers, who, in the absence of regulation, could choose to "self-regulate"—or not regulate much at all, really.

Under Thomas, standard practices at the EEOC to prescribe goals and timetables for greater representation at companies found responsible for discrimination were done away with. The tendency for the EEOC to take on cases with implications for many employees and large groups reversed under Thomas to focus instead on cases with a narrow focus and narrow implications. And many discrimination cases, under Thomas's own admission, were simply allowed to expire due to bureaucratic inaction.[28] The impact on the fledgling DEI industry was dramatic: with pressure from government regulators suddenly nonexistent, businesses reprioritized their expenditures. Racial sensitivity training that had formerly been mandatory for all employees was dismantled and scaled back, if not completely removed. For most companies that kept training in some form, the scope of training often shrank to managers-only or shifted focus entirely to train women and non-White populations on how to assimilate into male and White-dominated workforces that were now unlikely to change for them.[29]

As affirmative action fell, the impact on the racial representation in college admissions—the original battlegrounds of affirmative action policies—was dramatic. Gains in enrollment stagnated, then reversed. More than forty years later, the percentage of college-age Black and Latine Americans represented in top colleges and universities is lower than it was in 1980.[30]

The Business Case for Diversity

Then, in 1987, a new publication named *Workforce 2000* shook up the struggling racial sensitivity paradigm. Its authors noted that newcomers to the labor market would increasingly include women and non-White populations and that "workforce diversity," to build on a definition of diversity first established by the *Bakke* decision, should be a priority for future-focused companies looking to succeed. Workplace leaders, hoping to adapt to this new paradigm, began reexamining their options in racial sensitivity trainers and renewing their relationships with race and gender experts.

Enter R. Roosevelt Thomas Jr., a thought leader with a doctoral degree in organizational behavior. A masterful speaker, Thomas persuasively argued that if companies truly wanted to achieve the organizational benefits of a more diverse workforce, they needed to do far more than simply hire them—companies needed to manage the differences of their new, diverse workforce, create an organization-wide shared rationale for diversity as a business priority, and equip all of their employees with the learning necessary to unlock the benefits of diversity.

Thomas's work was a one-two punch for the newly birthed diversity *industry*.[31] The Thomasian core ideas of the new industry: managing diversity was good for business; people could be trained to do so; approaches to diversity that only focused on helping one group were out. Thomas' new "managing diversity paradigm" completed the shift from "outcomes to benefit disadvantaged groups" to "outcomes to benefit corporations."

Thus, the behemoth of racial sensitivity training and encounter groups was given new life. Even *more* training methodologies were developed during this period. Jane Elliott, an elementary school teacher, developed a widely publicized and controversial exercise that subjected largely White audiences to a proxy for racial discrimination based on the color of their eyes.[32] Lucky Stores was famously subject to a racial discrimination lawsuit after a diversity training asked participants to write out harmful racial stereotypes about racial groups to reflect on them, and material from that training was used as evidence of harmful intent in court.[33] Some companies invested in theater-based learning, with professional actors demonstrating the reality of discrimination and its impacts in the hopes of fostering empathy. Some training sessions were days long; others were an hour or less. Some training used newer techniques informed by research; some used the methods most familiar to their seasoned facilitators (welcome back, encounter groups!); others relied solely on the facilitator's imagination. A few characteristics stayed constant across these new types of training: They were voluntarily requested from organizations and corporations rather than required by any external source. They focused on the experience of the training itself, the input, rather than the outcome of training or the impact over time. And they trusted implicitly that the more companies applied themselves to DEI, the more inclusive and equitable they were guaranteed to become.

Data Without Experimentation

I could write an entire book on just telling story after story about the many different methodologies, tools, and techniques applied by DEI practitioners in the years since the business case was first developed, but in my opinion, the most interesting development in the last forty years has been the relative lack of desire from the DEI industry to coalesce around the data at our disposal.

Researchers painstakingly conducted post hoc analyses to measure the effectiveness of the Department of Defense's race relations training, which cost millions of dollars to implement—and yet, I was unable to find any even remotely mainstream publication even mentioning that this work had ever happened, let alone that there was useful data from it. The same goes with encounter groups—after multiple studies revealed mixed findings regarding encounter group methodologies,[34] their proponents simply insisted that "the benefits far overshadow the casualties" and continued carrying on as they always had done until encounter groups simply fell out of fashion.

Race denial, the belief that the best way to solve identity-related inequity was to act like identity did not exist, faltered when put to the test as well. In a 1986 study conducted at a desegregated school that deployed identity denial with Black and White students, race denial appeared on its surface to avoid many of the outright manifestations of racism but, in fact, enabled de facto discrimination and mistreatment in practice.[35] Optimistically, race denial espoused an ideology of equality that did not live up to its ideals. Cynically, identity denial was a means by which racism, racial hostility, and inequity could evolve and survive virtually undiminished under a new coat of paint. Other studies found that exposure to identity-denying ideologies lowered people's ability to perceive racism when it happened.[36] The research literature strongly suggests that race denial and other identity-denying ideologies sustain or even hide discrimination without meaningfully creating equity or inclusion in any sense; yet even today, many workplaces request this framing, and many practitioners willingly provide it. There continue to be workplaces where people proudly claim to not "see" race, gender, sexuality, ability, age, or size—despite ongoing realities of inequity and discrimination that undeniably suggest they do.

In the late 1980s through the 2000s, a rival social movement emerged against identity denial: multiculturalism, which aimed to name explicitly and positively recognize historically underserved and marginalized groups, including ethnic and religious minorities, Indigenous peoples, disabled people, LGBTQ+ communities, and more. By focusing on the positive representations of these groups and their contribution to culture and history, multiculturalism aimed to secure greater political power for these people beyond legal nondiscrimination protections.[37] There's some interesting data here for sure: multicultural approaches to discussing difference are connected to at least a temporary dip in prejudice[38] and boosts to workplace engagement[39] for all parties. Does multiculturalism directly benefit women and non-White groups? Yes, at least by some measures—women and non-White groups report feeling more accepted when their leaders espouse multicultural beliefs.[40]

But there's a catch. There always is. White people exposed to multicultural language that highlights the value of non-White contributions have a lower tolerance for disagreement or conflict.[41] They are more likely to feel excluded and thus respond by showing less support for diversity efforts or with frustration or hostility.[42] And in general, multiculturalism has been repeatedly linked to greater stereotyping and pigeonholing, with people viewing members of different cultural groups through a narrower lens.[43] "Multicultural" practices that might appear harmless, like highlighting notable achievements from non-White racial groups, thus run the risk of inadvertently contributing to the behavior they are aiming to reduce.

It's clear from the extensive research that neither rigid identity denial nor rigid multiculturalism can lower discrimination and prejudice. Achieving these outcomes by walking the line between the two requires thoughtfulness and nuance.[44] Yet, I've met only a few practitioners that navigate this line with the intentionality it requires. More often than not, practitioners pick a camp, wedge themselves into an ideological box, and offer their services with the righteous air of someone who thinks that the moral goodness of their mission all but ensures their positive impact.

History Repeats Itself...Again

In 1998, psychologists Anthony Greenwald, Debbie McGhee, and Jordan Schwartz developed a short assessment to measure the unconscious beliefs, associations, and biases regarding different social groups within individuals: the Implicit Association Test (IAT).[45]

The test, which measures the speed at which test-takers can match words into categories, compares whether test-takers are faster at matching identity labels with positive versus negative terms. If a person takes longer to match words or makes more mistakes when "White" and "Unpleasant" are paired compared to when "Black" and "Unpleasant" are paired, the test concludes that they have an unconscious bias toward White people and against Black people.

As a student of social psychology, I can tell you that quite literally hundreds of tests and measures like these get developed and collect dust in the deep recesses of little-read academic journals throughout the years. But the IAT emerged at the right place and time for many people to see in its simple test a promise that was too good to be true: an "objective" assessment, once and for all, of whether they were a racist. And not just that, either. The IAT claims to measure preferences for lighter or darker faces, gay or straight people, fat or thin people, old or young people, transgender or cisgender people, "Arab-Muslims" or people from other nationalities and religions, Native Americans or White people, disabled or nondisabled people, and Asians or White people.[46]

Individuals scrambled to take these tests, eager to learn if they were as progressive as they believed. And, according to the test, most people weren't—75% of adult White Americans, for example, showed a significant preference for White people over Black people.[47] And in one high-profile study, the test was deployed in hospitals and showed that IAT scores appeared to be correlated with racial discrimination.[48] Ten years after its introduction, the IAT website has been visited more than 5 million times.[49] Diversity practitioners responded to these developments like they were the universe's answer to the identity denial versus multiculturalism debate. "If we could only be made more aware of our biases and trained to acknowledge them," practitioners believed, "then we could finally make progress as organizations and a society on inequity."

By 2005, more than 65% of companies in the US offered some form of diversity training, whether out of a genuine desire to create more equitable and inclusive companies, prevent lawsuits, create a positive public image, or some mix of the three.[50] Many were unconscious bias training, but included in the mix were classic Thomasian "managing diversity" workshops, "business case" framings of diversity, identity denying approaches, multiculturalism, and even encounter groups, which had been rebranded at some point into "courageous conversations."

And quite literally, none of this training did what it promised to do.

A 2006 systemic analysis of diversity programs found that, of everything that had happened in the corporate world in the many decades prior, the old affirmative action programs—weakened and undermined by *Bakke*—were most effective, with the trendy programs of the time largely ineffective.[51] According to this analysis, moderately successful programs established leadership accountability for achieving diversity and created new structures in the form of mentoring and networking programs for underserved groups. In 2009, an even larger review of the research concluded that field experimentation and research were woefully lacking. Only a few kinds of interventions worked to do the bare minimum of reducing individual prejudice, let alone changing behavior.[52] These interventions include **cooperative learning**, working together to achieve a task or goal; **perspective taking**, thinking and acting from others' perspectives; **social norms**, framing inclusive behavior as widely common and normal; and **self-affirmation**, affirming positive depictions of the self to protect against feelings of threat.

And there's more. In the last few decades, we've only acquired more research showing that the business case doesn't promote equitable behavior (and, in fact, may undermine it, as support for diversity in business-case-using environments wanes as business performance drops[53]) and may even make underserved communities feel, paradoxically, devalued.[54] Diversity training, awards, and policies make people from advantaged groups (e.g., men, White people) *perceive* the organization as more fair without meaningfully improving fairness in reality and paradoxically make people from advantaged groups react with greater hostility to people from underserved groups who bring up experiences of discrimination.[55] How about unconscious bias training, the latest darling of the diversity industry? Unfortunately, that doesn't work either. It doesn't change workplaces. It doesn't change the behaviors of individuals. And the ironic cherry on top is that it doesn't seem to change people's biases.[56]

Pragmatic Hope

I took a deep breath after writing the previous sections. This is my profession, my chosen field, and frankly, what feels like my life's work. But *damn*, are we in trouble—a whole lot of trouble. I'm not so much a cynic that I believe that every encounter group, unconscious bias training, business case argument, identity denying, or multicultural approach will automatically fail, but our record has not been stellar, and the impatience and cynicism at the continued failure of DEI work are only mounting.

You might be wondering, "Lily, if you're so frustrated with all this, why the hell are you in this industry at all?"

Fair point. I did just take you through a fairly depressing run-of-show, and if you're anything like me, you're feeling a little uneasy about the prospects of this whole DEI thing.

I'm in this industry because I genuinely believe that the only way we can have hope for the future is by pragmatically understanding the past. And I don't think the failures of our past mean that failing is an inevitability. What I see from all of this research is a narrow path through the minefield of ineffectiveness that, if taken, can allow this rapidly growing industry to evolve beyond its problematic roots. To do that, we need to coalesce our understanding of history into some learning.

1. **Accountability is achieved only by centering outcomes.**
   Affirmative action made enormous progress in desegregating
   and integrating American schools and workplaces expressly by
   mandating certain outcomes through quotas. The allergic backlash
   to mandating outcomes meant that practically every intervention
   that came afterward failed. Unless outcome-centered interventions
   are put into place, using the wealth of data we have at our disposal
   on effective practices, accountability via intentions alone will never
   create the impact we seek.

2. **People are strongly motivated to protect a positive self-image.**
Interventions and framings that threaten a positive self-image
and make people feel disempowered (e.g., teaching that "women,
non-White people, and other socially underserved groups are inherently marginalized" or "men, White people, and other socially
advantaged groups are always at fault") tend to trigger unexpected
and undesired reactions and backlash effects. To avoid these failure
modes, interventions must tread carefully and intentionally around
people's perceptions of themselves.

3. **Seductively simple solutions rarely succeed.** There are no
"get-equitable-quick" strategies in the DEI space that work, and
those that exist (e.g., one-off workshop models, truncated/short-
ened workshops, standalone DEI talks) should be reimagined and
redeployed as part of larger, more comprehensive change-making
efforts. Those planning and budgeting for DEI work should
conceptualize it not as a serial, disjointed set of one-shots, but as
an interconnected and cumulative set of interventions building
toward change.

This chapter is titled "To What End?" My own answer: diversity, equity, and inclusion achieved as outcomes at scale. In every workplace
and organization. In every community. In society at large.

But doing that will require that we recognize that the very foundational tools we've inherited—that we must use to create change—are
rusted over, old, and brittle. In the US, the EEOC, which in the early
2020s continues to prioritize the needs of employers and businesses
over those of workers who have faced discrimination, is a toothless
watchdog.[57] Affirmative action is long gone. Businesses, which have
had free rein to "self-regulate" in the years since Reagan, have all the
time to inch toward change. In Western Europe, gender parity will take
fifty years; in America, sixty.[58] The DEI industry? We'll be fine so long

as there exist problems that can be smoothed over with an inspirational talk, which is to say, forever.

For those of us who want to mix up the status quo: it's not pretty, but these are the tools we're working with. What can we do, given what we've got, but learn from the many failures of those who have been tasked with success? We know what to do better now, and we're not heading forward with naive idealism but pragmatic hope. There's no better time to get it right than now.

TAKEAWAYS

- **Early case studies showed that even well-resourced DEI initiatives could fail if executed poorly.** The US military's race relations training initiative is one of the most spectacular examples of a well-resourced initiative that failed to reduce discrimination or decrease racial tensions due to conflict-heavy training techniques and leadership defensiveness.

- **Effective programs existed, but they were assailed and dismantled.** While affirmative action was creating substantial and measurable gains in workplace representation for under-represented groups, substantial backlash embodied by new narratives of "reverse discrimination" led to the dismantling of these programs and regulations supporting them, ending and reversing the gains made.

- **The DEI industry rebranded to use a new narrative of "competitive advantage."** The DEI industry's revival was enabled by DEI practitioner R. Roosevelt Thomas Jr. and the new "business case for diversity" and "managing diversity" paradigms he introduced, widely embraced by the corporate world to fill the vacuum left when government regulation and affirmative action programs were dismantled.

- **DEI work can be accountable if we learn from history.**
  Achieving DEI is possible, even through the minefield of failure
  that constitutes this industry's history. If we hold organizations
  accountable to their outcomes, protect people's self-image to
  avoid backlash, and forgo simple solutions in favor of complex
  and thoughtful initiatives, we can succeed at creating change and
  positive impact that sticks.

EXERCISES AND REFLECTIONS

1. Do a quick internet search for publicly available DEI training
   content, or pull up any you may have from training you've taken.
   Briefly skim what you find, and try to identify the content you see,
   given the history of the DEI industry. Which aspects seem inspired
   by encounter groups? Thomasian managing diversity paradigms?
   Business case arguments? Knowing what you know now, how does
   that make you feel?

2. Affirmative action and quotas have significantly dropped in popularity in the US and some other countries despite research showing
   effectiveness. However, this isn't the case in every country,
   especially for gender quotas. Research a country that implements
   a quota system for workplace representation. How effective is this
   system, and what challenges does it face?

3. Identity denial is an approach to DEI work that deprioritizes
   the role of identity in creating equity. While many practitioners
   oppose a rigid interpretation of this approach, people have varying
   opinions on what to do instead—how much, when, and in what
   contexts to talk about identity versus not. What feels to you like the
   right balance of the two? In what circumstances do you believe we
   should talk about identity versus not? Why?

4. If DEI work was implemented ideally from your perspective, what might the future look like? Describe a few aspects of the future—it doesn't have to be polished or perfect—that you hope for DEI work to achieve. What might organizations, leaders, and practitioners have to do for DEI work to get there?

◾ FOUR ◾

Real Change

"Social media didn't like it," the PR professional announced at the video meeting, their comment underscoring the slides displayed next to them. One executive frowned; another looked down, clearly thinking through the implications. The company in question, a growing start-up with a strong online presence, had put up a statement on social media denouncing anti-LGBTQ+ hate crimes at the urging of their customers. Following a recent major news event, they had received a torrent of messages urging them to take a principled stance on the issue and more effectively support their LGBTQ+ customers and the broader community.

So, after talking it over, internal leaders called up their favorite media-savvy vendor to draft the statement. The final copy looked pretty good. Its tone seemed heartfelt. It used all the right terms and demonstrated a solid understanding of the issue. It promised greater future attention to LGBTQ+ issues, stronger relationships built with LGBTQ+ communities, especially non-White LGBTQ+ women, and a commitment to doing good by this community.

Social media didn't like it.

"The most common sentiment observed in negative responses was that our statement was 'performative,'" the presenter continued.

"People accused us of spending more money on making this statement than we were willing to spend following up on it."

"That couldn't be further from the truth," the CEO quickly interjected. "What do they actually want us to do?"

It wasn't a rhetorical question but a pointed one clearly directed at the DEI professional in the room—me. Heads turned toward me, and I knew I had to deliver the unwelcome news.

"If 'they' means your customers? They don't want you to commit to doing anything at this point. They want you to have *already done it*."

Performative Allyship

In 2021, Dictionary.com's Word of the Year was "allyship"—what they defined as "the status or role of a person who advocates and actively works for the inclusion of a marginalized or politicized group in all areas of society, not as a member of that group but in solidarity with its struggle and point of view and under its leadership."[1]

Remember that we defined "allyship" somewhat more pointedly: "A strategy to achieve any DEI outcome whereby people possessing socially advantaged identities utilize those advantaged identities to create change."

Either way, optimists will hold this recognition up as evidence that the social movements of 2020 and beyond have created the critical consciousness needed to push our societies forward. The word didn't even exist in the online dictionary until 2021, to begin with. Surely that indicates that the tide is shifting in favor of greater equity, right?

Not exactly. According to Dictionary.com's own data, the word that most commonly precedes "allyship" is "performative: relating to ways of behaving that exhibit a socially acceptable belief, trait, or quality, often making a superficial impression."

I don't see a society newly hopeful that allies will help usher in a new era of change. I see instead a growing wave of skeptics that believe, more than ever, that *performative allyship* rather than actual change or actual solidarity defines our present day.

Do a quick web search of "examples of performative allyship," and you'll quickly become inundated with stories of individuals and organizations doing "the wrong thing," as it's so often described. Maybe they shared a black square on Instagram during the infamous "Blackout Tuesday," a tactic intended to show support for the Black Lives Matter movement in 2020 that instead was criticized for overwhelming the #BlackLivesMatter hashtag with useless information and hampering the information-sharing activities of actual organizers.[2] Maybe they wore a safety pin after the election of Donald Trump and Brexit to show that they didn't condone or support the violence associated with these events.[3] Maybe they adopted temporary rainbow logos or flew rainbow flags in June during Pride Month,[4] sang a widely mocked rendition of John Lennon's "Imagine" with their celebrity friends to "boost morale" during COVID-19 quarantines,[5] or canceled a controversial show only to resume production to screen in different countries, instead.[6]

What makes an action performative? Common answers to this question touch on the intentions behind it. "If an action is intended to gain social media clout or make a person look good, then those are dead ringers for performative allyship." Other answers call out the perceived lack of impact. "If an action is limited to social media without changing the material conditions of inequity, or solely related to personal growth via book learning, or even small-scale donations on a scale unlikely to make 'real change,' then that's all performative."

One writer argues, "If you're unwilling to confront your uncle who blurts out during Thanksgiving dinner that he 'can't believe the gays get to adopt now,' you don't get to post a picture on Instagram of yourself covered in rainbow paint at a gay pride parade."[7]

The intention behind these kinds of arguments seems, ostensibly, to set a bar or standard above which efforts at allyship become seen as genuine, and below which efforts at allyship are seen as performative. That's all well and good, in my opinion. The problem? The bar tends to move—all the time.

Doing nothing? That's being part of the problem; that's being complicit in harm.

Posting support on social media? That's performative allyship; you should be educating yourself instead of just repeating empty words.

Sharing the books you read that year to educate yourself? That's performative allyship; you should be doing something in the real world to make a difference.

Donate some money to a nonprofit or spend some time volunteering for a cause you care about? That's performative allyship; you should have addressed the deep, structural issues instead of just surface-level "band-aid solutions."

And if you somehow manage to solve an enormous, thorny issue by playing your part? That's still performative allyship; you should be solving your next issue rather than flaunting your "easy wins."

"Wait, Lily," you might ask, getting reasonably frustrated. "Isn't *everything* performative, then??"

Perhaps. One consulting firm argues that *any* public action taken by a company is likely to be performative allyship if the company's leadership team lacks representational parity, lacks metrics tracking DEI goals, or continues to exhibit discrimination and bias in its internal operations.[8] Frankly, that's every company I've ever interacted with in my career.

That's the truth behind the critique of performative anything: it's less an effort at correction and more an ambient expression of frustration. The actual substance of the "performative" critique *doesn't matter* because audiences want corporations to repair far more than a single corporate statement, action, or impact. People want corporations to repair the damaged social contract and earn back the *trust* that they lost through continued failure.

Want Trust? Get Accountability

Consider how it feels from the consumer's side. In 2018, the Edelman Trust Barometer reported a 37-point aggregate drop in trust across all US institutions, putting the US below Russia.[9] These trends worsened in 2020 due to the COVID-19 pandemic, the failures of political leadership, and global outcry against continuing gender, racial, and income inequity,[10] and unless big things change, they are likely to continue worsening over the decade. Worldwide, media became the least-trusted institution as a result of the explosion of media misinformation disseminated by social media platforms and search engines.[11]

Business hasn't been spared from these trends.

According to a global survey, brand trust in 2021 is at an all-time low, with only 47% of brands seen as trustworthy.[12] Scarcely a third of respondents believed that brand's promises to better the world were fulfilled in any way. The vast majority doubted brands' commitments, and only a small minority believed them to be transparent. Would respondents care if brands disappeared from the earth? For 75% of brands, the answer was a resounding "no." A corporate transparency study of the largest 124 companies in the world found that more than 80% scored less than 5/10 in transparency, measured by anti-corruption practices, organizational transparency, and country-by-country reporting.

Looking at the US, recent data from the EEOC shows that the lack of accountability for corporate discrimination remains steady. Only 18% of workers filing claims to the underfunded agency receive any assistance.[13] Legal redress occurs in only 7% of cases. Most cases are closed without ever finding out if discrimination occurred. The act of filing is also intensely dangerous for workers, 40% of whom experience retaliation after doing so—with 63% of this group eventually losing their jobs.[14] Employers in the US already spend billions each year to prevent lawsuits, and even when they happen, it's clear that the process intensely favors them.

And, of the most highly publicized efforts undertaken by corporations to genuinely impact change by opening their wallets, few of these are accountable, either. The staggering $49.5 billion donated by the fifty biggest public companies in America to racial inequity efforts between 2020 and 2021 look far less impressive when $45.2 billion are allocated in the form of loans (mostly mortgages) and investments that the two banks behind them, JP Morgan Chase and Bank of America, stand to benefit from.[15] Only $4.2 billion went to direct donations and grants for organizations. Of those, only a minuscule $70 million—a tenth of one percent of the overall total—focused on criminal justice reform. The entirety of these grants is less than 1% of the net income earned by these companies each year.

Take it this way—the *entirety* of tangible corporate donations to racial equity between 2020 and 2021 equated to a little less than *three weeks* of Jeff Bezos's average increase in net worth.[16] To make matters worse, few organizations are even tracking these promises, let alone holding corporations accountable for following through on them. They could withdraw their pledges at any point in the near future or quietly decide not to carry them through and be ignored for doing so. The news cycle has moved on. Barring high-profile grassroots movements demanding accountability, long-term tracking with regular updates from internal and external accountability groups or watchdogs, or voluntary reporting from organizations that have made these promises, the result will simply be another empty promise to earn short-term praise that people quickly forget.

This is the harsh reality for any organization that really, genuinely cares about achieving diversity, equity, and inclusion as outcomes any-time soon: goodwill and trust, and the patience these engender, has long since eroded. And so, when you say "we will make an effort soon," or "we commit to," or "in 202X, we plan to," all people will hear is blah, blah, blah. Cynicism is a way of protecting their expectations in a world where optimism has left them hurt and disappointed too many times to count.

I frequently share this and related information with leaders and often get the same bewildered responses. They say things like, "when did things get this bad? Why is everything so suddenly broken?" These are important questions to ask. To answer them and understand how to fix them, we need to track how corporate accountability has evolved alongside DEI accountability—because the two movements have now converged and present significant challenges for leaders looking to solve them.

Corporate Social What?

Business functions by public consent, and its basic purpose is to constructively serve the needs of society—to the satisfactions of society....Business is being asked to assume broader responsibilities to society than ever before and to serve a wider range of human values. Business enterprises, in effect, are being asked to contribute more to the quality of American life than just supplying quantities of goods and services. Inasmuch as business exists to serve society, its future will depend on the quality of management's response to the changing expectations of the public.

—Committee for Economic Development, 1971[17]

This argument embodied a new ideology, Corporate Social Responsibility, that first emerged in the 1950s[18] and found new life in the '70s as it was academically conceptualized. CSR was inspired by the

Civil Rights Movement and reflected the needs and sensibilities of the times. Corporations, argued proponents of CSR, should fulfill the increased economic, legal, ethical, and discretionary expectations of their societies.[19] Those expectations were often to take greater responsibility for their impacts on local communities they engage with, root out corruption and unethical business practices, and address inequity and discrimination within their organizations. Many new corporations founded during this decade were inspired by this new paradigm, including several that to this day embody best-in-class CSR approaches: Ben and Jerry's in the US[20] and The Body Shop in the UK.[21] Some existing businesses, out of a mix of social pressure and desire to proactively address these concerns, embraced a new social auditing movement seeking to operationalize the social impact of corporations.[22]

But there was another ideology co-present during this decade that diametrically opposed that of CSR: the Friedman Doctrine, espoused by American economist Milton Friedman and best defined by the *New York Times* headline that introduced it to the world: "The social responsibility of business is to increase its profits."[23] Friedman's ideas were seized upon by the coalitions that put both Ronald Reagan and Margaret Thatcher in power in the US and the United Kingdom, respectively, and upon their elections, the Friedman Doctrine gained enormous influence—helped out by the fact that Friedman himself advised both leaders.[24] As the Iron Curtain rose post–Cold War, the Friedman Doctrine found new influence in the policies of the World Bank and International Monetary Fund and thus reached as far as monetary policy in Asia and Latin America.[25]

One might assume that, with the advent of shareholder capitalism, the young CSR movement would die an early death as businesses embraced a "profit maximization at all costs" rationale. But it didn't. Sensing the unease of the general public in response to corporate misbehavior—whether accounting fraud,[26] environmental disaster,[27] defective and unsafe products,[28] bribery,[29] or racial discrimination—businesses looked for a way to address these concerns, lest continuing undisguised corporate greed provoked greater public backlash.

CSR, the darling of the 1970s, was an appealing set of ideas ripe for co-optation. Through a powerful combination of strategic investments, partnerships, and marketing, businesses leaned into the rhetoric of "self-regulation" to fill the vacuum that governments had left. This decade saw the activation of NGOs as a key player in corporate activities to legitimate CSR efforts,[30] an explosion in "green" marketing,[31] and the activation of the "business case" argument for CSR, an idea building on Keith Davis's original model formulated in the 1960s[32] (sound familiar?). As the 1990s and 2000s passed, CSR continued to evolve to reformulate the face of businesses in response to new social concerns and events like the anti-globalization protests of 1999[33] and the growing salience of "human rights" as a framework for driving global accountability.[34]

So, did it work?

If you mean, "Did companies rebuild consumer trust through CSR?" the answer is yes, for a little while.[35]

CSR activities across the board, even when initiated by companies with a poor reputation, succeeded in shaping consumer perception of brands, increasing their feelings of trust,[36] and thus winning back their business. This was also true for companies in industries associated with social or ethical issues, like tobacco, gambling, alcohol, weapons, and petroleum.[37] Thus, CSR became increasingly seen as a "best in class" strategy for defending the bottom line against moral and ethical attacks. Companies everywhere—especially large multinational ones—began creating CSR programs to do just that. By 2011, 20% of companies on the S&P 500 Index had CSR programs. By 2019, this percentage had risen to a staggering 95%.[38]

No story better exemplifies the power of CSR programs than that of multinational footwear company Nike. After a whistleblower revealed sweatshop-like conditions at a Nike factory, including below-minimum wages, child labor, and appalling working environments, the multibillion-dollar company was roiled in protests, boycotts, and fierce public critique.[39] If what Nike did next sounds familiar to you, it's because it became the playbook for addressing these kinds of criticisms for the entire corporate world.

In 1998, then-CEO Phil Knight publicly promised that Nike would change its practices, end child labor, apply US health and safety standards to factories outside the US, and allow outside labor and human rights groups to audit these overseas factories.[40]

That same year, responding to continued pressure from labor activists, Nike established a Corporate Responsibility department to manage its actions. After continued bad press in the media, including a highly critical documentary that aired in 2001,[41] Nike began shifting its procurement methods and adjusted its business model, releasing its first Corporate Responsibility Report later that year.[42] Throughout this time, Nike began intensive efforts to cast itself as a sustainability leader by voluntarily pledging to reduce emissions, and engaging in initiatives to conserve water usage and eliminate hazardous chemicals from its global supply chain.[43]

Long story short, these efforts worked to recover Nike's reputation, and it has enjoyed enormous success—and far diminished controversy—in recent years. It has been lauded for its CSR as a hero,[44] celebrated for its CSR reporting,[45] and closely studied for insights into organizational change[46] and innovation.[47]

Success! But wait, success at what?

Nike was in hot water in 2009 for failing to pay factory workers severance pay until pressured by student protests and media coverage to do so.[48] In 2017, it was again criticized for pulling production from factories with a strong union presence[49] and blocking labor rights experts from making independent audits.[50] In 2018, it came under fire from a scathing report on the continued poverty wages of the workers in its supply chain.[51] Most recently, in 2020, it was accused of using forced labor in Chinese factories.[52] The Fashion Transparency Index, a tool intended to encourage brands to be more transparent with their CSR efforts, scored Nike in the 51-60% range in 2021.[53]

I have no personal beef with Nike (for fairness's sake, I will also note that one of its chief competitors, Adidas, is no stranger to social justice controversy either[54]); in many ways, Nike's CSR program is indeed one of the most rigorous and thoughtful in the world. But answer me honestly—which of the above controversies would you have been aware of had you thought abstractly of "Nike" a few days ago? I wasn't well-acquainted with a single one myself; in my head, Nike had solved its CSR problem in the early 2000s and was simply coasting on its continued success. That I could think this is a testament to the power of modern CSR: amid controversy, CSR is organizations' way out; outside of controversy, CSR is their moral shield.

This is a problem because CSR doesn't necessarily create the impact it says it does.

A survey of 800 CEOs by the Economist Intelligence Unit found that 80% would characterize their company's supply chain as responsible—while less than a quarter of these supply chains addressed issues of child labor or climate change, and almost a third of these CEOs had recently *decreased* their focus on supply chain responsibility.[55] While over 9,500 companies and 3,000 nonbusiness participants have signed the UN Global Compact[56] and committed to sustainable practices, social justice, and a bevy of other ambitious commitments, data and documentation has consistently shown that doing so has little to no impact on these organizations' actual CSR efforts.[57]

A global analysis of companies that either conducted a human rights due diligence process or attempted to address human rights issues by integrating concerns into pre-existing CSR processes found that 77% of companies using the due diligence process found human rights abuses—while only 19% of companies using an umbrella CSR process found abuses. In other words, the very usage of CSR processes was strongly associated with failing to identify problems.[58] Another analysis using data from twenty leading garment companies and publicly available information concluded that companies front with their CSR initiatives while making only modest changes to their supply chains, insufficiently changing business models, outsourcing living wage commitments to multistakeholder initiatives without strong enforcement mechanisms, and diluting the definition of "living wages" to more easily meet strawman definitions of it.[59]

The evidence critiquing CSR's actual impact continues to mount. Some researchers find that CSR initiatives erode state-based regulation by outsourcing governance to opaque corporations.[60] Others show that CSR efforts weaken labor unions and worker-led campaigns.[61] In other words, modern CSR efforts almost always involve the expansion of unregulated and uncontrolled corporate power without necessarily changing many or even any of the issues that prompted them. While in many situations a reactive move prompted by activist or advocate pressure, CSR activities can quickly become relatively stable self-sustaining initiatives that recapture and maintain public trust while putting activists in the unsustainable position of needing to play watchdog constantly.

Do CSR programs do any good at all? Likely, some. No one is saying that we should return to the time before CSR or that corporations have achieved absolutely nothing with their initiatives. But CSR remains unaccountable through its lack of transparency and oversight and is far too easy to deploy for corporations with no intention of meaningfully creating real change. More importantly, the rewards of CSR—increased consumer trust and a stronger bottom line—are increasingly achievable without generating the impact it promises; even if CSR is conducted with positive intentions, its activities have become decoupled from its impacts. Modern CSR has thus morphed from a tool to make change into a tool used to sustain and obscure the status quo.

In that sense, it's quite like corporate DEI, isn't it?

We've had ample time to give "self-regulation" the benefit of the doubt, but it's clear that the status quo is far from enough to solve the world's current problems. We need more people to recognize this, recognize the power they have as stakeholders, and work collectively to hold organizations accountable for following up on their pretty words. And if the last few years are any indication, we've already taken the first few steps toward doing just that.

Performativity Hits Its Limit

As the COVID-19 pandemic spread across the world in 2019, it took millions of lives, disrupted food systems and supply chains, and drastically increased the number of people at risk of falling into extreme poverty.[62] Those most affected by the pandemic included members of historically disadvantaged groups like women, non-White people, disabled people, poor people, and LGBTQ+ people. In the US, Black, Latine, and Asian American women are far more likely to be essential workers, are overrepresented in the industries hit hardest by the pandemic, and have been additionally disadvantaged by the loss of childcare and educational services.[63] Disabled people experienced steep declines in mental health, physical well-being, and access to services.[64] LGBTQ+ people were more likely to have been laid off and similarly experienced declines in their mental health.[65]

Many companies with physical facilities and supply chains scrambled to respond to the pandemic's impacts on their operations. Every company was forced to rapidly address the concerns of both their consumers and their workforce amid changing conditions. For many companies, managing the transition from in-person to fully remote, then hybrid workplaces for all non-essential workers[66] created an enormous new set of challenges in logistics, coordination, management, and company culture.

Then, the murder of George Floyd in late May of 2020 ignited a new racial reckoning that swept up the corporate world. Almost overnight, expectations of corporations shot upward. US-based corporations, in particular, were expected almost universally to take decisive action on topics of racial injustice. In the short term, that meant saying "Black Lives Matter" on social media—and many did,[67] effortlessly taking a stance most had failed to take explicitly in the seven years since the start of the Black Lives Matter movement.

But the demands kept coming. It wasn't enough to say "Black Lives Matter"; companies had to also "open their purses,"[68] fire employees caught on video fabricating threats of violence to the police to intimidate a Black man,[69] and hold their employees—including even CEOs—accountable for racist and prejudiced behavior.[70] The conversation turned to many of the demands that racial justice organizers had levied at the corporate world for decades: better conditions, an end to discrimination, more racial diversity in leadership representation, and greater responsibility for their impact on the world.

The DEI industry saw a surge of interest at this time—a story on exactly this surge opened this book. DEI rocketed to prominence as the number one topic of interest on a survey of philanthropic donors in 2020 (it wasn't even mentioned in 2016).[71] The number of DEI job postings and open roles, which had plummeted by 60% at the start of the pandemic, rapidly climbed back to their former level and then some, with a greater number of roles for DEI leadership positions like chief diversity officers than ever before.[72]

When these moves happened, I remember cynically thinking that they were simply the latest efforts by corporate America to recapture an upset consumer base. It's what the research certainly suggests would happen: a terrible thing happens, companies are maligned, CSR efforts proliferate, the news cycle passes, and people settle down.

As I am writing this book in early 2022, I can certainly say one thing: the original news cycle might have passed, but people are *absolutely not settling down.*

Employee survey data from 2020 shows that, while the actions of employers during the summer of 2020 meaningfully improved employees' perception of their company's DEI work, that halo effect quickly diminished.[73]

In June (LGBTQ+ Pride Month in the US) of 2021, the typically celebratory atmosphere from the LGBTQ+ community members in my network, where the majority of individuals would at least tentatively express appreciation for companies flying rainbow flags, was notably absent. Instead, even mainstream news outlets were running cautionary articles about the perils of rainbow-washing and performative support for LGBTQ+ disguising ongoing harm.[74] Similar critiques were made throughout the year for autistic people,[75] especially during Autism Acceptance Month in April.[76]

If the experiences of my own clients are anything to go by, the righteous anger and indignation of 2020 have simply given way to a persistent, single-minded impatience. Talking about DEI but moving "too slowly" on putting commitments into action is increasingly a fast track to scathing critiques of "performative DEI." Past a certain point, additional commitments are less likely to increase trust and more likely to prompt probing questions about the accountability of prior commitments. Issue communications are increasingly scrutinized as being smokescreens for inaction.

If I'm right, we're headed into a *very* different new paradigm, one where "performativity" isn't simply an indictment reserved for the worst DEI or CSR offenders but a condemnation of both playbooks in their entirety. Consumers, employees, and even institutional investors and other stakeholders want real change.

Not talk, but real change.

Not commitments, but real change.

Not good intentions, but real change.

Not naive interventions, but real change.

So how the *hell* do we create "real change"?

From Proxies to Problem-Solving

The critique at the core of "performative" anything is that when people or organizations say they are addressing an issue by taking action, those commitments or behaviors don't translate into a measurable impact on the issue.

For simple issues, these kinds of critiques don't make much sense. Tell me to take out the trash, and you'll clearly be able to check whether I've done so: Is there still trash in the trash can? If yes, then I haven't taken out the trash. If I respond with something like, "I've committed to taking out the trash!" or "I've allocated some mental energy to take out the trash," or "I've opened the lid of the trash can," even if all of these things are true that doesn't change the fact that, well, I still haven't taken out the trash.

But tell me to "fix the rat problem," and accountability is much harder. It's much more difficult to assess whether my efforts have truly succeeded, and so you're likely to be satisfied with a proxy—maybe, the number of rats you see in the house a month. Sure, I could drive that number down to zero by identifying the source of the infestation, setting out rat poison, and finally calling an exterminator. But I could also seal up the most egregious holes in the house and keep you out of the basement, where they're congregating. I could aim to draw your attention away from where I know they nest. I could even try and convince you that the rat you saw the other day was actually a squirrel, and are you sure you didn't imagine things from all the stress?

Big, messy issues like systemic inequity are tough to pin down and fully operationalize with metrics.

Take LGBTQ+ inequity: we know, first, that the acronym itself amalgamates identities related to sexual orientation (lesbian, gay, bisexual, queer) with identities related to gender identity and expression (transgender, nonbinary, genderqueer, agender, etc.), and that their inclusion within the same acronym originated from an act of political solidarity.[77] While the issues of these two categories of experiences are often lumped together, to achieve accountability, we need to disaggregate the experiences of sexual minorities from those of gender minorities.

For sexual minorities in the US, inequities in housing,[78] education,[79] health care,[80] and workplaces[81] are directly linked to lower access to services, higher discrimination, and lower rates of utilization—often due to perceived or actual discrimination. Individuals may be outright singled out for being in same-gender partnerships or for having same-gender attractions and face interpersonal harassment, discrimination, or violence; targeted by laws or policies excluding them from services or civic life;[82] or denied access to infrastructure or support available to heterosexual people.[83]

For gender minorities in the US, inequities in housing,[84] education,[85] health care,[86,87] and workplaces[88] can be similarly linked to lower access, discrimination, and utilization. Individuals may face hostility, harassment, discrimination, and violence for their physical characteristics or mismatch between their appearance and legal documentation.[89] Similarly, they may be targeted by exclusionary laws and policies[90] and face hardships navigating infrastructure and systems not designed for them.[91]

Additionally, other dimensions of inequity complicate the experiences of LGBTQ+ people: the experiences of White, nondisabled LGBTQ+ men tend, on average, to be far more positive than the experiences of non-White, disabled LGBTQ+ women or nonbinary people.

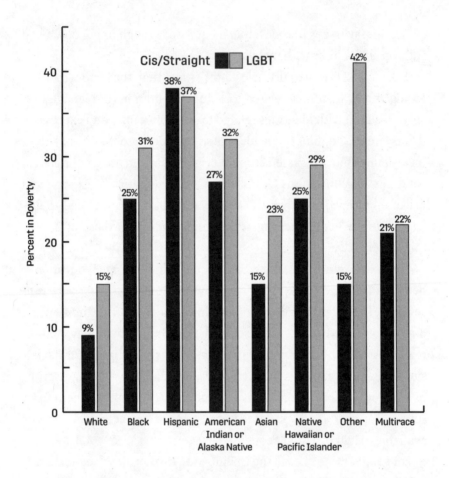

Source: Data is from the Behavioral Risk Factor Surveillance System (BRFSS) survey 2014-2017.

Notes: All race/ethnic groups are mutually exclusive. The "Other" race category represents respondents who did not select any of the racial groups on the BRFSS and also did not select Hispanic (e.g., "Other, Non-Latinx/Hispanic") and is exclusive of respondents selecting "Don't know" or "Refused." (University of Wisconsin-Madison, 2021; "The Complexity of LGBT Poverty in the United States," Wisc.Edu. June 2021.)

FIGURE 2. Rates of poverty for LGBTQ+ people of color are close to, or higher than, those for cis/straight people of their own racial or ethnic group and are notably higher than for White people, whether straight or LGBTQ+.

The real impact of these inequities? LGBTQ+ people have a comparable or higher poverty rate than cisgender (nontransgender) heterosexual people for every racial category, as shown in Figure 2.

Similar disparities can be seen in health outcomes,[92] educational outcomes,[93] incarceration rates,[94] workplace representation,[95] and more. And while the above data concerns the US, similar disparities exist in Europe,[96] East and Southern Africa,[97] Asia,[98] and Latin America,[99] with anecdotal data from all across the world.

These are the problems that LGBTQ+ people refer to when they talk about the need for "real change." This is why stakeholders are increasingly losing patience with visible but ultimately ineffective gestures like adopting rainbow logos and selling rainbow merchandise for one month out of the year.

I only explored a single issue, and there are dozens upon dozens, all of them similar battlegrounds. Whether CSR or DEI, stakeholders everywhere increasingly believe that corporate success isn't and has never been measured in terms that overlap even a little with their own—and they're not wrong. It's not that corporate intentions haven't yet materialized into impact. The intentions themselves have always been to meet goals that underserved communities have never cared about and every single one of them is a poor proxy for positive impact.

Employee engagement, dollars of corporate giving, revenue growth, brand awareness, reputation: *who cares*? Not community members, that's for sure. Increasingly, not even your own employees. These carefully constructed "business case" metrics, Thomasian arguments for the value of DEI, and "doing well by doing good" statements have already faltered in the academic literature, and the general public is simply catching up.

They're done with proxies—they want problem-solving, and they won't trust any organization that doesn't get it right. If we're leaders who care, this should be a loud, alarming wake-up call.

Success Is Possible

For organizations that have historically focused more on their reputation with stakeholders than their stakeholders' well-being, these new developments should be seen as concerning. But the flip side of this is that, increasingly, something like "real" success is possible. We just need to disassemble big challenges into clear and simple problems that can be readily measured and readily solved.

If working-class contract workers push to be treated and paid equitably, we can break that down into wanting an end to harassment, discrimination, and underpayment. We can further break that down into proxy metrics: comfort sharing feedback, employee net promoter score (the likelihood that an employee would recommend the organization to others), pay satisfaction, psychological safety, and satisfaction with interpersonal relationships. We can further identify the real behaviors and outcomes behind these proxy metrics: proactive feedback shared, usage of conflict-resolution processes and positive resolutions for these processes, employee referrals, objective pay equity, and worker health and well-being.

In other words, if contract workers are paid competitively and fairly for their labor, go about their daily work without encountering safety risks or interpersonal harassment, have positive interactions with management and employees, have their needs considered in decisions, and readily recommend people from their networks to apply for positions— all with a baseline foundation of pay equity and well-being—those are all signs of real success.

Suppose older employees push to be valued and respected for their unique talents. In that case, we can break that down into wanting a greater feeling of inclusion and belonging and an end to age-related discrimination and exclusion. We can further break that down into proxy metrics: employee net promoter score, satisfaction with management relationships, participation in conversations about age as a valuable dimension of diversity, perceptions of support, and feelings of authenticity. We can further identify the real behaviors and outcomes behind these proxy metrics: participation rate in meetings and organizational processes, rate of usage for employee benefits like vacation time or flextime, promotion and turnover rates, employee referrals, and amount and frequency of professional development opportunities offered.

In other words, if older employees have a high degree of participation in the organizational process, have a variety of continuing career and growth opportunities, are frequently recognized and promoted for their work, experience levels of turnover no higher than that of younger demographics, and readily recommend people from their networks to apply for positions—all with a baseline foundation of pay equity and well-being—those are all signs of real success.

Success is possible, and if we keep ourselves focused on the right problems, we can truly achieve the following:

- **Equity:** the measured experience of individual, interpersonal, and organizational success and well-being across all stakeholder populations
- **Diversity:** the workforce demographic composition in an organizational body that all stakeholder populations trust to be representative and accountable
- **Inclusion:** the felt and perceived environment in an organizational body that all stakeholder populations trust to be respectful and accountable

To do so, we must regain the trust of populations inside and outside our organizations, especially those that are and have been underserved and marginalized, who have lost patience with decoupled and performative corporate actions that fail to meet their needs or address systemic barriers and inequities.

We know from the history of the DEI and CSR movements that this work is far harder than it looks. Beyond the challenges of accurately understanding the extent and scope of our charge, we also need to address obstacles in the way of creating change. We need to avoid backlash effects from powerful incumbents and rank-and-file employees alike. We need to execute interventions informed by solid science and drive lasting behavioral change. We need to maintain the right balance between focusing enough internally to be actionable while engaging enough externally to be accountable. And the whole time, we need to stay focused on the right outcomes and the right problems, so we design the right solutions.

Whew.

Let's get to it.

TAKEAWAYS

- **There are no hard and fast guidelines for efforts or behaviors that are "performative."** Stakeholders' trust in a person's or organization's efforts determines the label. If stakeholders trust organizations or individual people, actions are given the benefit of the doubt. If they lack trust, actions are more likely to be seen as performative—regardless of what the actions are or what they achieve.

- **Stakeholders' trust in organizations and institutions has eroded due to a lack of accountability.** Despite heavy usage of the CSR playbook (pledges, commitments, external-facing reports, and celebration of proxy metrics), organizations' enduring lack of progress on important issues, ongoing controversies, and persistent inequity has expended goodwill and patience from stakeholder communities. Stakeholders are increasingly skeptical and cynical toward corporate DEI efforts not rooted in outcomes.

- **To create "real change," organizations need to prioritize the same outcomes that their stakeholders do.** These outcomes are not just organizational inputs or even outputs, but stakeholder health, well-being, success, and discrimination rates, among many others, for stakeholders including employees, contractors, local communities, the environment, and more.

EXERCISES AND REFLECTIONS

1. Think about the last time you saw a celebrity, public figure, or organization speak on a social issue. How did you feel about what they said? What indication did you have that they were being genuine or not? How was your own perspective different from or similar to that of others you know?

2. Which organizations do you trust, if any, and why? What in particular sets them apart from organizations you distrust?

3. Fill in the blanks for the following two sentences. "The purpose of a corporation is to _____.
All corporations should be responsible for _____
_____."
Replace "corporation" with the type of organization you work within or with most frequently (nonprofits, volunteer groups, government entities, etc.), if needed. What was your thought process in filling in those two blanks?

4. How would you know that a DEI effort has succeeded? Think about a measure of success, then examine it more closely to see if there are ways you can break it down further into specific and measurable indicators rather than proxy metrics. Repeat the process until you have a list of specific behaviors and actions you want to see that can "prove" that a DEI effort has succeeded.

PART 2

PILLARS

FIVE

Knowing, Using, Ceding Power

"I don't have enough power to make change," the employee shared, frustrated.

"What power do you have, then, and why isn't it enough?"

They looked quizzically at me like I hadn't heard what they said. "I don't have any since I don't have a leadership title."

I pushed them a little. "Do you have any control over your work products or your process?" They nodded yes.

"Do you ever lead meetings or present on your work?" Another nod.

"Do people listen to what you have to say or look to you for advice?"

They nodded again but looked impatient. "Yes, yes, sometimes. But none of that lets me make or weigh in on the decisions that matter."

"Perhaps. But power comes in many forms, and it sounds to me like you've got a fair amount of it. There are lots of things you can do to influence your workplace in the direction you want, formal authority or not. Tell me, does your manager have any close friends at work you know well?"

Suddenly, they broke out into a smile. "Yes. I know a guy; we're on the same committee…and, and! He owes me a favor."

I smiled back. "Keep going."

When I first started working with one client, the phrase "power dynamic" put people on edge—to leaders in the organization, who frequently referred to the organization as a "family," talking about power felt like a particularly repugnant flavor of conflict. It invoked an image of an autocratic leader forcing their employees to toil away against their will, held hostage by their need for a paycheck. This was an image they rejected vehemently. At their organization, conversations were all smiles, and dissent felt minimal. Why talk about "power dynamics" if there seemed to be no problems to begin with?

But perhaps the biggest indicator of the power dynamics in that workplace was the trepidation with which other employees described speaking up and the expectations that felt unchallengeable. The youngest and most junior employees were always expected to take on undesirable tasks. The most senior leaders responded poorly to constructive criticism and had historically worked to silence critics rather than change their behavior. The lack of outright conflict was, in fact, a manifestation of power dynamics rather than an indication of their absence.

To make any progress on DEI in that organization, the differing perceptions of the status quo needed to be brought into alignment. And to do that, the concept of a "power dynamic" had to be defined in neutral terms that everyone could understand: as the explicit or implicit set of expectations and abilities to influence outcomes at scale.

Senior leaders can make broad decisions that impact the entire company, while other employees must simply just abide by them? That's a power dynamic.

The most tenured employees never have their decisions questioned, while newer employees must prove themselves? That's a power dynamic.

White employees feel comfortable discussing their hobbies and interests at work, while employees of other races and ethnicities hold back for fear of mockery or awkwardness? That's a power dynamic.

None of those power dynamics were good or bad just by being power dynamics. But they all had a substantial impact on the workplace and its diversity, equity, and inclusion outcomes. And yet, no one felt comfortable saying any of this out loud. Fear of the very concept of power dynamics was the very thing sustaining them.

It took a comprehensive set of DEI surveys, numerous all-company conversations, and frankly uncomfortable conflict to bring these power dynamics out from behind closed doors. And when everyone could see these dynamics for exactly what they were and discuss how they impacted everyone, suddenly the notion that they could be changed didn't seem so unrealistic. Some people had power they weren't using that they now knew to use. Some people who had little power learned that gaining more would help them and the entire organization. And some people realized they had too much power—too much responsibility—and took steps to cede and share that power with others.

It took knowledge and awareness of power and power dynamics to begin changing them for this organization, which is also true for individuals. So we'll start from the top: what is power?

Like many deceptively simple terms, it has many formal definitions: Power is the potential to influence.[1] Power is the possession of control, authority, or influence over others.[2] Power is the ability to control people and events.[3]

If we are to achieve DEI in the organizational sense, we will need to engage critically and often with power. With power, organizational priorities, goals, and strategies are set, and with power, individuals navigate conflict, self-advocate, and collectively organize. Power isn't just a function of individuals, either. It's not just a tool wielded by state leaders or CEOs, but also deeply embedded within institutions, culture, structure, policy, and process. As Foucault argues, wherever we look, "power is always already present"; we are never truly "outside it."[4] And so, when we consider any aspect of the complex and varied systems around us—from the standard human resources policies in our workplace to the norms of social interaction between colleagues—we can do so understanding that they always exist at least partially to achieve some end, that power is always already present embedded within them, and that perhaps most importantly, there's always something we can do about it. We cannot ignore power—because if we do not choose to act on power, power will always act and be exercised on us in some shape and form.

Know Power

I advise the vast majority of my clients in at least some way about power, but their situations are often wildly divergent.

Some feel, for lack of a better term, disempowered. Maybe they report to a manager who repeatedly commits microaggressions and has shown a willingness to retaliate. Maybe they're a recent hire debating disclosing that they are both a new parent and gay. Maybe they've endured one unproductive meeting too many and are giving up on trying to make change through the internal DEI volunteer committee. These folks are all intimately familiar with power because power is the low ceiling constraining their choices, the leverage others have that they don't. They want to understand how power works so they can navigate the power dynamics they experience—and gain enough to protect themselves from others abusing it.

Another group of people feels lost. Maybe they're a longtime executive who feels like the rug's been pulled out from under them, that times have changed too quickly for them to keep up, and that the skills they learned over their career as a leader are suddenly outdated in our increasingly DEI-centric world. Maybe they're a director tasked with achieving an ambitious DEI strategy with little guidance and are overwhelmed by the scope of the work. Maybe they're a social media manager swept up in the new wave of DEI-related external pressure and unsure how they should now use the platforms at their disposal. They all have a great deal of formal power but no idea how to deploy it to achieve DEI-related goals. They want to be told what to do in unambiguous, exacting detail and be reassured that they'll meet the expectations that others are piling on them by following the right instructions.

Everyone else is somewhere in the middle. Some folks are DEI advocates or employee resource group (ERG) leaders with some access to power but not nearly enough to make decisions that matter. Some are mid-level managers who are already being run ragged getting their normal workload cleared and dread DEI as another set of lofty but unattainable goals. Some are new DEI leaders asked by their senior executives to "spearhead DEI" for an organization of thousands of employees and don't know where to start, let alone what they have the authority to do. They're not disempowered, but they also don't have enough power. They're not burdened with power, but they're also not lacking in responsibility.

There are common themes in how I address the needs of each one of these groups. I typically ask folks to dive deeper into what they mean when they say, "I don't have (enough) power."

See, "power" isn't just the formal authority conferred by a job title. Scholars of power typically understand it as an umbrella term encompassing *six* distinct variations:[5]

1. **Formal power:** the right to request behavior from another

2. **Reward power:** the ability to promise (monetary or nonmonetary) compensation to influence behavior

3. **Coercive power:** the ability to threaten punishment to influence behavior

4. **Expert power:** the ability to influence behavior by possessing greater expertise or ability

5. **Informational power:** the ability to influence behavior by possessing greater information

6. **Referent power:** the ability to build rapport and influence behavior through charisma

Job titles and formal authority certainly confer power, especially formal power. Your manager, for example, can give you directions just because they are your manager. Formal power is often also accompanied by coercive power—your manager can fire you for noncompliance—and reward power by giving you bonuses to reward good work.

But depending on the topic and issue in question, every person in every environment has some degree of access to all six types of power.

Formal power is granted based on organizational recognition, and there are many more kinds of recognition in the workplace than that given based on titles. Executives and managers, by definition, have formal power by dint of their role and title. But organizational entities, including informal or volunteer efforts like DEI councils and employee resource groups (ERGs), can also gain formal power, even when not given the blessing of organizational leaders. If the majority of people in an environment perceive an entity to have legitimacy, it can gain formal power on that basis alone.

Reward power is similarly flexible. While many people may not be able to formally offer monetary compensation for certain behaviors, each and every one of us can offer respect and gratitude—valuable things in the eyes of many and powerful enough to impact workplace environments for the better.[6] And depending on the person or group offering it, like, say, a well-respected employee-led DEI council, approval can be a powerful reward indeed.

Coercive power, or punishment, is also surprisingly accessible to all of us, whether or not we have formal power or authority. While we may not be able to fire our managers, employees are increasingly taking to internal company platforms or even social media (at times breaking non-disclosure agreements to do so[7]) and airing out their employer's dirty laundry for the public to see. These strategies aim to use public shaming as a tool for accountability. They are very much an expression of coercive power—aiming to hurt brand perception and trust to influence behavior.

Expert power isn't just attached to skills and competencies but can also be inferred from simply possessing particular social identities and experiences. For example, most women are assumed to have at least some degree of expert power regarding women's experiences in the workplace, even though no woman can speak for all. Expert power goes beyond identity-based expertise as well. Many people have what could be called expertise in some way, even if it's in a niche skill or body of knowledge that, on its surface, seems unrelated to a given context. You wouldn't normally call medical knowledge "expert power" when it comes to piloting commercial planes—until a passenger falls ill or gets injured mid-flight.

Informational power is also increasingly accessible as organizations navigate crises and unexpected situations. While informational power is short term compared to expert power, any solution to pressing problems has a high likelihood of adoption regardless of who it comes from in time-sensitive situations. When it comes to a DEI-related crisis, for example, an individual with the most up-to-date knowledge of the work schedules of the senior leaders best suited to make a public statement might temporarily find themselves quite powerful.

Finally, referent power is charisma, and anyone can have—or lack—it. It's the ability to control the attention of a room, make fast friends and connect with anyone, and effectively communicate, compel, and persuade. Influence is a science, and anyone can learn or deploy it regardless of their role, title, or experience.[8] While each of these six types of power boosts the power of all others when they exist in tandem, referent power is, in my opinion, the greatest force multiplier. Power without charisma is brute force. Charisma is what turns crude power into influence.

As important as it is to understand individual power, few workplaces are as straightforward as "X number of people running around deciding everything through interpersonal interaction." Small workplaces have unspoken ways of working that people become accustomed to, and the largest workplaces are well-oiled machines involving a complex interplay of people, processes, culture, and policies. For this reason, it's impossible to prescribe a one-size-fits-all way of making change or creating outcomes that will work similarly in every setting (sorry to those who were hoping to hear one!). Nor is it possible to illustrate an exhaustive list of how to make change in every conceivable environment—there's no practitioner in the world, no matter how pragmatic, that has that kind of knowledge.

Instead, I help the folks I work with reverse engineer the outcomes they want to change or create and, through that process, understand the unique structure, culture, and strategy of their organization. They learn how power in their organization functions: how decisions are made, how intentions translate (or don't) into impact, and how change is received. With that knowledge and a clear understanding of their own individual power and its limitations, they can start using that power to get things done.

Structure

Every organization has a structure: a set of formal and informal rules, roles, and responsibilities that coordinate behavior and facilitate achieving the organization's goals. While structure alone is rarely enough to predict or control organizational outcomes, it plays a critical role in helping us define the boundaries of the problems we aim to solve and understand how we might deploy our power most effectively.

When it comes to "types" of organizational structures, there are as many as can be imagined by an organizational founder[9] or a thoughtful pundit. Rather than attempting to make sense of the many classification systems that exist, I'll share what I believe are the three most important dimensions through which to understand any organization's structure: centralization, formalization, and complexity.

Centralization

One of the most classic and well-studied dimensions of difference, organizations vary immensely by the degree to which decisions are made from the top-down. On one extreme are pure command-and-control models, which give one person the sole authority over people and resources to make decisions that cascade down through the organization.[10] On the other are the extremes of decentralized organizational structures like decentralized autonomous organizations (DAOs), which could theoretically run without any managers or leaders at all.[11] Nearly every organization exists on the continuum between these two extremes and contains a hybrid of centralized and decentralized processes.

For example, *functional organizations* are organized by relatively independent departments that all report to the same core group of centralized leaders, *matrix organizations* introduce multiple reporting relationships for all employees,[12] *flat-archies* include temporary flat and ad hoc structures like a skunkworks inside a typical hierarchical structure,[13] and *agile organizations* involve loosely connected autonomous "self-organized" teams working on their projects under only the highest level of hierarchy.[14]

Rather than simply attempt to sort your organization into one of the categories above, it's more important in the process of understanding your organization to answer the following questions accurately:

- What is the process by which everyday decisions are made? Big decisions?
- How does decision-making differ for people situated at different places in the organization?
- How does the organization respond to crises or emergencies, and what aspects of the normal decision-making process change, if any?
- Where in the organization is power situated?

The more top-down the decision-making, especially for even small decisions, the greater the burden for those toward the top of the reporting structure, the more controlled and standardized the response to crisis, and the more concentrated power is among upper echelons, the more centralized an organization is.

Understanding centralization clarifies the process of making change and achieving DEI outcomes. In a highly centralized organization, for example, the chain of command is a powerful but singular lever of change—it is difficult to activate, but once decisions are made, they are difficult to stop as they cascade down; they lend themselves well to highly controlled, consistent, and standardized interventions.[15] Decentralized organizations rarely change in this linear way. They are more effective at addressing complexity, ambiguity, and variation and optimizing employee autonomy and independence; thus, highly flexible and variable interventions may be more likely to achieve success.[16]

Formalization

Formalization describes "how the organization works" is enshrined, institutionalized, and documented in a permanent and accessible way. Those formal processes are made part of the daily functioning of the organization. You most likely are familiar with formalization by another name: "bureaucracy," said disparagingly, or "red tape." Highly formal organizations like government agencies or NGOs have no shortage of rules, regulations, documents, forms, instructions, and formal processes governing behavior. In contrast, highly informal organizations like small family businesses, many quickly formed advocate or activist grassroots groups, or a clique of friends embedded inside an organization operate more on a shared and unspoken set of norms and practices.

While not all highly formalized environments can compel all their members to *follow* explicit rules, the presence of formalization is nevertheless associated with achieving consistency and information transfer within organizations.[17] Too much formalization, however, and organizations lose the flexibility to deal with changes in their environment or new challenges.[18] On the other end, too little formalization and organizations become inconsistent and unregulated in their functioning, a phenomenon common enough to be given its own organizational form by sociologists: *organized anarchy*. In these environments, regardless of the formal structure on paper, processes, rules, and systems are poorly understood by the participants in them, participation of stakeholders is fluid, and decisions are made as chaotic outcomes emerging from a "garbage can" of choices, problems, issues, and decision situations.[19]

To understand the formalization of your organization, ask yourself these questions:

- How commonly are standardized formal processes used to achieve outcomes in the organization?
- To what extent do all members of the organization understand the formal rules for operating in your organization?

- How does the organization react to individuals or entities who do not know or follow the formal rules?

The more commonly standardized processes are used, the greater the shared understanding of formal rules, and the harsher the sanctions for those who do not follow these rules, the more formalized the organization.

Understanding formalization allows you to identify the degree to which power operates formally versus informally. If your organization is high in formalization, the formal rules gatekeep all possible change: if they run against your efforts, you are unlikely to succeed; if they complement your efforts, they become an accelerator. If your organization is low in formalization, your path for change will be messier though more rewarding for discerning and opportunistic change-makers able to identify and jump through windows of opportunity when they arise.

Complexity

Organizational complexity describes how organizations divide their functioning into jobs, internal groups or entities, and locations. Organizations highest in complexity have many jobs, each performing a narrow set of tasks, and many divisions, departments, or units, many of them requiring specialized education or training, divided across many roles with differing supervisory responsibilities, spread across many physical (or increasingly, remote) locations and geographies.[20] One might imagine a small start-up working out of one office, in which only a handful of formal titles exist and the people possessing them perform every task imaginable, as an organization low in complexity when compared to a multinational corporation with hundreds of thousands of employees, thousands of roles and titles, with dozens of layers of managers and supervisors, spread around the world.

Of course, as with centralization and formalization, organizational complexity can differ wildly between these two extremes. Your organization may have many jobs but spread over only a few departments. You may be operating in different contexts and environments worldwide but have a relatively standardized set of tasks and a small number of departments. In general, however, you can assume that the complexity of an organization tends to increase as the external environment becomes more complex[21] and as organizations grow in size.[22]

To get a rough handle on the complexity of your organization, you can ask yourself the following questions:

- What is the ratio of managers and supervisors to individual contributors?
- How many discrete responsibilities are listed in job descriptions?
- How many different groups of internal stakeholders must coordinate for an organization-wide initiative?

The higher the manager-to-individual contributor ratio, the greater the discrete responsibilities in job descriptions, and the greater the number of stakeholder groups required for coordination, the more complex an organization is.

If centralization helps define the "process" of change and formalization defines the "flavor," complexity describes its magnitude. DEI outcomes are intended to create change across the entirety of an organization, and that takes different forms depending on the organization's complexity. The more complex an organization, the more complex an intervention must be to reach all corners of it successfully.

Culture

If structure describes "how things work," culture describes "how things feel." It is a shared but often unspoken understanding of the assumptions and expectations for behavior and thought within an environment and manifests in the form of rituals, myths, and stories that embed a core set of unspoken rules.[23]

Management scholar Mats Alvesson makes this definition explicit with an example: Let's assume that in an organization, a certain level of management is allowed to make investment decisions up to $50,000 and must receive permission from more senior leaders for decisions beyond that amount. That is a rule—an example of what we've learned can be called "formalization."

But all rules are subject to interpretation, and this is where culture comes in. Is it a hard and fast rule, heavily enforced, and punishable by termination if broken? Or is it possible to interpret "investment" loosely or use $50,000 as a ballpark? Or perhaps, is it widely understood that while the rule exists for a reason, to prevent misuse of authority, asking permission is a hassle and not worth upper management's time—and so the rule is more of a "suggestion"? Maybe the rule only applies to fresher managers who haven't proven themselves but disregarded for more tenured managers who hold upper management's trust.[24]

Think about your own experiences working in an organization— faced with a formal rule like this, how would your organization have treated it? Maybe you've worked in a highly centralized and bureaucratic organization where the rules are always followed to the letter, to the displeasure of everyone—or maybe you've worked in a nominally decentralized and flexible organization led by a bureaucrat who nonetheless requires everyone to follow an arbitrary set of rules. In this way, we can see that structure can influence culture but not necessarily predict it. In some organizations, structure and culture complement each other, mutually reinforcing the behaviors and outcomes the organization wants. But more often than not, they clash—the structure dictates one thing that the culture undermines, or the culture holds up an ideal that the structure disincentivizes.

What kinds of organizational culture exist? Because there are an infinite number of unique "kinds," it's more useful to describe the key dimensions by which they vary. I've included below what I believe are the most useful ones for DEI.

Power Distance

Power distance refers to the degree to which a large distance between the most and least powerful is accepted and normalized. In high-power distance cultures, hierarchies are normalized and seen as desirable; there are few attempts to change power imbalances that exist. Those with more power are seen as deserving that power due to their greater responsibility, and those with less power are seen as needing to meet the needs of those with more power. In low-power distance cultures, hierarchies are less normalized or seen as undesirable; there are many attempts to challenge and rebalance perceived power imbalances. Equal power dynamics are legitimated through moral or ethical arguments, and those with less power expect to be consulted or have a role in decision-making.[25] You can gauge power distance in an environment by asking the following question:

- How comfortable do people with the least power in a given environment feel sharing potentially critical or negative feedback?

In a high-power distance culture, for example, if it is evident that senior leadership overrepresents men of socially advantaged races (for example, White men in the US and Han Chinese men in China), there might be little impetus among the workforce to disrupt that dynamic. A lower-level woman employee that protests these dynamics in a high-power distance culture might immediately face repercussions from not only men but also other women in the workplace for doing so. If the same situation took place in a low-power distance culture, senior leadership would likely feel greater pressure to acknowledge the woman's concerns and take action to remedy the representation gap.

In(ter)dependence

In(ter)dependence refers to the degree to which people perceive themselves as part of a larger whole. In independent cultures, greater focus is put on unique individuals making their opinions known, striving for personal achievement, and standing out. Conflict in these cultures is encouraged as an arena for personal expression. More interdependent cultures focus on relationships and groups, with group well-being, achievement and responsibility considered more important, and fitting in as a useful tactic for success. Conflict in these cultures tends to be avoided for worry that it will damage group cohesion.[26] You can gauge independence or interdependence by asking the following question:

- To what extent do people in a given environment act to share their personal views versus deferring to the widely understood views of a larger group, especially when the two diverge?

Independence versus interdependence inform divergent and varying reactions and approaches to many things, from hypocrisy[27] to well-being[28] to innovation.[29] Cultural psychologists Hazel Markus and Alana Conner note that independent versus interdependent beliefs in individuals can lead to significantly different reactions to the same event. For example, for independently oriented upper-class MBA students, if a friend purchased the same car as them, it was threatening and offending—it diminished the uniqueness of the student. But for interdependently oriented working-class firefighters, that same act was a positive act of solidarity befitting starting a car club.[30]

Uncertainty Avoidance

Uncertainty avoidance speaks to the degree to which uncertainty or ambiguity is avoided or embraced. In cultures with high uncertainty avoidance, there is a greater preference for stiff rules and formal structure. There may be a greater belief in "objective" reality or truth, greater efforts taken to fully understand or conceptualize situations in unambiguous terms, and fear or dislike of the unknown or unexplained. In cultures with low uncertainty avoidance, there is a greater acceptance of ambiguity and greater comfort with multiple informal (at times conflicting) rules or norms for behavior.[31] There may be greater value accorded to activities that call into question seemingly "known" or "understood" things, and less satisfaction with "entirely explained" outcomes or situations. You can gauge uncertainty avoidance in an environment by asking the following question:

- What happens when people in an environment encounter something new or unknown?

In a culture with high uncertainty avoidance, a disabled person bringing up the value of sign language recordings and text transcripts to accompany prerecorded video content[32] may face resistance due to the uncertainty represented by the decision. Leaders may bring up concerns with quality control, anxieties about the potential for inconsistency between older videos lacking accessibility features and newer ones with them, and worries regarding how these efforts might be perceived as outside the norm by their competitors. In a lower uncertainty avoidance culture, leaders might instead embrace the opportunity to set a new working standard for future produced content, create a new process for phasing older standards out, and use the occasion to advocate for similar changes in their industry.

Failure Avoidance

Failure avoidance relates to the degree to which failure and imperfection are avoided or embraced. High failure-avoidance cultures are often perfectionist and offer little patience for errors, mistakes, or setbacks. Failures or even small mistakes are seen as directly reflective of individual skill or worth, and one individual's failure can be seen as an opportunity for others to take advantage. So, when failures occur, they are more likely to be suppressed or hidden. Individuals in more perfectionist cultures may be more likely to work alone, set and strive for overly ambitious goals, and overwork to give the impression of working hard.[33] In low failure-avoidance cultures, there is a greater premium put on learning, growth, and experimentation. Risk-taking is often higher because the fear of failure is lower; if risks do not pay off, they do not threaten the status or well-being of the risk-taker.[34] (Note, though, that even in these cultures risk appetite is rarely infinite; if risk-taking is not adequately managed and swings too hard in the opposite direction, catastrophic failure becomes a possibility.[35]) You can gauge failure avoidance in an environment by asking the following question:

· How do people react when a person fails or exposes another's failure?

In a culture with high failure avoidance, few people are comfortable taking risks of their own volition and often make "safe" decisions that are unlikely to fail. For example, in a high failure-avoidance culture, ideas put forward by leaders are unlikely to be questioned, even if they are faulty or likely to fail—the fear of being associated with failure and punished, as a result, prevents many from speaking up or getting involved, even if doing nothing would cause the entire group to fail as a result.

Strategy

While structure and culture play large parts in understanding and tracing outcomes, they aren't deterministic. Otherwise, we could easily predict any outcome using only the context of the structure and culture behind it. The wild card here is **strategy**. While strategy is typically defined as the rationale or intentions behind those in and with power, in keeping with the spirit of our outcomes-centered approach,

I am choosing instead to situate my definition in something more observable. When I use the term, I am referring instead to the *choices themselves that people with power make.*

In this way, we can understand that every choice backed by power is in some way a strategy. In the classic sense, when organizational leaders convene a meeting with a slide presentation titled "Strategic Plan," their upcoming choices constitute a strategy. But so too is the choice of a middle manager to ignore a directive from the top, or the choice of the DEI committee to CC the CEO in an email to a Human Resources leader. Why do people make the choices they do? Sometimes, they're incentivized by the organizational structure or culture. Other times, they're acting in their own interest against or per the structure or culture. And sometimes, choices simply happen for reasons unknown even to the person or entity that makes them. They're the final piece of the puzzle needed to understand and reverse engineer outcomes—for DEI and for anything else an organization can undertake. You can gauge any strategy of people in an organization by answering the following questions:

- What choices do people make, and when do these choices appear to conflict with what is normalized by the organization's structure or culture?

- If choices are strategies, what are people trying to achieve through them, and why?

- Strategies can complement or conflict with each other. Where do you see people making the most complementary choices in the organization, and where do you see people making the most conflicting choices?

Strategy, structure, and culture are the trifecta that collectively explains how organizations get from intentions to outcomes. Let's put some of these ideas into action using a story of a fictional company inspired by some of the clients I've worked with over the last five years.

Zorm

A large US-based tech company named "Zorm" is in full-on crisis response mode after an anonymous whistleblower leaked an internal document to the Associated Press implicating the corporation's leadership in a controversial DEI issue. The document itself was only recently made available on the company intranet—the dates on it supported this—so speculation abounded that a current employee was the whistleblower. Zorm's PR team quickly took to social media to spin the story, discredit the document, and argue that the facts were being taken out of context. At the same time, the CEO made statements denouncing the leaks and minimizing the leadership's responsibility for the DEI issue. Immediately after the leak, employees—many of whom were unfamiliar with the information in the document until seeing it on social media—vented their shock and frustration on the internal communications platform. The information in the document contradicted many employees' understanding of the company's values and how it operated.

The next day, a company-wide email came out from the CEO expressing disappointment in these events and announcing that the company would be working to find the person responsible for leaking the document and holding them accountable. As senior leaders instructed all their direct reports and the HR team to restrict the information shared with employees more tightly, employees hastily deleted their open discussion threads on the internal platform regarding the leak. Several months later, the company had still not announced the results of its internal investigation into the leak, if any, though several employees had been terminated in the intervening months. Some employees whispered that the whistleblower was one of these fired, that the campaign had arbitrarily targeted outspoken activists, or that the whistleblower was still employed. Senior leaders, regardless, had stopped talking about the issue.

Eventually, the controversial issue reappeared in the news cycle, and senior leaders decided to administer an employee poll to gauge their workforce's opinions. They instructed their direct reports to cascade down the survey link, as was the standard, and waited patiently for two weeks as they collected responses. The survey results at the end? The overall sentiment was ambivalent and inconclusive on the issue, but more importantly, the overall response rate was dismal: just 23%, with almost no qualitative comments shared. Leaders were stunned—their past surveys had typically received 80-90% completion. Moving quickly, they contracted with a third-party employee assessment company to get a more comprehensive understanding of their workforce and again surveyed their employees, this time on a bevy of important issues. The initial data was sobering: low engagement, low confidence in leadership, warning signs with retention rate, and still, alarmingly, a low response rate despite a much more ambitious campaign—only 65%. What had happened here?

Let's go step-by-step to reverse engineer and understand the structure, culture, and strategy that resulted in this outcome.

- What is the process by which everyday decisions are made? Big decisions?

- How does decision-making differ for people situated at different places in the organization?

- How does the organization respond to crises or emergencies, and what aspects of the normal decision-making process change, if any?

- Where in the organization is power situated?

Zorm had a fairly centralized structure with a powerful senior leadership team at the top, with its functions divided into departments. While each department varied in form, function, and culture, the tight-knit senior leadership team treated these departments in the same way: as tools to carry out their strategic plans. All but the smallest decisions were made in their regular closed meetings and cascaded down through the company's departments, with middle managers serving more as logistical coordinators rather than decision-makers. Individual contributors, especially junior ones at lower levels of the organization, had little control over their roles and tasks.

When the crisis occurred, business continued as usual for all parts of the organization while senior leadership rapidly consulted a small number of PR consultants and experts. They were able to decide how to proceed after one efficient meeting and act accordingly. Members of the communications team were deputized to draft a statement, external relations teams reached out to their media connections, and HR leaders instructed their teams to identify which teams had access to the leaked documentation.

- How commonly are standardized formal processes used to achieve outcomes in your organization?
- To what extent do all members of the organization understand the formal rules for operating in your organization?
- How does your organization react to individuals or entities who do not know or follow the formal rules?

The company had all the formal rules one would expect of its size. It had a sizable employee handbook and a bevy of processes in each department to facilitate efficient work—though not all of them were always followed. The most important rules, those governing decision-making processes, were never formalized but known by everyone:

Senior leaders call the shots. What they say goes. What they don't know doesn't exist. These rules, more so than anything written in a manual, guided the de facto processes of the organization and were among the first things that new employees learned.

- What is the ratio of managers and supervisors to individual contributors?
- How many discrete responsibilities are listed in job descriptions?
- How many different groups of internal stakeholders must coordinate for an organization-wide initiative?

For a large organization, Zorm wasn't a particularly complex one. Managers often had far too many direct reports to be able to mentor or provide guidance effectively; the majority of their time was spent simply delegating tasks and holding their reports responsible for their execution. Individual contributors' jobs were fairly narrow and specialized, allowing them to understand the scope of their individual roles easily but giving them little information about other work occurring in the organization or even in their own departments. This was why employees were so genuinely shocked by the information shared in the leak: they had zero reasons to believe that the company leadership was even aware of the controversial DEI issue, let alone being implicated in it. They were similarly surprised by the company's swift public statements and communications. At the same time, many understood that decisions were made at the top, and the speed of the response made it clear that truly no one but the senior leaders needed to coordinate to make decisions for the entire organization.

To the senior leaders, the decisions they made to forcefully speak out against the leak publicly while internally denouncing it were part of a strategy to do damage control and dissuade future leaks. They wanted to present a solid presence to internal and external stakeholders alike and control the narrative.

- How comfortable do people with the least power in a given environment feel sharing potentially critical or negative feedback?

- To what extent do people in a given environment act to share their personal views versus deferring to the widely understood views of a larger group, especially when the two diverge?

- What happens when people in an environment encounter something new or unknown?

- How do people react when a person fails or exposes another's failure?

To most employees, leadership's response was a perfect embodiment of what a growing number perceived as a toxic internal culture. Senior leadership perceived their culture as one of high-power distance, in which most people accepted and tolerated the need for leadership to have vastly more power and control than other employees. Yet, that view wasn't widely shared by others in the organization, who resented the lack of control they had over their day-to-day activities and the direction of the company, and hoped that leaders would eventually distribute their power down the chain of command.

Additionally, while the culture of the senior leadership team was more independent—they encouraged vigorous debate, differing opinions, and even conflict when useful—that culture stopped as soon as you looked one level down in the organizational chart. Perhaps informed by the widespread perception that conflict would put one at risk, most employees acted more interdependently, sticking to their teams and departments and subduing conflict when it occurred. The whistleblower, similarly, initially felt unable to report their concerns to their direct manager for fear that they would be punished for it. Junior employees simply weren't expected to engage with these sorts of critical questions, but even middle managers were rarely seen to elevate concerns from within their teams and departments to the attention of senior leadership, and stories abounded of those who did so being reprimanded. Those stories only proliferated following the punitive approach suggested by internal communications and the termination of employees following the leak.

And so, when senior leadership sent out the survey to gauge employee sentiment, employees were viscerally reminded of what had happened the last time the topic was raised. Fearing that their responses would be identified, traced to them, and used as leverage to punish or fire them, employees chose the safest option: not to respond at all. They didn't trust that the process was transparent, that they would be safe no matter their answer or that leadership would listen even if they answered truthfully. Zorm was not known for listening or elevating junior employees' concerns. If the decision was between taking a risk for potential zero payoffs or doing nothing, it was an easy choice for most to make.

Use Power

When you're able to reverse engineer outcomes in the context of an organization's structure, culture, and strategy, you start to gain insights into how you might use power to create different ones. The first step in this process? Knowing what kind of organization you're in. You can use the resources below (Figures 3 and 4) to identify and note your organization's structure and culture.

Then, with an understanding of structure and culture, you can start to think about the stakeholders in your organization, their objectives, and the choices they make to achieve them—their strategies.

Recall the various types of power I opened the chapter with:

Organizational Structure and Culture

Aspect	Description	Low	Medium	High
Structure	The rules, roles, and responsibilities that coordinate people.			
Centralization	The degree to which decisions are made from the top down.	☐	☐	☐
Formalization	The degree to which organizational function is documented and follows strict rules.	☐	☐	☐
Complexity	The degree to which organizations divide work across jobs, divisions, and locations.	☐	☐	☐
Culture	Shared assumptions and expectations for behavior in an environment.			
Power Distance	The degree to which power differences are normalized and accepted.	☐	☐	☐
Interdependence	The degree to which people see themselves as connected to a broader group.	☐	☐	☐
Uncertainty Avoidance	The degree to which uncertainty or ambiguity is avoided or devalued.	☐	☐	☐
Failure Avoidance	The degree to which failure or imperfection is avoided or devalued.	☐	☐	☐

FIGURE 3. Structure and Culture Chart. Each dimension of structure and culture can be low, medium, or high.

- **Formal power:** the right to request behavior from another
- **Reward power:** the ability to promise (monetary or nonmonetary) compensation to influence behavior
- **Coercive power:** the ability to threaten punishment to influence behavior
- **Expert power:** the ability to influence behavior by possessing greater expertise or ability
- **Informational power:** the ability to influence behavior by possessing greater information
- **Referent power:** the ability to build rapport and influence behavior through charisma

Stakeholder Power and Strategy

Stakeholder	Formal	Reward	Coercive	Expert	Info	Referent
You						
Objectives/Strategy						
Objectives/Strategy						
Objectives/Strategy						
Objectives/Strategy						
Objectives/Strategy						
Objectives/Strategy						
Objectives/Strategy						
Objectives/Strategy						

FIGURE 4. Stakeholder Power and Strategy. Different aspects of power can be indicated for each stakeholder with their objectives or strategy.

The power that individuals and groups have is contextualized by their relationship to an organization's structure and culture. If a person has a management role with many direct reports in an organization that is mainly top-down, they would have a large amount of formal, reward, and coercive power. If a person has an extensive network and is well-connected in a highly interdependent culture, they would have a large amount of referent and informational power.

When this kind of analysis is done for many stakeholders in an environment, we can get a sense of where power is located in the organization and how we might create change. You can use the Stakeholder Power and Strategy resource (figure 4), also included in the Resources section at the end of the book, to identify and track the different aspects of power that the stakeholders in your organization hold.

Why do these exercises? Because identifying all of this information gives us the means to plan our own strategy in our own organizations. With this information, we can more deftly understand workplace power dynamics, secure opportunities, deploy our own power, and navigate organizational politics. This "knowing" doesn't just have to be abstract, either—you can literally draw out your understanding of power and its major stakeholders in your organization,[36] using the Stakeholder Power Map (Figure 5) to guide your thinking, and map out the many forces working toward, versus against, your goals.[37]

Let's return to our hypothetical example, Zorm. If you worked at Zorm and wanted to achieve DEI outcomes given its current environment, how might these frameworks help you do so? If you're a non-senior leader, you likely won't have much access to reward power or coercive power, so for now, we'll leave those off. It's clear, though, that DEI is not something existing leadership has much experience with or knowledge about.

Thus, if an outside DEI practitioner were to come in, they'd have outsized expert power given the dearth of expertise on the inside and the willingness of senior leadership to take them seriously.

But there are many more opportunities than just that one. Because of the structure and culture of the company, Zorm struggles to assemble and integrate the information across its many departments easily. Accordingly, there's a large and unrealized opportunity for well-informed employees to leverage this knowledge for each other and the organization.

If there's greater interest in helping the organization, well-informed experts from each department could create a new channel in the internal communications platform, using their informational power to

Create a Power Map

Use this chart to map stakeholders related to your change effort.
The x-axis represents the stakeholder's position toward your goal.
The y-axis represents their amount of power relative to your goal.

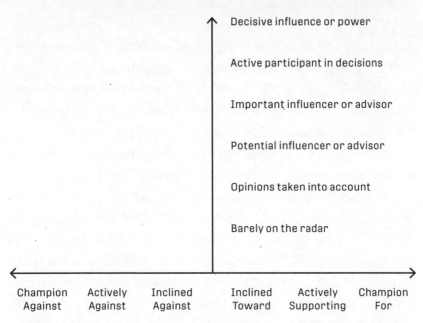

FIGURE 5. Stakeholder Power Map. A sample visual framework for mapping stakeholders along two axes, by power and support/opposition to an agenda.

facilitate information transfer and create alternative sources of information not tied to senior leadership.

If there's greater interest in helping each other and junior employees, well-informed experts from each department could contact each other outside of work, pool knowledge, and use their informational power to benefit employee organizing or unionizing efforts.

Because there are few formal entities within the organization that can request or even influence the behavior of the organization, this also represents a ripe opportunity to create a new source of formal power. While a successful union might achieve this, there are other options as well that would gain legitimacy from the employee base, even if they weren't met with enthusiasm by senior leaders.

An employee union or non-senior-leadership-led volunteer organization, like a DEI council, working group, task force,38 or an employee resource group,39 would likely accrue a large amount of legitimacy through the perception that this group represents the employee voice.

In the short run, given low morale across the organization, thoughtful middle managers could draw on their formal power, as well.

Middle managers could deploy their formal power to create safer environments on a team or department level for their direct reports.

Finally, any employee from across the organization with close connections to the senior leadership team could directly make a case for change if they felt safe and empowered enough to do so.

Any employee with referent power and the ability to hold the attention and consideration of the senior leadership team could use that power to influence the leadership team and shift the organization toward desired outcomes.

Cede Power

What if, like many of the clients I work with, you see yourself at the very top of that power structure? In my experience, many resources on DEI treat you like a constant obstacle that cannot change, that change-makers have to organize around, or conversely use an overly patronizing approach and treat you like an amateur.

Especially if you are reading this book, neither of these assumptions is true.

The leaders of Zorm weren't bad people but built an organization on a few assumptions. They valued their own skill, knowledge, and decision-making ability over all else and did everything in their power to enable it. They expected their workforce to deliver on their decisions and trusted heavily in their ability to make the right ones. To these assumptions, I'll say: that's fine. Remember, the approach doesn't matter, but the outcomes do. And in Zorm's case, the outcomes were clear: engagement, confidence in leadership, and retention rate were all down. A solid third of the workforce didn't even want to fill out an important survey, and only a fourth felt comfortable sharing their opinion on a controversial issue. Something about the status quo that senior leaders had built and maintained just wasn't working.

These outcomes made it clear that leadership couldn't ignore the problem. Their poor outcomes were unlikely to go away on their own. These outcomes would likely be made worse if leaders decided to double down on their punitive approach. As painful as it was, before anything could be done, senior leaders at Zorm had to admit that they had done something wrong—and that now they needed to make it right.

But how? They needed first to know what they didn't know: what people were feeling and how things had gone wrong. Thankfully, their survey—even with lower-than-ideal response rates—gave preliminary answers to this. Employees overwhelmingly believed that senior leaders were behind the curve when it came to DEI comprehension, managing company culture through growth, and empowering early-career and junior employees. They raised as pain points numerous incidents when leaders responded poorly to conflict originating outside their team, struggled with maintaining good boundaries with their junior employees, and poorly communicated corporate stances on important issues. And most damningly, employees just didn't trust their leaders to do the right thing.

Leaders considered a number of options to fix their issues. One appealing option was to bring in experts, educators, and coaches to help the leadership team bridge their gap in knowledge and experience. They could learn enough about DEI to be competent communicators of it, talk to some experts on scaling and company culture, and get coaching to become better mentors and leaders.

But lingering still was the elephant in the room: their employees' loss of trust from numerous incidents, not least this latest one. How would they regain that? An apology wouldn't be enough. Closing their doors and promising that they'd "educate themselves" might not be enough, either. Should they change how they ran the organization?

As the group discussed among themselves, they started considering what different approaches to running the organization might look like and the new benefits and challenges these ideas entailed. They could give individual departments more autonomy, changing the role of the senior leader in charge of each department from a "commander" giving instructions down the chain of command to a "translator" connecting the realities of the department to the needs of the rest of the organization, communicated by other senior leaders. They could create alternative decision-making structures like advisory boards, committees, and councils, on which a greater mix of employees from different areas of the organization or different title levels could serve and delegate important decisions to these entities. They could slowly shift the culture by pushing decision-making down, letting go of some control from the top to better empower folks at the middle and bottom. Most dramatically, they could reorganize the company and start again from the ground up with a different structure, potentially flatter, more complex, and more decentralized—though that would significantly disrupt their operations and may not necessarily fix their problems.

What did the senior leaders at Zorm do? Truth be told, I don't know—they're a hypothetical example, after all. But many senior leaders that I work with, while rarely in the exact same situation as those at Zorm, take a hybrid approach that blends elements of both these directions. They often act first with the understanding that their workforce wants to see something different from them and that closed-door interventions—even effective ones—don't inspire confidence or regain their workforce's trust. They often encourage the formation of groups like employee resource groups, DEI councils, and advisory groups explicitly for the legitimacy they bring, start engaging these groups in the decision-making process, then start the much slower work of learning as individuals and as a leadership team. Over time, they try through a blend of better communications, tweaks to decision-making practices, and relationships built with new stakeholders to rebuild trust. This continues until the next big crisis—during which the changes implemented in the organization get put to the test.

This chain of events is far from the only one that might happen, but it's more common than you'd think. If you're a leader facing a situation like the one here, contemplate how you'll deploy the power you have.

Thus far, we've covered what, in my view, are some of the most foundational aspects to doing pragmatic and effective DEI work—centering outcomes, taking a systemic approach to understanding challenges, and deploying power critically. But we haven't addressed yet perhaps *the* largest set of challenges that have plagued this work since its inception: the matter of identity and the power associated with it.

Making organizational change in the broad sense can already feel like rolling a boulder uphill. Doing so while also keeping identity and DEI in mind can feel more like rolling a house.

TAKEAWAYS

- **Power is not only held by people but embedded in systems.**
  Power is the potential to influence or compel people or events, and
  we are always engaging with power in some way, shape, or form,
  whether or not we want to. Achieving DEI requires that we engage
  intentionally with it, to know it, use it, and cede it as needed.

- **Power comes in many forms.** There are many different types
  of interpersonal power, including formal power, reward power,
  coercive power, expert power, informational power, and referent
  power. These types of power, if deployed thoughtfully given an
  understanding of an organization's structure, culture, and strategy,
  can be used to achieve DEI outcomes.

- **An organization's *structure* describes the rules, roles, and
  responsibilities that coordinate the behavior of those in it.**
  Important things to understand with structure include *centralization*, or the degree to which decisions are made from the top down;
  formalization, or the degree to which the organization's functioning is documented and enshrined through formal processes;
  and *complexity*, the degree to which organizations divide their
  functioning across jobs, divisions, and locations.

- **An organization's *culture* describes its members' shared
  understanding of its assumptions and expectations for behavior.** Important dimensions by which cultures vary include *power
  distance*, the degree to which a large separation between most
  and least powerful is accepted and normalized; *interdependence*,
  the degree to which people perceive themselves as part of a larger
  whole; *uncertainty avoidance*, the degree to which uncertainty
  or ambiguity is avoided or embraced; and *failure avoidance*, the
  degree to which failure and imperfection are avoided or embraced.

- **An organization's *strategies* describe the sum of what people choose to do with their power.** The choices that people make can complement or conflict with each other. Understanding how power is used, gained, or ceded amid these choices helps us understand the most unpredictable factor in how organizations function.

- **Knowing how strategy, power, culture, and structure interact allows us to reverse engineer outcomes.** If we understand each piece's role in creating a status quo, we can work effectively to create different results by reshaping and rearranging those pieces.

EXERCISES AND REFLECTIONS

1. For an organization you are familiar with, whether your own workplace, an organization you volunteer with, your school, or any other, work through the exercises presented throughout this chapter to understand its structure, culture, and strategies. A selection of them is included below.

   a. Where in your organization is power situated? How much is the operation of power exercised inside formal structures? How much is exercised outside of formal structures, such as in personal relationships?

   b. How does your organization react to individuals or entities who do not know or follow the formal rules?

   c. How many different groups of internal stakeholders must coordinate for an organization-wide initiative?

   d. How comfortable do people with the least power in your organization feel sharing potentially critical or negative feedback?

   e. To what extent do people in your organization act to share their personal views versus deferring to the widely understood views of a larger group, especially when the two diverge?

f. What happens when people in your organization encounter something new or unknown?

g. How do others react when a person fails or exposes another's failure?

h. What choices do people make, and when do these choices appear to conflict with what is normalized by your organization's structure or culture?

i. If choices are strategies, what are people trying to achieve through them, and why?

j. Where do you see people making the most complementary choices versus the most conflicting choices in your organization?

2. Pick any issue that matters to you in your organization. Try following the Stakehold Power Map (figure 5) to map out stakeholders in your organization. What new insights emerge from your power analysis?

SIX

Identity and Difference

"You're all experts in how gender works in your workplace," I said. I looked around the room, and many women were nodding. The men looked like I had mistaken them for celebrities—confused and somewhat embarrassed. So I called on one.

"Why the look?" I prodded.

The man I called on stood up. "I know a lot about how my workplace works," he commented slowly as if carefully choosing its words. "What to do if you want a promotion, how to resolve problems, how decisions get made. But...my wife is teaching me that things don't work the same for her. She's the gender expert, not me."

It was a humble admission, and many other men nodded, some looking more appreciative, others looking somewhat frustrated.

"Thanks for sharing that," I responded. I knew how hard it was for him to admit that knowledge believed to be expertise wasn't as correct as he had previously thought. It can't have been easy to swallow his pride and admit ignorance.

But he was being a little too humble.

"You honestly know plenty about gender."

He looked up, puzzled.

"Everything you said earlier about your workplace knowledge was true, at least for some people. You're saying your wife knows a lot about how your workplace works *for women*. Well, you know a lot about how your workplace works *for men*. How promotions, conflict resolution, and decision-making all work *for men*. You're both gender experts, even if you've never thought of it that way."

Who Gets an Identity?

White. Man. Nondisabled. Neurotypical. Heterosexual. Cisgender. Wealthy. Christian.

Pause for a moment and let yourself experience how it feels to process these words. Are you bristling? Tense? Do you feel exhaustion, reluctance, frustration, shame, or anger? Perhaps neutrality, or not much emotion at all?

The majority of people in the world fall into at least one of these categories. For many, they are passive markers of physical and social characteristics that impact their lives without receiving much active thought.

Black. Latine. Asian. Indigenous. Mixed. Woman. Nonbinary. Disabled. Autistic. Neurodivergent. Lesbian. Gay. Bisexual. Trans. Queer. Poor. Muslim. Jewish.

The majority of people in the world *also* fall into at least one of these categories. While some people with these characteristics may see them as neutral markers, many do not. For many people, their race, gender, disability, sexuality, class status, religion, and more go beyond passive identifiers to become an active source of social identity.[1]

Many of these latter identities have a long history of persecution or marginalization, continuing into the present day. Because powerful entities and people singled out groups based on specific characteristics, people with those characteristics found community, safety, and solidarity together—and thus, over time, developed unique cultures, subcultures, and languages related to their communities. It is at least partially because of the unique interactions between shared hardship and community-building that we have such (at times controversial and well-debated) concepts like "womanhood,"[2] "Asian American culture,"[3] and "autistic self-advocacy."[4]

Even the identity terms themselves evolved to reflect histories of solidarity through hardship. For example, the term "LGBT" and its later variants "LGBTQ," "LGBTQIA," and beyond were developed by communities specifically to recognize solidarity between different groups of people persecuted for their sexualities, gender identities, and gender expressions.[5] Similar things can be said for "people of color" (POC) and its more recent evolutions like "Black, Indigenous, and people of color" (BIPOC) emerging to symbolize racial solidarity[6] and a desire to center anti-Blackness and decolonization when discussing race, respectively.[7]

Historically, workplaces have been no stranger to referring to their workforce in terms of social categories—at least when it came to explicit discrimination[8] or segregation.[9] But in most workplaces, that kind of discrimination, where an employer could say "no women" or "no Blacks" or "no Asians," eventually became both socially frowned upon and, in many workplaces, illegal.[10] Did banning explicit discrimination end it? Certainly not. As we covered earlier in this book, hiring and workplace discrimination simply persisted in more subtle forms.

But banning discrimination did provide the rationale to empower the first wave of race-focused, then gender-focused workplace training, like those the US military created in the 1970s. These trainings were formed around the key premise that, because prejudice and discrimination originated from certain groups of people (White people, men), those groups should be targeted in an effort to eliminate it. As such, race relations trainings and similar examples of proto-DEI work largely focused their efforts on compelling White people and men in workplaces to become less prejudiced and therefore engage in less discrimination.

Consider it this way: it's one thing to notice that a friend comes from a family with drinking problems. It's another to take that friend, forcibly enroll them in a recovering alcoholics program, and tell them that they've been the source of pain and hardship for their other friends and colleagues—even if it's all true.

Whether or not you're correct, that approach is an almost guaranteed fast track to defensiveness and resentment. When it comes to DEI training, taking away the agency of participants and framing learning as a remedial effort is more likely to make recipients increase their animosity toward those delivering training and even *increase* their negative feelings toward women, non-White groups, and other underserved communities.[11] And there's good evidence that, over the last few decades of less-than-effective DEI work, that's what happened exactly.

Workplaces that faced a backlash to identity-based blaming, in later iterations of DEI work, then tried to address the challenge of identity by simply ignoring it. If we didn't talk about identity, didn't mention race or gender or sexuality or ability or age, and discouraged anyone who did, our workplaces would become post-identity paradises of equity—or so the idealist belief went. This identity-denying approach was in vogue for quite a long while in the US, and in some European countries, it continues to be the standard enforced by law.[12] It manifests in statements like, "people who talk about race are the real racists" or "gender doesn't matter."

If discrimination had ended and inequities had disappeared, identity denial might have found a more permanent home within the working world and broader society. But inequities didn't disappear from workplaces, and they didn't disappear from society; the only thing that changed was the social permissibility of being explicit about prejudice. Underserved communities thus felt even *more reason* to talk about identity because if they didn't call attention to discrimination in the newly identity-denying environments they found themselves in, even fewer people would notice it.[13]

So new approaches emerged, most notably multiculturalism: a 180-degree reversal in the previous approach to identity that denied difference. Multiculturalism was, more than anything else, a celebration of those different from the social norm. Women's contributions were celebrated. Non-White communities' historical achievements and cultural heritage got the spotlight. And newly visible and politicized dimensions of difference like religion, disability, neurodiversity, LGBTQ+, immigrant status, and motherhood further extended the celebratory focus on "difference as positive."

The problem here was that "difference" was a code word. Multiculturalism didn't truly celebrate every dimension of difference—it celebrated specifically all experiences that weren't "cisgender, heterosexual, nondisabled, Christian, White, or male," a fact that was blisteringly obvious to cisgender, heterosexual, nondisabled, Christian, White men and others with one or more of those identities. This was pointed out in the often sarcastic complaints about multiculturalism by members of socially advantaged groups: "Why don't we get a White History Month?"[14] "When do we get to celebrate men?"[15] and "Where's Straight Pride Month?"[16]

These questions have become some of the favorite punching bags of academics and experts; it's easy and cathartic to (at times rightfully) castigate ignorant members of socially advantaged groups for not understanding history and power. The arguments are similar: "We don't celebrate your identity because every single day of every single month is already a celebration of cisgender, heterosexual, White, Christian masculinity. Your identities are plastered on all our media,[17] embedded in our value system,[18] and even hard-coded into our national holidays."[19]

I agree with this critique from a bird's-eye view, but it's missing something important. Our society *does* value some identities over others, but it's fully completed the transition to doing so in implicit and subtle, rather than explicit and crude, ways. *And so, we can all exist within societies that benefit cisgender, heterosexual, White, Christian men while simultaneously never talking about cisgender people, heterosexual people, White people, Christianity, or men in neutral terms.* The many cisgender, heterosexual, White, Christian men I talk to mention this often. They point out that in recent times, the only time they hear the word "White" is immediately preceding the words "privilege," "fragility," or "supremacist," and that the only time they hear the word "male" or "men" is immediately preceding a critique or criticism about their implication in sexism. In the best of times, they are unmarked, lacking an identity. In the worst of times, they suddenly receive an identity as a marker of shame or culpability.

And, understandably, it pisses a lot of them off.

Pragmatic Identity

There are now, in fact, many movements and communities that "celebrate" members of majority groups. "Men's Rights Activists" promote a vision of masculinity as powerful and positive but under attack from women and those wishing to restrict men. White supremacists do similar things, positioning Whiteness as under attack from a progressive, "woke" society looking to shame White people for characteristics out of their control. These groups and communities are some of the few that promote an unapologetic, positive, and highly visible depiction of the social majority or advantaged identities. The problem with them isn't that they frame having an advantaged identity in positive terms— it's that they intentionally weave in fascism, nationalism, and calls for violence with the positive framings. This is one of the reasons why groups like these only continue to gain traction in the US,[20] Europe,[21] and worldwide.[22]

They make arguments directed at other White people, along the lines of, "why be a constantly apologizing, self-flagellating, Robin-DiAngelo's-White-Fragility[23]-reading White person when you can be a strong, confident, unapologetic one?"

"Why be a disempowered, meek, always-stepping-through-minefields, terrified-of-feminists man when you can be a strong, confident, unapologetic one?"

These are not good-faith arguments. And yet, I can't deny that there are far more ways to be a "bad" man or a "bad" White person in DEI circles than there are ways to be "good" ones. I am frustrated but not surprised when I hear of people who, considering their choices, gravitate toward the more comfortable option for their identity.

We are severely messing up as an industry and profession if we can't present a more appealing identity alternative for the people we work with than *fascism* can.

That isn't to say we haven't tried.

One of the major appeals of unconscious bias training, for example, is that it avoids some of the overly simplistic finger-pointing of some prior DEI work. It doesn't matter what your identity is; if you have bias, you're part of the problem. This approach may be identity denying, but it replaces "identity" as a proxy for discrimination with "bias" as a proxy for discrimination, arguing that while we can't change identity, we can certainly change bias. A shame that these efforts have not yet borne fruit and may never be able to, but an intriguing angle nonetheless.

Ibram X. Kendi's *How to Be An Antiracist*, a wildly popular book amid the racial reckoning of 2020, presents another model: racism as situated in policy (which I like), and "antiracist" versus "racist" as designations for people who oppose or support racist policies (which I don't like).[24] Kendi similarly avoids inherently connecting membership to a privileged racial group with the implication of harm but doesn't go far in identifying a proxy. "Unless you oppose gerrymandering, you're a racist" is unlikely to be particularly compelling or do anything new to avoid defensiveness and backlash for people who aren't already amenable to the idea.

Complementary to Kendi's framework is one that's been espoused by DEI and social justice practitioners for decades: being an antiracist (or an "antisexist," or an anti-[insert oppression here]-ist) isn't just about having the right beliefs, it's about *doing the right work*.[25] By making and following through on plans for self-improvement and being a more conscious, aware, and intentional individual, we can blossom into our own as burgeoning antiracists. This is an interesting approach, too—it, like Kendi's, identifies "antiracist" as a positive status symbol that can be earned through hard work and dedication, as a badge against accusations of racism. The problem with it is that literally, no two writers can seem to agree on what "doing antiracist work" looks like and how much is "enough." Without a clear or consistent pathway to acquiring the status of "antiracist," the designation can easily become either a check-the-box exercise an individual can sell (e.g., "Take my class to become an antiracist!") or a moving goal post to dangle always just out of reach for social cred (e.g., "You'll never be an antiracist unless you _____!"). Making "antiracist" a positive status symbol without aligning on how people can attain it simply sets up a circus for people already committed to antiracism, without doing anything to incentivize changed behavior from those routinely committing racist acts.

Am I an antiracist yet if I call in my family members for their racism?

How about if I advocate in my workplace for new policies?

What if I volunteer in my local communities and show up to protests?

Imagine me saying this in my best "antiracist influencer" voice: "antiracism isn't about identity. It's about constant and principled movement in the right direction, to move the status quo and dismantle systems of oppression." Cue the applause.

Now imagine the cisgender, heterosexual, Christian, White man in the audience who raises his hand.

"So, if I do all these things...will I still get called a racist if I ask a question about why we need a chief diversity officer?"

Yes, John. You probably will. And that's why we need a new way to tackle this shit.

The problem with every single one of these approaches is that they don't acknowledge the messy reality of DEI work in our workplaces—not just around race but around every dimension of difference. If I were to characterize the complications that we have to design around, these would include:

- We have little shared understanding of DEI impact or outcomes in the workplace and thus have to rely on proxies that connect systemic outcomes (e.g., the workplace well-being of all disabled people) to individual behaviors (e.g., the usage of inclusive language). Accordingly, "get-woke-quick" frameworks centered on individual absolvement or empowerment easily validate our egos—and our wallets, if the *New York Times* bestsellers list is any indication.[26]

- We are strongly motivated to avoid approaches that make us feel bad about ourselves. Thus, historical and present-day framings of change work blaming those possessing advantaged social identities and exhorting them to self-flagellate have tended to elicit backlash, hostility, and resentment from the very people they should be shifting toward greater understanding, inclusion, and empathy.[27]

- We need to be able to name identity to even talk about power, let alone recognize the many ways that power and inequity work to marginalize many people, especially those with marginalized identities, in our workplaces.

What would a new approach to identity and DEI work, taking these challenges into account, look like?

No Racists, No Antiracists

We should scrap these labels because there's no compelling or consistent way to define them, their pursuit and avoidance tend to drive unhelpful behaviors, and they don't do us good at scale.

Is a sexist someone with sexist beliefs? Then we're all sexists because, to some extent, we all hold sexist beliefs. Is an ableist someone who supports ableist policies? Then quite a few of us, regardless of what work we do to create change, are ableists because a policy we support has ableist implications. Is a "trans ally" or "antiracist" or "feminist" someone who meaningfully improves the lives of trans people, non-White people, or women? Then either a great deal of us fit these categories, or none of us do, depending on where we set the bar.

Whatever we define a "racist" as, people will do everything in their power to avoid. If racism is defined as using slurs, then people will rush to attend antiracist language workshops. If racism is defined as refusing to hire diversity professionals or organize diversity training, then people will rush to make DEI leader hires and bring in diversity trainers. And more importantly, if one practitioner prescribes a 10-step plan for "becoming an antiracist" and another practitioner claims that they can do it in 5, where do you think people will go? Actions motivated by the avoidance of a negative label or the achievement of a positive one are easily decoupled from real outcomes.

In workplaces, too, there is little benefit to knowing "how many (anti)racists" exist on a team or in a department. If you're trying to understand what's happening in your workforce, you should be collecting quantitative and qualitative data on psychological safety,[28] engagement,[29] access to opportunity,[30] enablement,[31] (comfort with reporting[32]) discrimination,[33] and more across different demographic categories. If your workplace has no disparities on any of these dimensions, what does it matter if no one's ever even heard of Ibram X. Kendi or Robin DiAngelo or any DEI expert? If your workplace has enormous disparities on these dimensions, conversely, what difference does it make if everyone has read *How to Be an Antiracist* or *White Fragility* or even this book?

So forget about the labels, and focus on what matters: the outcomes. We don't need to call ourselves "antiracists" to dismantle racism. Same goes with ableism, Islamophobia, xenophobia, and so on and so forth. Either we've solved the right problems and achieved the outcomes we want, or we haven't and have work to do. Is it that hard to imagine cutting the crap, and just doing the work, instead?

What of our social identities, then? Our race, gender, sexuality, age, size, religion, and so on?

Identity as Incomplete Insight

We all have identities, and they meaningfully make us all different from each other. I'm a millennial, second-generation Chinese American, queer, trans, neurodivergent, areligious, nondisabled, upper-class, nonbinary person. Statistically, your combination of identities is probably different from mine, and even if it's not, our differing relationships to our identities would mean that we *still* perceive and are perceived by the world differently. No two millennials have the exact same shared experiences or perspectives, though we might see some things similarly in the broad sense. Same with two queer people, two nonbinary people, and so on. No matter who we are, our identities and our unique relationships with them give us valuable insights into the world.

That's a strength for all of us.

My identities and experiences undeniably give me a unique set of insights, expertise, and knowledge: I'm more familiar with navigating largely White and East Asian suburbs, universities, and online millennial and Gen Z–adjacent LGBTQ+ communities, for example. But I was *not* naturally familiar with talking to Black and brown people in high school or early college. Nor was I comfortable at all talking about religion of any kind at first. I spent a large portion of my life steeped in rhetoric that I now know is called the medical model of disability,[34] and accordingly, it took me a while to understand disability in more social terms. I am still working to understand men, manhood, and masculinity in different racial contexts than my own, and I am still learning about different generations, social classes, and identity-related experiences that I did not and could not have had myself. Are there aspects of the world I understand better than you do because of the identities I have? Yes. Are there aspects of the world you understand better—far better—than I do because of your identities? Absolutely.

That's identity—it's inherently value-neutral but always insightful for every dimension of difference, whether privileged or marginalized. Having a marginalized identity is valuable because it gives you insight into that identity and the experiences informed by it. Having a privileged identity is valuable because it gives you insight into that identity and the experiences informed by it. But no matter what mix of identities we have, they give us only a partial or incomplete understanding of the world.

A nondisabled person won't have the same understanding of the world as a disabled person—and no two disabled people will have the same understanding of the world, either. Women, men, and nonbinary people all experience the world slightly differently: they see different things; they're treated in different ways; they draw different conclusions. If we want to design a world for everyone, then *we need everyone*. We need non-White people, women, LGBTQ+ people, disabled people, neurodiverse people, Muslim people, Jewish people, and so on to create a world that interrupts inequity and designs for the difference in mind. We also need White people, men, cisgender people, straight people, nondisabled people, neurotypical people, Christian people, and more—to make sure that the world that we design together doesn't just put new people in charge of broken systems but truly designs something better for everyone.

The notion that everyone has a place in DEI work is, unfortunately, not always apparent in the mainstream DEI movement, and that ambiguity is often felt most by people with privileged identities. In a survey of White men's responses to DEI work, almost 70% shared that the biggest obstacle to their participation in DEI efforts was uncertainty around whether they were even "wanted" within the work itself. This should be a sobering statistic for anyone who cares about this work. For us to have so polarized the concept of identity within DEI that a supermajority of otherwise like-minded individuals feels shut out of DEI by dint of their privileged identities alone should be a travesty. Many DEI advocates feel no qualms about bluntly stating the role of people with privileges in the problems we face in our organizations and societies, so I'll do the same for the solutions. *Of course,* White people, men, nondisabled people, cisgender people, heterosexual people, Christian people, wealthy people, and people with other privileges have a part to play in the solutions we're building. We couldn't succeed otherwise.

Harm and Impact

While the framework I'm building here avoids the blaming and shaming inherent to many of its predecessors, it lacks accountability. Previous frameworks have all featured some kind of "boogeyman": unconscious bias training has its specter of "bias," and much of current DEI discourse has its "racist," "sexist," and "bigot."

In this framework, the outcome to avoid is **harm**: the negative physical, emotional, economic, or social impact—whether damage, suffering, devaluing, or otherwise—of an action or decision. We can think of harm as affecting individuals, groups, and/or society more broadly.

It can result from both intentional acts (e.g., a hate crime intending to terrorize a group) or unintentional acts (e.g., an accidental misnaming of an individual). Harm can result from both proximal causes (e.g., a viral video of police brutality circulates on social media, prompting widespread distress and outrage) and distal causes (e.g., a law passed decades ago continues to disproportionately restrict the behavior of certain groups of people). And finally, harm can originate from individuals (e.g., offensive comments), organizations (e.g., inflexible working policies), institutions (e.g., racist laws), and even objects and environments (e.g., inaccessible apps; hostile architecture). Harm at scale is the impact of homogeneity, inequity, and exclusion—the opposites to the outcomes of diversity, equity, and inclusion we're trying to achieve.

Previous DEI frameworks have often focused on the level of the individual. The premise of "unconscious bias" or "allyship training" is that individuals can gain greater awareness of their own biases, shift their behavior, and become better people. The premise of targeting "racists" or "sexists" or "bigots" is that changing the behavior of the worst offenders through individual interventions—whether shame or education—will make them better people.

What I am proposing is that we look beyond the scope of the individual, to focus instead on the larger *systems* around us.

When I use the word "system" in a DEI sense, I am referring to the broad and interconnected policies, processes, and practices, the structure, the culture, and the strategy, within a given environment that create and maintain outcomes.

In other words, a concept like "systemic sexism," or in social justice language, "patriarchy," communicates a large number of things simultaneously.

1. **Policies like laws, rules, and workplace guidelines that explicitly or implicitly advantage men and disadvantage women.** For example, laws that regulate access to reproductive health,[35] laws

restricting clothing that is "too religious" *or* "too secular,"[36] and the lack of laws guaranteeing paid parental leave.[37]

2. **Standard and normalized processes and procedures embedded in society and its institutions that explicitly or implicitly advantage men and disadvantage women.** For example, hiring processes that reward characteristics beyond merit,[38] board selection processes with narrow criteria for a women's "fit,"[39] and decision-making processes within heterosexual relationships (e.g., for division of household chores) that benefit men.[40]

3. **Everyday practices and routine activities that explicitly or implicitly advantage men and disadvantage women.** Examples include street harassment, catcalling,[41] victim-blaming sexual assault survivors,[42] and sexist workplace practices—from taking credit for ideas or achievements to the assignment of office housework.[43]

4. **Organizational structures that enable discrimination or multiply its effects in ways that explicitly or implicitly advantage men and disadvantage women.** For example, gender-segregated job ladders in hierarchical structures,[44] organizational networks,[45] and department assignments.[46]

5. **Organizational cultures that devalue femininity and other traits associated with women and/or normalize casual sexism that explicitly or implicitly advantages men and disadvantages women.** For example, the normalization of sexist and objectifying jokes,[47] discrimination apologism, rationalizing abuse and inequity,[48] and the tightrope women must walk between being punished for being "too masculine" or punished for being "too feminine."[49]

6. **Strategies and decisions that reinforce other aspects of inequitable systems resist efforts at change and maintain or worsen the status quo that explicitly or implicitly advantages men and**

disadvantages women. For example, decision-makers choice to utilize HR policy or not based on personal gender biases,[50] avoid women, or attempt to minimize different-gender interaction[51]or any other actions that continue supporting policies, processes, practices, structures, or cultures that are known to have inequitable gender outcomes without change.

Apart from my complaints about practitioners who use the term "systemic" without understanding what it means, there's a good reason why the shorthand term is so much more prevalent compared to, well, this.

"That's all well and good Lily," many of the folks I work with say, "but what am *I* as an individual supposed to do in the face of all this… of changing a system?" And the prospect certainly feels daunting. Unconscious bias training makes a far more seductive sell: take a 90-minute training, question your biases, change your behavior, and absolve yourself of blame. When the harm surrounding us is so comprehensive, pervasive, and systemic, taking action can feel overwhelming.

But us exploring what "systemic" really means helps us be as specific as possible when we ask the question, *"what role do individuals play in changing systems to reduce harm and achieve DEI?"* To that, I answer: **individuals must be stewards of the system within the environments they hold responsibility in.**

Every single person is responsible for creating positive outcomes and reducing or eliminating harm, but that responsibility isn't the same for every person. Within a workplace, who is responsible and accountable when data shows that Muslim employees aren't being promoted at similar rates as others? On some level, we can say that the individuals applying for promotion bear some responsibility for having the right skills and competencies and performing at the same level as their peers. We can also say that those responsible for promotion decisions bear the responsibility for making unbiased decisions based on valid metrics and that direct managers bear some responsibility for mentoring, supporting, and equipping their direct reports for success. HR professionals are responsible for making and stewarding policies and processes that work for the whole workforce. Every employee is responsible for creating and maintaining inclusive environments on their teams and respect in their interpersonal interactions.

So, when harm occurs, whose responsibility is it? That's the question we should ask as we examine the roots of these issues within organizations, looking into all of these dimensions and more. Maybe our investigation identifies the biggest problem: a combination of unconscious bias in promotion decision-makers and the lack of a standard decision-making process within the organization. Or perhaps it identifies a particular skill heavily weighted in promotion criteria that Muslim candidates for promotion are less adept at for whatever reason and that managers don't know to provide support for. Perhaps it identifies a culture that normalizes Islamophobia and microaggressions against Muslim employees or a lack of infrastructure to validate belonging, like prayer rooms. Maybe it's some mix of all the above or other factors not listed here.

Thus, depending on the origins of inequity, responsibility may fall mostly on HR leaders, senior leaders, or direct managers, or all of them to some extent for a given inequity. That means it's their responsibility to make things right and rectify the parts of the inequity they own— whatever it takes.

That's it.

"Wait, but what about their identities?" Well, what about them? Unless these leaders happen to be Christian *and* have explicit anti-Muslim attitudes, *and* these attitudes result in behaviors that result in inequitable outcomes, I couldn't care less what identities these people have. It doesn't matter if they have privileges. It doesn't matter if they have marginalizations. All I care about is that they do their jobs, eliminate inequities, and make things right within the environments they hold responsibility for.

With this firm grounding in impact and outcomes, we can then treat identity the way most people perceive it—not as a high-stakes proxy for harm or accountability, but as just another facet of difference that we can use to understand each other and our work better. And when it comes to accountability, no longer should we ask, "am I biased?" or "am I racist?" Instead, just ask:

"Am I fulfilling my responsibilities to eliminate harm and make my environment diverse, equitable, and inclusive?"

Identity Is a Language

There's a lot about early 2020s DEI that makes me groan. Perhaps my biggest pet peeve is the language we've developed to talk about identity "without talking about identity." Take the following sentences:

"We need more diverse employees."

"We're looking for intersectional identities."

"Our board of directors is 30% minorities!"

Diverse employees? Given that diversity is a quality of a group rather than of an individual, might you be referring to something else? Are you trying to say, "employees possessing identities other than cisgender, heterosexual, White, Christian, men?" Isn't that, well, most people in the world? Is there a reason why you're being so cryptic and unspecific in your wording, so much so that your call to action is completely un-actionable?

Intersectional identities? Given that intersectionality is just an analytic lens to understand different social identities in tandem and that every individual in the world by definition has their own "intersectional identities," are you perhaps trying to say something else?

Are you trying to say "women of color" or "disabled trans person" or "low-income Jewish person over 50," and if so, which, and why?

30% minority? What kind of minorities? Assuming you mean racial minorities in your country, which ones? Is there a reason you're combining the categories, and who are you appealing to?

Can we say what we mean?

I spoke with a colleague years ago who scoffed at an engineering team for being "all dudes" when what this colleague meant was that they were all misogynists. The two words are *not the same.*

I spoke with a different colleague who lauded a team for being "all LGBTQ," when what they meant was that the team was immune to bias (they weren't).

Identity isn't morality. Being privileged or marginalized on one or more dimensions of identity doesn't make us any better or worse as people; it simply positions us differently and offers us different advantages and disadvantages within broader systems. It changes the power we have access to and our ability to understand experiences similar to and different from our own.

But it doesn't make us any better or worse as people.

And, as useful as identity is in understanding the world, it's far from a perfect tool. Knowing everything about a person's social identities, from their race to their gender, class, sexuality, disability status, religion, age, and so on and so forth, can give you useful information to analyze their experiences. But if you somehow got two people whose identities exactly matched in every way and put them next to each other, they'd still be different people because identity isn't deterministic, and people are more than just the sum of their parts.

I like to frame identity like it's a language, one of many. It has its own rules and peculiarities. Some things it excels at describing; others, not so much. Being fluent, or at least proficient, in identity as a language lets you speak to more people and understand a greater swath of the world, even if you don't speak it all the time.

With a bit of homework, you can learn that many autistic self-advocates are increasingly preferring identity-first language ("autistic person") over person-first language ("person with autism") and that there are ongoing debates over the distinction.[52] You can learn too that these trends are paralleled in some[53] but not all[54] disability communities and that preferences may range from person to person.

You can learn the historical complexity of the term "Asian American" and the evolution of its political implications over time[55] to be more intentional about how you describe and gather data on this complex group of communities.

You can learn that acronyms like people of color (POC) and Black, Asian, and minority ethnic (BAME) emerged from similar histories of political solidarity between racial groups in the US and UK, respectively, before becoming watered down over time into less-than-helpful umbrella terms and becoming a target of critique.[56]

You can learn that "Jew" as a noun isn't a slur and that most Jews take no aversion to the term when used respectfully.[57]

You can learn about the conflict between trans people and trans-exclusionary radical feminists (TERFs) over what constitutes womanhood and gender (identity or genitalia?).[58]

"Lily, that's a lot to learn," you might say. You'd be right. Any language is—and is worth it for the understanding, access, and connection that comprehension brings. If there's one reason to increase your literacy of identity, it's to stay connected and in communication with the many communities around the world who increasingly speak this language. You don't need to become fluent overnight. There's no arbitrary bar you need to meet. Just stay humble, correct your mistakes, and hold yourself accountable as you continue learning.[59]

Does that mean identity needs to be the *only* language you speak?

Hell no. If I'm being honest, most people fluent in talking about identity rarely want to speak it all the time, either. Can you imagine if I introduced myself in every conversation to every person as a "queer nonbinary Chinese American nondisabled millennial" every day? It'd get old, awkward, and unhelpful very, very fast. Sometimes, I just want to be seen as "Lily." Sometimes, I just want to be seen as "a DEI strategist." And yes, sometimes I want to genuinely lead with one or more of my identities because it's what I want to be seen as. When that happens, and I say, "as a Chinese American, anti-Asian violence impacts me on a deeply personal level," or "seeing another queer, trans person in media gives me joy," I want the people listening to be at least proficient enough in "identity as a language" to know what I mean.

TAKEAWAYS

- **Change-makers must take identity seriously if only because many people, especially marginalized populations, already do so.** Social identities on dimensions including race, gender, sexuality, religion, age, class, and more can often be deeply important to the individuals that hold them and heavily inform peoples' choices and decision-making. Denying or ignoring these identities can be more harmful than productive.

- **Many DEI practitioners default to discussing socially advantaged identities in purely negative terms.** People with socially advantaged identities can feel like existing in DEI spaces requires either relegating themselves to the back or publicly apologizing for having their identities—neither of which are particularly empowering, especially compared to far more unsavory movements that offer better options for maintaining a "positive" self-image. This approach may contribute to defensiveness and backlash from people whose contributions are important to successful movements.

- **Efforts to pursue non-identity-related proxies for outcomes have yet to succeed.** Some, like "unconscious bias," aim to establish impartial metrics to gauge prejudice and inclusion. Others, like "antiracist as a status symbol," aim to tie certain perspectives or behaviors to valued status designations. These efforts lack the consistency and accountability to make the change they promise.

- **We can avoid the pitfalls of past proxies with responsibility, positivity, and accountability.** Connecting inclusive behavior in organizations to personal and professional responsibility avoids tying it to status designations. Thinking of all social identities as value-neutral or positive by default avoids blaming and shaming privileged identities. Centering accountability on individual and organizational responses to harm focuses on an important outcome rather than the proxy of identity or status.

- **Identity is a language that leaders can build fluency in.** By approaching identity as a language to learn and become competent in (without mandating that it be the *only* language leaders speak), deploying identity-related interventions among a larger toolbox of DEI tools, and being humble with their incomplete knowledge, leaders can better reach their stakeholders and navigate identity-related issues.

EXERCISES AND REFLECTIONS

1. Think about some of the many dimensions of difference: race, gender identity and expression, sexuality, religion, age, class, nationality, disability, parental status, veteran status, citizenship status, education, size, and many others. Which of these, if any, are linked to identities you have? Which of these are dimensions of difference you don't think of often, if ever?

2. Individuals must be stewards of the system within the environments they hold responsibility in. Think of a situation in which you play a leadership role or hold responsibility, no matter how small. How might you use that responsibility to embody how you want your larger organization to be? How might you lead by example?

3. Think about the people you interact with most frequently in your organization. What identities have each person mentioned or shared with you? What identities have they not mentioned that you are inferring based on their characteristics? How might you react if they spoke frankly about an aspect of identity that you yourself do not possess?

4. Learning about different identities and dimensions of difference is a lifelong practice, and we're all constantly engaged in it. Think of one dimension of difference that you're interested in learning more about. How might you engage in that learning respectfully? Write down one action you'll take to do so, even a small one. You can commit to learning more about that dimension of difference over the next few weeks.

5. You likely have an identity that you wish others around you knew more about. Use your phone or another device to look up an article or resource about that identity that you like, and save it for the future. What are some other ways you can think of to help others learn about your identity respectfully?

◾ SEVEN ◾

Change-Maker: Everyone

The executive director I was speaking to was getting exasperated.

"They have no idea what it takes to run this company. I spent the entire day yesterday—the entire day—flying across the country and back to talk to the sources of our two biggest grants. Today my schedule is booked solid with meetings with our community liaisons and regional directors. You have to understand. I get that some of our staff are upset with how our gender representation is, especially at the top, but come on: 'firing all of our leadership and hiring women instead?' I hope I don't have to explain why we can't do that."

"No, you don't. So what would you have them say, instead?"

He sighed. "Anything else productive. A strategy, maybe? Some actually feasible thoughts and ideas on how we as an organization can deal with this issue…given the financial constraints and other constraints that we have," he added.

"What levels in the organization are these vocal employees? Help me understand, are they more early-career, more senior—?"

"Mostly junior employees. That's why they have no idea how things work; they're enthusiastic but don't have the experience."

"Who does?"

He paused. "Who does what? Have the experience that these

employees don't? Well, I suppose quite a few folks. But we're all busy. We're not going to educate these employees on every aspect of how this nonprofit works."

"How will they ever develop the sort of thoughtful, informed strategy you're talking about, then, if the thoughtful, informed people in the organization don't put in the time to teach them?"

Silence, for a long moment. I raised my eyebrows at him, and he eventually grimaced, but nodded.

"That's a polite way to say that I should be doing more if I want these people to stop making bad suggestions."

I shrugged and gave him a small smile. "Your words, not mine."

Know Your Role

Achieving diversity, equity, and inclusion in any organization requires widespread systemic change. And, contrary to stories you may have heard involving change-making "heroes," never does change happen with just one, two, or a few people. If you're trying to create new policies, processes, and practices, new structures, cultures, and strategies that work, then you'll need everyone in an organization to do their part. And I mean everyone—from the most senior and tenured employee who has been in the organization for decades to yesterday's new hire. From the most seasoned and passionate DEI advocate to the most new-to-this-topic learner playing catch-up. I'm not just saying that everyone "can participate" in a change-making movement. That's far too passive. Instead, I want to point out that if you find your sweet spot given your skills and position, you can find the change-making role for yourself that maximizes your impact.

I can already see some folks nodding prematurely. "'Maximize your impact' means we should all attend every protest and rally for change!" No. "'Maximize your impact' means we should all work to deliver the vision and follow the instructions that leadership shares!" No. Successful movements to create change in organizations involve everyone playing important and *different* roles. Each role has little impact in isolation, no matter how much effort even the most passionate individual pours into it. But when people work together to meet the different needs of effective movements, the gargantuan task of making systemic change becomes far more conceivable and achievable. Role clarity, not just hard work, allows us to coordinate our intentions into impacts.

Now, when I say "role clarity," I don't mean that everyone in a social movement gets formal titles that you write on their nametags in sharpie. Instead, I suggest you also critically consider the role you're best situated to play in DEI change-making efforts alongside your power analyses; structure, culture, strategy assessments; and reflections on your own identities. These roles aren't deterministic, but they help guide your work and help you set boundaries for yourself. Role clarity helps answer some of the biggest questions change-makers ask about DEI:

"What am I expected to do?"

"How much is enough?"

"How does the work I'm doing fit into everything else?"

No matter where we are in our organizations, we can play critical roles in achieving DEI. Note that these roles are far from mutually exclusive: individuals can and often do occupy multiple at once. What's most important is that all of these roles are filled in some way or another, if DEI efforts in organizations hope to succeed.

The Advocate

The advocate is perhaps one of the most well-known roles an individual can play in DEI work and social movements in general. They're the people who speak up most often and loudest about the issue at hand, forcefully arguing in no uncertain terms that the status quo must change—sometimes putting themselves at risk to make their point or expose inequity.

Advocates are often the first exposure many people get to an issue. They're compelling and attention-grabbing and are often highly effective at both building rapport with those the issue affects and forcing the engagement of those who have the luxury to ignore the issue. The best advocates utilize referent power (i.e., charisma) to surmount the activation energy required to "break the ice" on an issue many know of but few feel comfortable bringing up. They can also serve as powerful injections of energy and momentum to revive dormant movements or reenergize stagnant ones, reminding stakeholders of the urgency and magnitude of an issue.

The Educator

The educator is often less visible but no less important than the advocate. Educators aim to "change the hearts and minds" of stakeholders on the issue and ensure that even those unfamiliar with an issue can develop an accurate working understanding of it.

Educators take people from "interested ignorance" to "informed intentions." They are patient and creative, able to use various methods to reach stakeholders with varying levels of understanding and help each understand an issue. Well-informed educators can deploy expert power to convince those with differing opinions, utilize a wide range of persuasive framings, and truly "meet people where they are" to take them to where they need to be. Educators increase and refine the potential of stakeholders to create change, no matter where those stakeholders lie at the start, and ensure that change-making movements can both stay focused and resist misinformation. Educators thrive as movements increase their momentum and are important sources of sustainability for long-term efforts.

The Organizer

The organizer turns a group with good intentions into a critical mass for achieving specific goals. Organizers are skilled at reading a situation and moving quickly to utilize windows of opportunity to create change.

Organizers often dislike the limelight themselves, preferring instead to lift the voices of others and coordinate different stakeholder groups from backstage. Coalition-building is their bread and butter. Empathetic and thoughtful people able to see the same issue from multiple angles, the best organizers can build (at times unlikely) alliances and identify and take advantage of windows of opportunity to take collective action. Similar to advocates, the best organizers can utilize referent power to rapidly connect with and build partnerships between different stakeholder groups and use a range of tactics to sustain and empower movements. Their role is most important leading up to major decision points as they coalesce informed and energized stakeholders around key asks and goals.

The Strategist

The strategist helps ensure that movements trend toward effectiveness on a macro level. Strategists are those who preoccupy themselves with the "why" and "how" behind issues and solutions and work with other leaders to make effective decisions.

Strategists often work fully behind the scenes to coordinate those playing other roles. They take a bird's-eye view of an issue and its full context, identifying key information about stakeholders, power dynamics, and decision points to inform the approach that is most likely to achieve goals effectively. Skilled at synthesis and boiling down complex situations into straightforward and easily communicated strategies, the best strategists can increase the efficacy and intentionality of other stakeholder groups. Their role is important early on in movements, to inform the direction of future momentum-building, and especially near the peak of organizing efforts—to ensure that the momentum of a movement is being directed effectively with the right tactics to achieve the right goals.

The Backer

The backer is perhaps the least romanticized and visible role in movements and, ironically, one of the most critical. Backers serve as a powerful normalizing force in bringing a movement from the fringes into the mainstream and according a movement with the legitimacy it needs to become enshrined into a changed status quo.

Backers may not even perceive their work as filling a role in movements, to begin with. They are less likely to participate near the start of movements and often consider themselves part of the status quo that movements are trying to change. However, at a critical point in movements, backers endorse, legitimize, and therefore normalize movement efforts' framing, asks, and solutions. They are skilled at using their formal power to grant legitimacy and "normality" to movements and force decision-makers to take movements' concerns seriously. The "critical mass" that organizers build is made up not of the other movement roles but of backers, specifically. Backers additionally play an important role at the end of movement cycles—their retrospective and collective thoughts, interpretations, and reflections on the movement help imprint it in organizations' institutional memory.

The Builder

The builder makes things that don't yet exist, especially new structures, policies, processes, and practices. They have the important job of following through after commitments have been made and approval secured.

Builders are perhaps least focused on inputs and intentions and most focused on the process of execution and its outcomes. They are skilled at thoughtfully translating abstract and idealistic mandates and goals into tangible realities. Pragmatic and detail oriented, the best builders are able to bridge the gap between rhetoric and reality and draw on a wide range of internal and external knowledge to create working solutions that meet the needs of multiple stakeholder groups. Builders play the most important role near the end of a movement cycle, following through on and executing the vision of the wins secured by other stakeholders.

The Reformer

The reformer maintains and steadily improves the (new) status quo of organization, especially building on new elements created by builders. Reformers thrive on steady, ongoing, incremental change based on continuous feedback.

Reformers use the tools of a system to better it. Process oriented and likely to care about the long-term sustainability of their efforts, the best reformers utilize their formal power to drive steady and impactful change according to received feedback. Reformers are a powerful way to gauge the health of a given system: When the number of reformers is high relative to other roles, the system can be inferred to be self-regulating effectively. When the number of reformers is low, this is a sign that the system is either stagnant—indicating a likelihood of change in the near future—or in the process of a more tumultuous change effort already. Often, when reformers' impact grows too limited or ineffective, that can often be the impetus for advocates to break the ice and restart the movement cycle in service of more dramatic or radical changes.

No Role Is Replaceable

A *lot* of movements fail. Some fall victim to internal infighting, fail to secure a critical mass to create change, get sandbagged by leadership, and so on. Rather than list all of these failure modes as a checklist to avoid, I want to propose the following: **movements fail when they fail to activate even one of the roles I listed.** Let's explore that.

A movement without advocates isn't a movement at all, just the status quo continuing on and self-maintaining as needed. There's nothing *inherently* wrong with that, provided that the system as-is is perceived by all stakeholders as working "well enough." But more often than not, systems fall into disrepair and then dysfunction, and the power of inertia stretches that state of dysfunction for many weeks, months, and even years.

These are the workplaces that everyone working within knows are toxic, where sexual harassment, racist microaggressions, and daily abuse of power are on full display, but no one feels empowered enough to denounce them. Often, people worry—rightfully—that speaking up will paint a target for retaliation on their back, but because no one speaks up, many people falsely believe that no one else cares about or even sees these issues. In this way, when movements lack advocates, a toxic status quo can extend indefinitely.

How about a movement without educators? Without them, movements led by other roles will fail to bring audiences to the level of understanding needed to participate effectively. This means that, while some people may become interested in a movement due to, say, the actions of a charismatic advocate, they are likely to misunderstand or misinterpret the movement's goals without an educator's help. This failure mode is exemplified within failing movements where, when presented with an individual's ignorance or a lack of understanding, advocates or organizers continually respond with, "It's not my job to teach you!" or "Figure it out yourself!" Lacking those able to acknowledge their current level of understanding, neutral individuals or even interested people without a complete understanding of an issue can end up feeling discouraged, turned away, or even resentful of movements.

When this happens, movements often fail to grow beyond their usual starting reputation of "fringe disruption led by a few dissatisfied people." The initial jolt of momentum eventually fades when advocates burn out, and movements dissolve or go dormant.

Movements lacking organizers go through a similar set of challenges. Think of organizers as a lens that focuses the diffuse energy from an informed movement into a small number of simple, powerful asks. The "lists of demands" that effective movements coalesce around aren't laundry lists filled with every possible improvement but intentionally selected high-priority items that are easy to rally around for those in the movement and easy to comprehend for those outside it. They are specifically chosen because they can unite the many different stakeholder groups within the coalitions that the best movements are able to build.

Without organizers, movements often lack focus and direction. While many in the movement may have the knowledge they need to comprehend the issue, a lack of alignment on the highest priorities can cause movements to either aim to solve every problem at once or splinter into factions with differing priorities. Both of these outcomes significantly lower the likelihood that movements succeed. To decision-makers, movements that are unfocused or splintered indicate a significant risk that any decision they make will leave no one pleased and everyone disappointed; in these situations, decision-makers will be leery of acting. Though it takes longer to happen, movements without effective organizers will gradually lose steam and ultimately dissolve.

Strategists help ensure that movements move in the "right" direction while minimizing costly mistakes that drain momentum or political goodwill. Without them, even well-organized movements with powerful coalitions behind them can drag on long enough that morale within the movement begins to fall. For example, a movement that mistakenly directs its energy to sway the opinions of someone who turns out to be an inconsequential decision-maker can lose valuable time, energy, and support in the process. These resources are not infinite—too many missteps and a movement can undermine its own goals, use up the trust it needs to unite coalitions and take coordinated action, and run out of time to make change before its members lose faith.

As environments and issues get more complex, so too do the repercussions of lacking a strategist. In the most straightforward and simple situations, it can be easy to identify the stakeholders, the power dynamics, and the tactics required to make change without the need for a skilled strategist. But as any of these factors gets messier, an effective bird's-eye view of the problem goes from "nice to have" to "need to have."

Movements without backers haven't yet reached the people they need to. The reality of making change is that, even when fully activated and engaged, the population of people enthusiastic about the new vision is, in most cases, still a minority when compared to the entire population. In my experience, a movement within an organization of a hundred people can consider itself powerful if it activates thirty or forty in the movement itself. But until that movement reaches key backers like decision-makers, well-connected individuals, and respected leaders, it won't gain the perception of legitimacy from those in the organization who genuinely are neutral or have no opinion on the movement.

Contrary to popular belief, movement cycles don't end when decision-makers make commitments to change systems. They end when those systems get changed—and that work takes builders, who are the ones writing new policies, creating new processes, and piloting new practices, and reformers, who are the ones modifying the policies, processes, and practices that already exist. The challenge with this work is that, even in the most successful movements, actually changing a system can take more time and effort than the movement-building itself. There is usually a gap between the high point of a movement, in which leadership commits to doing better, and the point at which anyone in the movement can see tangible indications of whether progress has been made or not.

That "progress" can only be achieved with builders and reformers. And so, without builders and reformers, the follow-through of a movement never occurs. You'd imagine that, without seeing the outcomes they were promised, movements would hold decision-makers accountable and rally their members to redouble their efforts to influence change. However, this doesn't always happen. When movements achieve their highly publicized goals (e.g., they secure the approval of a critical backer, like a CEO or executive director), one of the common short-term consequences is that the movement rapidly loses momentum. Movement leaders might then turn their attention to other issues and may assume that the movement's goals will be procedurally achieved through builders and reformers.

If builders and reformers don't exist or aren't empowered to play their roles effectively, movements will fail to achieve their goals and lose the critical mass they once had with little to show for it. This can force movements to start over from scratch, but with a significantly-diminished feeling of trust toward the organization and each other. In other words, without builders and reformers, movements suffer a premature ending.

From my experience, virtually every failure mode of a change-making effort, DEI or not, can be traced back to the lack of or disempowerment of one or more of these roles.

I've seen an effort to increase the non-White representation of an organization fall apart because movement leaders overutilized advocates and underutilized educators, polarizing a previously neutral population to either take their side or "be an ignorant White supremacist."

I've seen a well-organized movement slowly drain the stamina of its members over several years trying to sway an unsympathetic backer to change rather than appeal to the far more powerful backer he reported to because it lacked strategists to inform the movement's advocacy efforts.

I've seen more than four movements start, grow, and dissolve trying to address a single issue in one organization over many years due to disregarding the importance of the builders and reformers who would be eventually building their solutions.

And I've seen countless would-be movements that never started because no individual was willing to take a risk and become an advocate in the first place.

If it wants to succeed, every movement must ensure that these roles are filled. And from an individual's perspective, if *you* want to contribute to a movement, consider which of these roles speaks to your skills, experience, and power most convincingly—and how you can coordinate those around you to fill the others.

The Best Roles for Your Role

It's one thing to talk about advocates and organizers and builders like they're items on a menu, but in most organizations, your roles on paper at least somewhat predict what movement role you end up occupying. Your formal titles and job descriptions give you different access to formal, coercive, and reward power (remember these?) and thus different opportunities to be most effective within a change-making effort. For example, you're not likely to be effective as a backer unless you already possess some formal power in the organization, say, as a manager or a more senior decision-maker. You're not likely going to be effective as a reformer unless your job description already involves changing and improving policy and process (e.g., Human Resources or an equivalent role), or you have enough influence and respect within the organization that your opinion has weight.

So let's revisit this conversation about movement roles, but this time consider the role(s) you already play within—and outside of—your organization.

Individual Contributor

I'm using this term loosely to describe "anyone who directly works on the product or service of the organization, without managing others." Depending on the organization, they might be called "frontline staff," or "assistants," "associates," "cooks," "engineers," or similar.

ICs, regardless of the organization they work in, are often the people most at the behest of rules, regulations, policies, and processes but with the least formal power to change them. ICs are more likely than other roles to be directly involved in an organization's day-to-day "work" and thus the most directly exposed to an organization's real culture and everyday practices. When there is a misalignment between what those at the top of an organizational hierarchy say and how the organization functions (e.g., "our organization is free from discrimination"), ICs are most likely to be aware of that discrepancy. That gives ICs enormous *informational power* when it comes to both the minutiae of organizational functioning and the needs of stakeholders outside the organization. For example, if productivity requirements drive workers to engage in unhealthy workplace behaviors for fear of losing their jobs, or long hours and a "constantly on" culture are keeping workers from spending time with their family, no one is more likely to be aware of that than the workers themselves. In the age of social media, ICs can also be accorded additional power: their understanding of the workplace is seen as *expert power*, more so than highly sanitized corporate PR accounts.

Thus, ICs are often uniquely situated as stakeholders that have the most internal information on broken systems and the most expertise when perceived by external audiences. This allows them to rapidly identify problems, rally others behind a cause, and convincingly represent movements. ICs are often more likely within movements to succeed as advocates and organizers.

On the flip side, ICs' keen understanding of their immediate environment is often offset by a lack of a bird's-eye view of the organization. Additionally, many ICs, often not being in leadership roles themselves, cannot change systems unless first formally granted that ability by decision-makers. ICs are often less likely within movements to succeed as strategists, backers, builders, or reformers.

An important exception to this general pattern is the senior IC, an individual near the top of the organizational hierarchy that isn't a manager or a senior leader. While lacking *formal power,* their seniority and the fact that their role sits largely out of an organization's hierarchy gives them enormous *referent power,* or respect, with which they can effectively enact change. Senior ICs are often uniquely effective as backers and reformers, roles that allow them to utilize their referent power.

Manager

When I say "manager," I refer to "anyone with at least one direct report." Especially within big organizations, this spans quite a wide range of roles, from the junior manager relatively low in the organization with only one or two reports of early-career ICs, to managers higher up in the organization managing other managers or senior ICs.

Managers are directly responsible for stewarding an organization's culture. They play the difficult task of taking the high-level set of aspirational values or goals of the organization (e.g., "respect others" or "scale sustainably") and putting them into practice on a day-to-day level. Alongside coordinating the basic execution of tasks, managers are at least hypothetically expected also to provide mentorship; lead inclusive and respectful meetings; ensure that mistreatment, conflict, and potential discrimination are handled efficiently, fairly, and accountably; and make everyday decisions at their discretion to achieve the latest corporate strategy. Yikes! Having worked with many organizations that expect these responsibilities of managers, offer them little in the way of training, support, or resources, and then lambast them as the "frozen middle,"[1] I'm well aware that this work is far harder than it looks.

If there is a movement role that managers should prioritize, knowing the constraints that many have on their time and energy, it should be to protect those members of their teams that are advocates, educators, organizers, and every other role. The ability of a manager to protect their direct reports is unparalleled within the organization. An effective manager can use their *formal power* to legitimate the efforts of an employee advocate or employee and shield an organizer from potential retaliation. Managers excel as key backers of movements, especially at their start. In addition, many managers have discretion over the structure and culture of their own teams and can exercise their authority to create team environments that may differ—for the better—from those of the rest of the organization. Managers are also able to be effective builders in a temporary capacity preceding larger organization-wide change.

What tends to be more difficult for managers? Typically, roles that require a large quantity of time in addition to their typical job duties. Managers are less likely to succeed as advocates, educators, or organizers within movements. And while managers can often carve out a team environment that is different from the organizational one, all but the most senior nonetheless lack the power needed to change organizations formally. Managers are less likely within movements to succeed as reformers.

Senior Leaders

I use "senior leaders" to describe the decision-makers at the highest levels of an organization or environment who have the authority to make and follow through on their decisions. Think most leaders with "chief" in their title in a corporation, leaders of all key departments in an NGO, or a presidential cabinet.

Senior leaders are unambiguously some of the most powerful people in organizations, with the highest levels of formal power. They have the responsibility for steering the organization, coordinating its activities at the highest levels, and stewarding its structure, culture, and strategy. Every senior leader's action on (and increasingly, off) the job is seen as a reflection of the organization. Suppose a leader accordingly acts with respect, is organized and timely, and holds themself accountable when they make mistakes. In that case, stakeholders will infer that the organization they lead will also be respectful, organized, and accountable. Suppose an individual leader ignores reports of discrimination, dismisses concerns about DEI, and refuses to change policies or processes that are contributing to inequity. In that case, stakeholders will infer that these must not be the organization's priorities, either.

This is one of the reasons that senior leaders tend to be thought of as the "object" of a movement's focus rather than participants in a movement. When leaders are perceived as untrustworthy and intent on preventing the movement's goals, this makes sense—leaders are the final backer to be swayed. Yet, that leaves little room for senior leaders who genuinely want to contribute proactively, who may not know what actions would be most effective.

Senior leaders have the most *formal power* in their organizations. They are able to formally drive change to structure, culture, and strategy from the top and coordinate the resources and political authority required to scale this change across the organization. Yet, they are the farthest away from the situation "on the ground" and require that their employees trust the organization enough to share their experiences. If senior leaders can build trust and gain the information they need, they can deploy the power they have at their disposal to change organization-wide strategies and direct those under them to build new systems or reform existing ones. In other words, skilled leaders holding the trust of their employees are most able to succeed within movements as strategists and backers empowering the builders and reformers under them to work.

With some exceptions, notably the small number of high-visibility "activist CEOs,"[2] senior leaders often struggle to have the expertise, trust, and time to thrive as advocates, educators, or organizers. Additionally, apart from perhaps senior HR leaders, most senior leaders may find it challenging to act in a builder or reformer capacity themselves. As senior leaders are typically most effective in leading the organization on a high-level, they thrive within or adjacent to movements when they can leverage this power toward movement goals.

DEI Professionals

This group describes professionals with DEI-related roles and job titles either embedded within an organization—including chief DEI officers, heads of DEI, and more junior DEI-related roles that report to either DEI leaders or other leaders in an organization, like DEI specialists— or the many third-party consulting firms and individuals that partner with organizations to do relatively short-term DEI work. Why did I lump all of these roles together? Because most organizations still aren't quite sure what to do with any of them.

Embedded DEI professionals are a relatively new species within most organizations. Nominally, they exist to help hold the organization accountable for achieving DEI in practice, and in some organizations, they directly work on DEI themselves. They manage other DEI-related entities, consult for departments or senior leadership teams, and put out DEI-related fires within organizations. They can be trainers and facilitators, change management experts, or data analysts. Accordingly, they make good advocates, educators, organizers, strategists, backers, builders, or reformers—depending, that is, on the extent to which the organization trusts them.

Trust and formal power really are the deciding factors with embedded DEI professionals. They occupy a strange middle between "insider" and "outsider": if they are leaders and employees distrust other senior leaders, embedded DEI professionals are likely to be distrusted as well. But as many DEI professionals work directly with underserved communities and are highly aware of their experiences, they have the potential to be "unicorn" change-makers that can play nearly every role, bridge the gap between junior and senior employees, and realize the success of movements. That is, if they're trusted by employees, granted power and authority by senior leaders, resourced with a budget and headcount, empowered to make change cross-functionally, and stick around long enough to see their vision through.

Unfortunately, that's a big "if"—and most embedded DEI professionals don't find themselves nearly empowered enough to succeed in all of these roles. In my experience, they typically find themselves most effective when involved in training the workforce, especially senior leaders, and spearheading organizational change following a successful movement. While embedded DEI professionals have the potential to succeed in all movement roles if supported by their organizations, they are most often effective within movements as educators, builders, and reformers.

How about external professionals like consultants and trainers? External DEI professionals are typically brought on to deliver a highly reliable service, like a DEI survey, training, workshop, or discussion group. They have the benefit of being unassociated with the organization and so are less affected by any existing negative perception associated with senior leaders or embedded DEI professionals. For example, employees who do not trust their leaders enough to give critical feedback may share this feedback in confidence with a DEI consultant. Unfortunately, external DEI professionals have key constraints: they cannot secure the organizational power, budget, headcount, or cross-functional authority like embedded DEI professionals can. This means that they often have *expert power* but not *formal power* and means that they are most effective when they can engage in tasks that are more easily achieved over a bounded period of time. External DEI professionals are most likely to succeed as educators, strategists, builders, and reformers.

DEI Groups

DEI groups describe any formal entity within an organization dedicated to DEI. I consider entities like employee resource groups (ERGs), DEI councils, DEI task forces, and DEI working groups all examples of DEI groups.

DEI groups occupy a similar "middle space" to that of DEI professionals. Hypothetically, each could play a powerful role in change-making efforts: ERGs, if appropriately resourced and supported, could coordinate efforts to create better working environments for their constituent groups. DEI councils, task forces, and working groups, if appropriately resourced and supported, could connect junior and senior employees together, coordinate change-making activities, and inform an organizational DEI strategy. But the devil is in the details, and organizations are inconsistent at supporting these groups—all of which are volunteer efforts that employees engage in, unrelated to their actual job responsibilities. Too often, organizations take advantage of their DEI groups' passion and enthusiasm to overscope their responsibilities and overwork their members, leading to individual burnout and group collapse.

DEI groups that are supported and operated sustainability tend to focus on a relatively small number of discrete responsibilities: helping their DEI-interested employees organize and find community, helping connect leaders with more junior employees, and using volunteer labor to improve inequitable aspects of the organization. Multiple groups often exist to fulfill different responsibilities on this list. While DEI groups have the potential to succeed in all movement roles if supported by their organizations, in most organizations, they play effective roles within movements as advocates, organizers, and reformers.

Change-Making Roles in Action

One of the most effective change-making movements[3] I've ever witnessed was one in which I played a small role. The movement started from the grass roots, as many do. A small group of employees with relatively little power of any type got together to voice frustrations with their organization's anti-harassment training, cold and clinical mandatory sessions steeped in racial, gender, and sexuality-related stereotypes that were more likely to intimidate, scare, or even just bore the daylights out of attendees without meaningfully changing their behavior.

These advocates took their concerns to organizational leaders and, importantly, coalesced around a single clear ask: "We need better trainings that focus more on positive, respectful, and inclusive behavior rather than using scare tactics to tell us what we *shouldn't* do." The leaders listened to the concerns, nodded, and responded with, "We'll see what we can do." And that was the last of it that advocates heard, at least for a little while.

Behind the scenes, sympathetic leaders—backers—passed down the feedback, alongside other related messages they had heard from other employees and stakeholders, sharing concerns from their teams to the internal department that offered training: "Focus on positive behavior."

That department, at the time, was in the middle of a hiring search for a new director-level employee to improve on training programs and develop new ones that was heading into its third month. The leading

candidates seemed largely cut from the same cloth as current employees, with the exception of a candidate with a unique background and
skills in, miraculously, tackling difficult topics of conflict and misconduct from a positivist and empowering lens. The directive couldn't
have come at a better time, and the decision was suddenly far easier:
the unique candidate was hired. The ball had started rolling.

Months after their meeting with organizational leaders, many of the
advocates who had originally shared feedback received an email from
a director they weren't familiar with, with a simple ask: "Can we chat
about harassment training?" The earnestness of the email, coupled
with the promise that this new leader would be less beholden to the
machine of organizational politics, prompted many advocates to say
yes. During the meeting, the new director spent a small amount of
time asking questions and the rest of the time listening, nodding, and
furiously scribbling down notes. They asked about all the ways in which
the current programs failed and about employees' vision and ideas for
a better replacement. They thanked folks for their time, packed up, and
headed off to meet with more employees and leaders about the same
topics to gather more information.

Weeks later, folks received another email, this one triumphant.
"We've received approval to add a new program to our yearly new employee orientation," it read. "We're looking for volunteers interested in
sharing their stories."

Behind the scenes, the director had been tirelessly working with
leaders across the organization, especially strategists who encouraged
them to look into HR programs and employee processes; the new
employee orientation was a tantalizing objective, though it was noto-
riously difficult to change. The director spent weeks identifying and
speaking to important allies—backers—about their vision for the event:
it needed to be through new employee orientation to reach *all* new employees and start changing the culture of the organization, rather than

just another opt-in program that would fail to reach the people who needed it most. They built a groundswell of support and ultimately *succeeded* in getting approval from the decision-makers who controlled the coveted orientation program. As the director started working with builders to create this program and make it effective in the context of the new employee orientation, they began reaching out to advocates to update them on the progress that had been made and for help building out the program's content.

The advocates who worked with the director had high standards for the program and its content, tone, and execution to ensure that it not only took a more positive spin on anti-harassment but also avoided many of the problematic pitfalls of the old program and was set up for success. One of the many additions to the program they implemented included, for example, coordinating and resourcing managers of new employees to follow up on the program with continued conversations on their wider teams. After months, happy with what felt genuinely like a radically new and effective program, advocates began tapping their networks for peers to volunteer as participants in the program and promote it as educators and organizers. Some wrote articles shared on the company intranet describing their excitement that such a program was happening. Others encouraged their managers to attend as spectators in the hopes that they would be open to similar conversations with their existing teams, new employees or not. There were skeptics and detractors, of course—some employees openly scoffed about the program and doubted that it would be anything other than a waste of time. "Wait and see," was the response from educators and organizers.

The first iteration of the program, months later, was an unprecedented success for the new employee cohort.

Interest in the program skyrocketed beyond expectations, partially thanks to the work of organizers and educators, and the director was flooded with interest from all corners of the organization. "It's not fair that only new employees receive this training," folks said. "Can we attend, too?"

And the movement took off. Strategists recommended expanding the program out to different cohorts on the organization's history, given their shared experiences, and creating new channels and groups to prepare for each year's new cohorts. Builders helped create these new programs and groups, and reformers tinkered with the original program based on feedback from advocates and other stakeholders. Educators helped inform resources for all managers to support conversations on this program, organizers rallied audiences to attend and participate, and backers continued to expand the reach of this program and institutionalize it as an integral part of the organization's DNA.

When I checked back in on the program years after its inception, I couldn't believe how normalized the once-radical idea had become. Conversations about inclusive behavior and eliminating harassment were the norm throughout the year. Leaders looked forward to each year's cohort and the insights that would come from the program and its many spin-offs and follow-ups. Years of constant refinement and improvement had produced a self-sustaining and effective program that had embedded itself into the fabric of the organization's culture and structure—a success in every sense of the word.

I share this story because it's far from the norm. Many change-making movements lack the sort of success seen here for many reasons. But I want to highlight that when the stars align—when people across organizations all play their roles effectively at the right place and time—the type of revolutionary change that transforms an organization is very much possible. If we strive intentionally and critically, it can be possible for our organizations, too.

Understanding both movement and organizational roles is useful for personal reasons in that it helps you figure out where your own

Stakeholder Roles

Stakeholder 1	Advocate	Educator	Organizer	Strategist	Backer	Builder	Reformer
You							
Notes	IC	Senior IC	Manager	Senior Leader	DEI Group	Embedded DEI Pro	External DEI Pro
Stakeholder 2	Advocate	Educator	Organizer	Strategist	Backer	Builder	Reformer
Notes	IC	Senior IC	Manager	Senior Leader	DEI Group	Embedded DEI Pro	External DEI Pro
Stakeholder 3	Advocate	Educator	Organizer	Strategist	Backer	Builder	Reformer
Notes	IC	Senior IC	Manager	Senior Leader	DEI Group	Embedded DEI Pro	External DEI Pro
Stakeholder 4	Advocate	Educator	Organizer	Strategist	Backer	Builder	Reformer
Notes	IC	Senior IC	Manager	Senior Leader	DEI Group	Embedded DEI Pro	External DEI Pro
Stakeholder 5	Advocate	Educator	Organizer	Strategist	Backer	Builder	Reformer
Notes	IC	Senior IC	Manager	Senior Leader	DEI Group	Embedded DEI Pro	External DEI Pro

FIGURE 6. Stakeholder Roles Chart. Stakeholders' movement and organizational roles can be indicated, along with a section to write notes for each stakeholder.

efforts fit into those of a larger movement. But you can apply this knowledge in action to not only yourself but all other stakeholders in an organization, and with this knowledge, start building a movement from scratch. Understanding stakeholder organizational roles empowers you to approach them with suggestions for movement roles. Understanding the movement roles of stakeholders you're currently engaged with allows you to identify which roles are lacking for a successful movement. You can use the Stakeholder Roles Chart (Figure 6) to identify and note the movement and organizational roles of stakeholders.

Coalitions Required

There's a reason why when my clients ask me, "What can I do?" My first answer is, "Not everything."

There are necessary limits to every movement role when it comes to making change, and every role is required for success. That means you need your workforce to speak up and advocate for what they need. You need your senior leaders to deploy their power and resources to strategize and coordinate. You need the help of DEI stakeholders to coordinate and organize employee enthusiasm. You need the help of trained professionals to guide, inform, and accelerate change. As the case study showed, it truly takes a broad set of stakeholders to enable a movement's success—and many of them may not initially know each other well, if at all.

This is not an idea that comes easily to many people. We're often enamored by the idea of the "hero advocate," an infinitely courageous individual that fights against the odds to single-handedly compel obstinate leaders to finally open their minds to the importance of DEI, or the "hero organizer," an infinitely charismatic individual that unites the masses behind their banner of change. Or perhaps we romanticize the "hero decision-maker," an infinitely wise individual that always makes the right choice in good times and in bad, or the "hero reformer," an infinitely insightful individual who fixes every organizational policy or process they touch.

These people are fictional. They don't exist outside the words of motivational speeches and inspirational clickbait internet articles. In the real world, successful movements that achieve their objectives succeed not through just the efforts of people in any one role, no matter how skilled they might be, but through multiple people and stakeholder groups who collectively occupy all of these roles, working together.

It's tempting to write about coalitions as formally emerging from top-down directives or a planned, joint problem-solving initiative where stakeholders meet in the middle. But more often than not, coalitions are *informal* groups formed for a specific purpose, without a formal structure, to achieve some external goal that nominally advances their members' wants.[4] They're often messy, emergent, irrational, and organic,[5] and their members may not even all join for the same reason.

In a DEI movement, ERGs may want to minimize the additional volunteer work their leaders take on while aiming to secure more funding for event programming. Senior leaders may want the approval of their workforce so that they can focus efforts on hitting an important growth milestone. Some people will participate because they want to look good, others will participate because they would do anything in the pursuit of what they feel is right, and still others will participate because there's something in it for them. Accurately understanding a stakeholder's needs is thus important—not to assign moral value, but to understand how and why they might join a coalition.

This shouldn't be unfamiliar to folks in the DEI space. In fact, many underserved identity groups themselves are based on historical coalitions. "Asian American" or "LGBTQ+"? Coalitions between different communities coming together to protect themselves from discrimination. "Neurodivergent" or "disabled"? Coalitions to build community while consolidating political power. The identity terms we use for ourselves exist because those before us recognized the power and solidarity that comes from naming the many as one.[6] We should treat movement coalitions similarly: as inherently heterogeneous and imperfect but nonetheless powerful.

We need to recognize that coalitions inherently involve conflict and disagreement. Members of any given coalition may disagree about ideology, approach, and even their ultimate goal. This conflict is normal, and thorny questions like these don't have to be fully resolved for coalitions to work together successfully and achieve objectives. That said, there is such a thing as "useful" or "positive" conflict versus potentially derailing or undermining conflict that threatens the existence of the coalition. The difference? Useful conflict is often **task conflict**, and focuses on the goals, process, strategy, and content of making change, while toxic conflict is often **relationship conflict**, and fixates on the people making change—their political opinions, beliefs, and values.[7] To achieve the former and avoid the latter, coalition leaders and members can take an interest-based and non-adversarial approach to conflict resolution, seeking to solve problems, fluidly shift positions when needed, and create potentially win-win outcomes.[8]

They may not always look neat or be ideologically pure, but when coalitions of stakeholders activate every role required for success, movements succeed. Advocates bring issues into the spotlight. Educators upskill the knowledge of those around them. Organizers focus abstract goals into clear and comprehensible goals, and strategists point those goals toward effective tactics. Backers give the movement credibility and legitimacy and ultimately commit the organization to change. Builders follow through, reformers refine what was made, and when new challenges and inequities arise, so do new movements to change them. Rinse and repeat.

So once again, know that when I say "movements require everyone," it's not aspirational but pragmatic. There is nothing we can do as individuals to create effective movements in isolation. Only when DEI work utilizes coalitions of stakeholders with shared goals, mindfully approaches naysayers and neutral groups to avoid backlash and polarization, takes a systems-oriented approach to understand issues and power dynamics, and builds a shared sense of trust between all stakeholders can it succeed.

TAKEAWAYS

- **Creating change requires movements of people playing different roles to succeed.** These rules include the well-known advocate, educator, and organizer, but also less-visible roles like strategists, backers, builders, and reformers. While people can play multiple movement roles at once, if even one of these roles goes unfilled, then movements will fail—with the failure mode changing based on which role is lacking.

- **Movement roles vary substantially.** Advocates "break the ice" on hard-to-discuss issues and inject momentum into movements. Educators use movement-related information to increase the ability of stakeholders at different stages in their learning journeys to make change. Organizers help well-intended groups attain the critical mass required to achieve specific goals. Strategists equip other roles with the big picture and facilitate decision-making. Backers make decisions that resource, support, and add legitimacy to movements. Builders create new policies, processes, and practices that don't yet exist, while reformers change and improve that which is already present.

- **Your formal role in an organization can guide your movement role(s).** Individual contributors (ICs) are most effective as advocates and organizers, with senior ICs additionally effective as backers and reformers. Managers are most effective as key backers and short-term builders. Senior leaders are most effective as strategists and backers, with activist leaders occasionally able to be effective as advocates. DEI professionals and DEI groups are most effective as educators, builders, and reformers.

· **Coalitions are powerful ways to organize effective DEI movements.** The interconnectedness of DEI roles requires that movements not only engage many people but actively create coalitions of folks that may not agree on every aspect of a movement but endorse its core goals. Movements composed of informal coalitions are imperfect by design but can be highly effective if united behind achieving the same outcome.

EXERCISES AND REFLECTIONS

1. Of the different movement roles—advocate, educator, organizer, strategist, backer, builder, and reformer—which role(s) might you be most effective in?

2. Thinking about a DEI-related movement or change effort you care about, is there a movement role that interests you that you may not have the skills, network, power, or resources to play effectively at the moment? If so, what are some ways in which you might be able to gain those things?

3. We can benefit from thinking about even the smallest change-making efforts as movements. Think about any initiative you've witnessed or been a part of. Which movement roles were filled? Which, if any, were missing? How did the people in these roles work together, or not, to achieve outcomes?

4. Change-making movements rarely succeed if we try to undertake them alone or only with our friends. Thinking about a DEI-related

movement or change effort you care about or find interesting, how might you envision a successful coalition to achieve the outcomes you want? Try to put yourself in the shoes of stakeholders that might participate in that coalition. What might be their rationale, angle, or objective for participating, and how might that overlap, complement, or conflict with yours?

━ EIGHT ━

Achieving DEI

You've just finished analyzing the data from an organization-wide survey, and one of your findings is clear: applicants with identities like "man" or "White" are advantaged over applicants with identities like "woman" or "Black" or "Latine" in the hiring process, all else equal. It can be tempting to look up "how to address hiring discrimination," identify the first intervention you find, like "deliver a bias training to your hiring managers," and eagerly deploy it with high hopes and little accountability.

I cannot stress this enough: taking this approach will jeopardize even the most carefully planned change-making movement. Do this, and you will fail dramatically and expensively. You'll be no better than the US military's expensive failure of a race relations program in the 1970s—the poorly executed product of an otherwise powerful movement to build awareness and galvanize change.

Throwing the first plausible intervention you find at a DEI problem is like hearing someone shout for help outside your window and throwing a fire extinguisher in the direction of their voice. It's sloppy, ineffective, and, most importantly, might not solve any real problem, to begin with.

Instead, when you know an outcome isn't what you want, you need to get deeply curious about the chain of events that caused it. Let's look at that hiring situation again and ask some questions. How do people come by your job postings? What factors do they consider, whether personal factors or aspects of the listing itself, before they decide to apply? How do candidates' applications themselves differ? Who are all the people within an organization involved in a hiring decision? What are their roles in the process, and what factors do they consider about the candidate when making decisions? How do they engage with candidates? How do interviews or skills tests feel to the candidates who take them? When candidates "fall off" of the hiring process, where and why does it happen?

Thoughtful change-makers, especially the decision-making backers and the strategists informing them, can find creative ways to ask and answer these questions. For example, an applicant tracking system (ATS) might already offer some insights into what stage of the process some candidates are eliminated more than others.[1] Let's say that it's the first interview—people of different genders might apply and make it to the interview stage at similar rates, but women and nonbinary candidates are disproportionately screened out from this point onward. Why?

Post-interview surveys or one-on-ones sent out to all candidates might help you collect additional quantitative data. Of course, since you can't require all candidates to participate in this additional data collection process, there might be similarities in which candidates choose to answer a follow-up request from you that you can't rule out. Nevertheless, suppose you collect and analyze post-interview survey data alongside your existing demographic and organizational data. In doing so, suppose you find something interesting: women candidates who interview with hiring managers working in a specific department, say, marketing, are more likely to be rejected.

After interviewing a few people in marketing, you're able to develop a tentative theory about why. Perhaps the department was led by a longtime employee of the organization who was influential in leading his department and others through a crisis many years ago. His department largely embraced his command-and-control leadership style, with many modeling their work and communication style off of him. That leader had a particular talking point that he repeatedly made: marketing, and the entire organization, was a place where only highly confident, assertive, ambitious, and extroverted individuals would find success. Many in his department, including many women, embraced the characterization. And so, when hiring managers from marketing took part in *any* interviews—even for candidates not interviewing for their department—they tended to carry over their beliefs about what an "ideal" candidate looked like and rejected candidates based on these arbitrary criteria.

Mystery solved. Does that mean it's time for unconscious bias training?

No, or at least not yet. You won't be able to achieve DEI until you move beyond a simplistic view of "best practices" as your default answer to DEI challenges. Achieving DEI requires that you understand your organization inside and out, that you accurately conceptualize the arc of change-making with the level of trust you're working with, and that you solve the right problems.

Recall again the outcomes we're trying to achieve with DEI:

- **Equity:** the measured experience of individual, interpersonal, and organizational success and well-being across all stakeholder populations
- **Diversity:** the workforce demographic composition in an organizational body that all stakeholder populations trust as representative and accountable
- **Inclusion:** the felt and perceived environment in an organizational body that all stakeholder populations trust as respectful and accountable

There's a reason that trust is a crucial component in these outcomes: because the perception of an environment by the people in and around it is as important as any "objective" achievement of representational parity or engagement. For this reason, this chapter will *not* be a simple laundry list of practices that you can deploy as off-the-shelf. Instead, it will feature three different strategic approaches divided by the level of trust in a given environment.

The Currency of Change

Structure, culture, and strategy delineate the parameters of an organization and guide change-making efforts to clear outcomes. Coalitions and movements describe the play-by-play steps individuals and collectives can take to create change. But there's one thing missing: trust, the extent to which stakeholders inside and outside an organization believe that the organization will do what it says. Why? Because in an organization without trust, coalitions and movements will never get enough steam to turn intentions into actions into outcomes. It is the fuel that every change-making initiative runs on, and it doesn't come easily.

Most organizations naively believe trust to be an infinite resource when it most certainly is not. Every time employees are asked to share their experiences in a survey or public forum, that expends trust. Every time employees utilize a formal feedback mechanism or participate in a hiring process, that expends trust. If their stories are respected, suggestions respected, feedback taken, and best efforts recognized and evaluated fairly, the expended trust is renewed with interest, enabling organizations to take even bigger actions. In this way, when trust is honored and respected, it enables a positive feedback loop of organizational functioning and change.

In high trust environments, no matter the organization's shape or size, stakeholders rarely question leaders' decisions and won't hesitate to lend their support when asked—organizations' positive track records speak for themselves. If stakeholders ask questions or challenge the directions the organization is moving in, it's always with the organization's best interests in mind.

However, trust in most organizations is not honored or respected. Employees who publicly share their stories are shamed and humiliated. Those who use formal feedback mechanisms that promise anonymity have that promise broken and are tracked down and retaliated against. Those who dutifully jump through the hoops set in front of them awaiting promotion kept waiting for years without explanation. Each time trust is broken, the trust expended is not renewed. And when enough of these incidents accrue, the consequences start to be felt on an organization-wide level.

In low-trust environments, it doesn't matter if decision-makers have all the awareness in the world of their structure, culture, or strategy— stakeholders simply won't cooperate. They'll be highly skeptical or cynical about organizational commitments, believing them only to be performative or decoupled. They'll distance themselves from participating out of self-protection or participate in bad faith to see whether new initiatives can be leveraged or undermined for personal benefit. Movements will fizzle and fail, and each failed effort further solidifies in the minds of skeptics that success just isn't possible, deepening a vicious cycle.

Gauging Trust

Given the extreme importance of trust, it's imperative to gauge whether an environment is high, medium, or low in trust. A high-trust organization may achieve DEI outcomes solely through leadership authority and formal power. However, the same strategies and tactics might fail in a low-trust organization, where stakeholders may simply ignore, disengage, or even actively undermine initiatives put forward by leadership.

How do you measure trust?

One approach is to conduct sentiment analysis of written or verbal content, from social media posting to internal communications about a company.[2] I use a simpler measurement in the form of one additional "Strongly Agree to Strongly Disagree" question that can go on a survey: "I believe that when this organization (or department, or team) commits to a goal, that it fully intends to follow through and achieve it." Don't have the means (or the trust) to conduct a survey? You can estimate trust by identifying its opposite—cynicism. Cynicism, when people believe that change can *never* happen and that outcomes will *never* be achieved, is a powerful and highly visible way to immediately identify challenges to trust. If cynical perspectives are few and far between or scoffed at when shared, that suggests at least a medium, if not a high, level of trust. If cynical perspectives appear occasionally but are accepted as true when shared, that suggests a medium to low level of trust. And if cynical perspectives are a dime a dozen and optimistic perspectives get scoffed at, that's a clear indication that trust is low to nonexistent.

In my own work, trust has such an impact on the effectiveness of DEI efforts that strategies for achieving DEI in a high-trust organization almost completely diverge from strategies needed to achieve DEI in a low-trust organization. The advice I give to leaders, similarly, varies depending on the level of trust present in their context.

High Trust

If trust is the currency of change, then high-trust environments are quite wealthy. And given that so many stakeholders now inherently distrust organizations of any kind, a high-trust environment doesn't come about from a stroke of luck; it must be built. How do you know if your organization is high-trust? When harm is done, it is rectified swiftly and without incident. Feedback is shared casually and proactively both up and down the chain of command. Stakeholders are patient when it comes to change, willing to extend the benefit of the doubt to each other and organizational leaders amid challenges, and expect that their interests are always in the mind of decision-makers.

If your organization is a high-trust environment, it has achieved this with a consistent leadership track record, effective responses to crises and controversies, and strong relationships with its stakeholders. When it comes to DEI, having that level of trust is a boon: it allows for much of the hard work to proceed relatively straightforwardly. This is because, in high-trust environments, the formal decisions of an organization's leadership are generally perceived favorably by stakeholders and accepted without major pushback. Keep this in mind to contextualize the following recommendations: with high levels of trust, achieving DEI is actually quite straightforward.

Prime the Organization for Change

DEI change-making is a process that involves just about every stakeholder in an organization. To ensure that people can understand and prepare for the role they are to play, leaders of the organization should actively work to set expectations for all stakeholders. Note that this isn't the same as making a detailed timeline—anyone who's worked to make a change in an organization can tell you that detailed timelines are the first thing to go wildly off the rails. Instead, describe the work that people can expect in general terms. Share that people can expect a period of assessment, where the organization will seek to learn from their experiences and perspectives. Share that people can expect interesting findings from that process, some of which will seem obvious and others that might be surprising. Share that people can expect a nonlinear period of growth, learning, and experimentation, where new solutions will be tried on. And finally, share that people can expect the process to be at times joyous or sad, at times high energy or boring, at times deeply affirming or deeply challenging, but at the end of the day, the organization created will be better, stronger, more intentional, more effective, and more inclusive.

By setting these expectations, senior leaders buy time to do the important backstage work to continue readying the organization for change. How? Ready the roles required for an effective movement—in reverse. As high-trust environments are best suited for the deployment of *formal power* to facilitate change, individuals with that power must be prepared to play their role effectively. Backers, reformers, builders, and strategists are those roles. To activate them, senior leaders should:

· Ensure that *every* senior leader is prepared to act as an effective backer and strategist on DEI. This is often a prime opportunity to involve DEI educators, coaches, and strategists to work with these leaders early on and help them understand their responsibilities: to legitimate the DEI efforts under them, to model inclusivity and respect for their departments and teams, to take the lead and/or empower leaders under them to experiment with new approaches that solve identified problems.

· Prepare all managers in the organization to both give useful feedback during the assessment process and exercise their power effectively on their teams and departments to empower advocates, educators, and organizers. This is often a prime opportunity to potentially revise, update, and redeploy manager training that exists to remind them of their role in stewarding structure, culture, and strategy. Anticipate that these leaders will be under an additional burden and prepare accordingly with greater budgets, additional growth and development resources, and modifications to workload.

· Ready leaders in the organization who are most likely to be working as builders and reformers later in the change-making process. This often includes Human Resources / People Operations and their equivalent. Prepare these leaders to potentially be working alongside new entities like ERGs and DEI councils to do this work if they don't already exist.

Assess the Present

Running parallel to the above work, senior leaders should set in motion efforts to assess and understand the present. The goal is to understand the current state of the organization's structure, culture, strategy, policy, process, and practice when it comes to DEI, identify strong foundations, and trace inequities that exist to their root causes. There's no one method to do this, and I typically recommend a hybrid approach using several.

Quantitative data is a powerful way to surface inequities in the organization and contextualize stakeholders' experiences. While the type of data you can legally collect varies by country, in general, you should ensure the confidentiality of your participants, the security of the data you collect, and compliance with laws and requirements where you operate. Quantitative data can include:

- Self-report survey data (using "Strongly Agree to Strongly Disagree" questions) on employee engagement,[3] well-being, inclusion and belonging, enablement, fairness, access to opportunities, and many others

- Self-report demographic data on race, gender, class, age, and other dimensions of identity

- Self-report organizational data on tenure, department, level, and other dimensions of organizational experiences

- Existing personnel data on employee networks, daily communications, work relationships, productivity, and workflow

- Existing personnel data on hiring, firing, feedback, promotion, and pay

When this quantitative data is put together, for example, in a survey that collects data on employee engagement on DEI, as well as employee demographics and organizational characteristics, analyses can identify statistically significant disparities in access to decision-making, for example, by employees' demographic or organizational characteristics.

Pay equity analyses, when combined with demographic data, identify whether pay disparities exist by race, gender, and other demographic characteristics.

Network analyses, when combined with demographic and organizational data, can identify disparities in complex patterns of interaction by members of different demographic groups and at different locations in an organization.[4]

Quantitative data is powerful, but it's often insufficient on its own. An analysis of survey data might reveal that West Asian, Latine, and Black women are evaluated more harshly by White managers in an organization, but it doesn't tell you exactly why or how this happens. Is it that White managers are more likely to be biased against people of specific races? Is it based on colorism or skin color, with racial identity as just a proxy for this more important variable? Is it that there are actually more performance issues for employees in these groups related to less access to support and resources starting from onboarding?

Understanding the "why" behind the "what" is essential, but no organization can afford to be perpetually surveying their entire workforce to answer increasingly specific questions. This is due not only to the difficulty of constantly revising surveys and reanalyzing data on the organizational side but also to the increased risk of fatigue and disengagement from survey respondents over time.

And few employees are willing to take a survey made up of hundreds or even dozens of questions—even in a high-trust environment. While more sources of quantitative data are likely to reveal increasingly useful and powerful findings (a pay equity analysis and organizational network analysis, in addition to survey analysis, can be enormously powerful), quantitative data has its limitations.

This is where qualitative data comes into play.

Qualitative data fills in the blanks left by quantitative analysis, and there is no limit to the amount of qualitative data one can collect. Comments on surveys. Questions asked during a Q&A at an event. Feedback from an anonymous online suggestion box. This data can support or even completely reframe the findings from quantitative data analysis. Does the quantitative data suggest a correlation in one department between women's promotion rates and their tenure within the department? If qualitative data from women in that department is flooded with references to the one discriminatory boss stopping women from getting promoted, there might be a more actionable solution to the promotion disparity beyond telling women to "wait it out." Does the quantitative data suggest that the number of people open about their disabilities on a team is related to the accessibility of that team's work products? Interview data involving numerous firsthand accounts of disabled team members holding their colleagues accountable might strongly support that claim.

Good data analysis should focus not only on the shortcomings and inequities of an environment but also on its strengths and successes. It's important to know, for example, whether a strong culture of belonging is the result of intentional actions taken by organizational leaders or simply a happy accident as a result of hiring the right people. The former situation might suggest the organization prioritize scaling these actions; the latter might suggest that the organization quickly find ways to institutionalize positive practices before growth destroys them.

Tell a Story

When was the last time you were motivated by a headline that said, "statistically significant disparity observed between Southeast versus

East Asians in resource usage rates"? Unless you live and breathe DEI data, probably not anytime recently. Quantitative and qualitative data collectively constitute all of the raw material to gain a broad understanding of a DEI environment, with its strengths and weaknesses, risks, and opportunities. Good data analysis ensures that the plot of that story is pointed in the right direction—for example, you wouldn't want to characterize a dearth of LGBTQ+ representation as a "pipeline issue" when it's an issue with the hiring process, and vice versa.

But in all but a few organizations, you'll need more than just a laundry list of statistically significant correlations to galvanize a workforce to make systemic change. To create a compelling story that stays true to the data, have DEI, data, and communication experts work together and coordinate with the senior leaders that will be sending out communications. The rationale for change should be aligned with the organization's ethos and its culture and strike a balance between powerfully honest and inspirationally hopeful.

Perhaps the organization prioritized rapid growth over sustainable growth, and that tradeoff had consequences that it's now in a good place to correct.

Perhaps the organization had strayed somewhat from its mission as it found its place in the market, and now it's ready to reaffirm it.

Perhaps the organization made some tough choices to survive, and now it's ready to go beyond surviving to achieve thriving.

A good story isn't just a headline on an internal report but also a driving rationale to unite stakeholders. It should flow easily off the tongue of change-makers, activate those who would otherwise have remained neutral, and at least attempt to convince those against change that the effort is both serious and needed for the organization. Importantly, a good story keeps in mind some of the core learnings from Chapter 3: accountability is achieved only by centering outcomes, and people are strongly motivated to protect a positive self-image. Stress accordingly in your story that we drive change to achieve an outcome that benefits us all and that it's all of us—not just one group being targeted—that must change. Done right, a good story will activate the movement roles needed to turn inspirational language into effective action: advocates, educators, and organizers.

Advocates can propagate the rationale for change throughout the organization far faster and more effectively than senior leaders and communications teams can do on their own.

Educators can ensure that members of the organization understand the findings from the assessment process and their implications for the present.

Organizers can coalesce groups of stakeholders around potential solutions to the challenges that advocates and educators have raised in the context of the story. Which solutions? Let's explore.

Experiment Carefully

At the end of the day, DEI is about problem-solving. Interventions are tools to achieve outcomes; just as you wouldn't use a tape measure as a screwdriver, you can't substitute different DEI tools for others. Once you have a basic understanding of a problem, like the story about a hiring disparity that opened this chapter, you need to remember that this work is about solving the right problems. Look closer at this example. On the surface level, a small number of employees with different views on candidates are influencing the hiring process to create inequitable outcomes. The clear, easy solution would be to see these hiring managers as the problem and train them on, yes, addressing their biases—or simply remove them from the hiring process altogether.

But hold up; if the interview process is so subjective that a hiring manager's beliefs about ideal candidates can create such obvious disparities, isn't that a bigger problem? Simply addressing the biases of a few individuals after such an extensive learning process doesn't change the fact that any number of other hiring managers could be influencing hiring outcomes with their own biases, as well.

And what about marketing; isn't its culture significantly different, almost alarmingly so, compared to the rest of the organization? If the actions of their hiring managers are so problematic, and those hiring managers are relatively aligned with the department in general, there's a bigger challenge to address than just bias.

At this point, decision-makers have to start getting creative and experimenting—carefully.

Perhaps they decide that formalizing the organization's hiring criteria is a useful goal but are uncertain about the extent to which they want to include or remove assessments of candidates' personality, communication, and working styles. While tasking HR to develop and implement best practices like common grading rubrics and structured interviews, senior leaders might put together a task force or a working group dedicated to operationalizing organizational culture within the hiring process and ensuring that "culture fit" is being deployed effectively and not as a smokescreen for discrimination.

Perhaps they decide to explore the variations in culture between marketing and the rest of the organization, using data gathered from previous assessment work, with the intention of coming to a shared understanding of the culture that the organization is trying to build. Individual departments, then, could each undertake their own pilot programs to embody that new culture using new practices and processes, collect data, and gauge the effectiveness of their efforts.

And perhaps they decide that hiring managers do require training, not just on unconscious bias, but on how to use hiring rubrics, collaborate on important decisions, and steward the new processes they're using. They might contract an outside firm to deliver this training, but ensure that the training was bookended by data collection and follow-up several months later to reassess whether the training achieved what it promised.

Iterate, Celebrate, Reiterate

All that was for one single disparity in outcomes. Just one. In a real organization, there will be potentially dozens of these disparities, dozens of potential solutions, and dozens of change-making efforts all happening more or less simultaneously. In 2022 and beyond, a high-visibility example of this is the experimentation that many organizations are undergoing with hybrid workplaces.[5]

All this effort takes a significant amount of momentum to sustain, and this is where, even in a high-trust environment, movements shine. Advocates, educators, and organizers help translate organizational learning into stories of success and failure that deeply resonate with a workforce and temper excitement with wisdom. They help maintain excitement and a steady tempo of DEI-related change throughout the many other day-to-day activities of an organization. And most importantly, they help ensure that the people who are often executing the strategies created by others are being treated equitably throughout the process, and any feedback they have about the process of change is taken into account by decision-makers. Strategists use every success and failure to refine the direction of future initiatives, to lower (but never eliminate) the likelihood of experiments failing. Backers, builders, and reformers are the ones tinkering with the building blocks of organizations to make them better, and the ones at least formally responsible for success and failure.

As an organization activates all of these roles within a movement, senior leaders and respected individuals can sustain change-making by not only iterating and delivering on new initiatives but also leading the organization in celebrating what they've achieved. And, because these moments celebrate not the input (a training or new policy) but instead the outcome of a successful intervention (higher retention rates, greater representation, or pay parity), they build and reinforce trust over time. This is the final step required to achieve the outcomes of DEI: a demographic mix that holds the trust of its stakeholders, an environment that is felt and perceived to be respectful and mutually beneficial, and individual and organizational success in all ways.

Medium Trust

The vast majority of organizations don't have the kind of spotless track record needed to sustain the trust of all of their stakeholders. Leaders might have made amends, but that doesn't change actions they might have made throughout the organization's history that were harmful or discriminatory. Some might have made racist, sexist, or homophobic jokes that were later brought to light and had to apologize to their workforce extensively. Some might have brushed off or dismissed incidents of mistreatment when reported to them before realizing their mistakes and attempting to make things right.

How do you know if your environment is medium trust? The presence of doubt. Enough to call into question the ability of organizational leadership to actually achieve what they say they will, but not so much that people assume change will never happen. Stakeholders are skeptical but not yet cynical and will often challenge the official narrative put out by an organization, whether in public, private, or both. There are two core tensions present in medium-trust environments that define them: the tension between legitimacy and power and the tension between stakeholder patience and intervention effectiveness.

Stakeholders will inherently doubt the intentions of organizational leadership and call into question its ability to make the right decisions for the workforce—yet, they are often forced to grudgingly acknowledge that these leaders have the power needed to make DEI-related decisions. Stakeholders lacking trust will be far less patient or forgiving of change-making efforts that do not immediately show results—yet, most effective and high-impact efforts take weeks, months, or years to show results. These tensions both help identify medium-trust environments and contribute to achieving DEI in them more complicated than the relatively straightforward path of doing so in high-trust environments.

Get Skin in the Game

Where senior leaders in a high-trust organization can drive behavior simply by setting an intention, those in medium-trust organizations need to stake more than just their word to budge their workforce. Yet, people in this position often are highly aware that it's a chicken and egg problem: a substantial commitment must kick off any effective change process, but the details of that commitment rely on at least some knowledge of present challenges—knowledge that results from engaging in that very process. One way to break this impasse is to ditch the overly positive tone of typical organizational commitments for a balance of earnest and honest while making organization-wide commitments to achieve specific outcomes. For example:

> As a leadership team, we recognize that embarking on this effort as
> an organization is going to be uncomfortable for many of us. We're
> grateful for your comments and feedback about things like our
> promotion process, the representation of our leadership team, and our
> company's engagement with hot-button issues and current events.
> To show that we not only mean well but are committed to doing well,
> we'd like to make an additional commitment: our organization *will*
> achieve parity in people processes like hiring and promotion and
> outcomes like pay and flexibility. Our organization *will* diversify at
> all levels, including the executive. This process that we are engaging
> in will help us gain clarity around timelines, tools, and the scope of

efforts needed to succeed, but know that even before we have these things, as a leadership team, we are aligned on our commitment to getting this right.

I can already see many senior leaders reading this getting worried. "Lily, this sort of public commitment puts us at risk." "Lily, we shouldn't make promises we can't keep."

Exactly. And your stakeholders will feel similarly, as well. By going beyond a mere PR announcement to showing that you have skin in the game, you open the door to your stakeholders holding you accountable. Feelings of accountability build trust, and trust is the currency of change.

The challenge with making a public commitment like this isn't in your stakeholders. It's in getting the agreement of the *entire* senior leadership team, some—or in many organizations, many—who will be direct contributors to stakeholders' trust issues. Building alignment among this team isn't an easy task and often requires significant investment in executive coaching, DEI-related learning and development, and leadership training to upskill the team on not only DEI but their responsibilities as senior leaders. The goal of this work is to get every member of the team to a place where they can individually articulate (even reluctantly) their role as a senior leader in the DEI efforts to come. How long will this take? It depends on the team. There's a reason why this step is first—because it's so important to have this alignment that formal DEI change-making shouldn't proceed without it.

Prime—or Create—Additional Accountability Groups

Senior leaders in medium-trust environments can proceed according to "Prime the Organization for Change," with one twist: they should explicitly promise the creation of additional *grassroots-led* accountability groups like DEI councils, committees, task forces, and working groups.

Why? Because these entities (when led by employees without prior leadership titles or existing reputational associations) are perceived to have large amounts of legitimacy when it comes to DEI and powerful accountability mechanisms for an otherwise dubiously accountable leadership team. The less trust stakeholders have in the organization, the earlier these entities should be created. On the low-trust side, a DEI council can be organized to steward the entire assessment process. On the high-trust side, a DEI working group can be organized to follow through on the findings from the assessment process. Which of these should your organization do? It depends on the answer to this question: *"How would the response rate and quality of responses differ in an employee survey if senior leaders versus an employee-led group administered it?"* If the answer is "slightly," then you might be able to wait and create these groups with the insight from an employee survey. If the answer is "dramatically," then you can't wait: a group like this is a necessity to learn anything of value from your workforce.

If you do create an entity like a DEI council to steward the assessment process, it should have a large degree of sway over decisions like which third-party DEI survey to use, who will get access to sensitive employee data from quantitative and qualitative sources, and what role the entity will take in delivering and following through on feedback. Importantly, build alignment on keeping this group's scope of work limited and temporary until after the assessment process. Formalizing a structure too early is likely to create conflict if the results of the assessment suggest a better or more effective accountability mechanism: a passionate group of friends makes a great informal volunteer group to spearhead initial efforts but are a far cry from a representative and effective DEI council when efforts get more serious.

Additional accountability mechanisms can include consulting firms or experts from outside the organization. While these third-party stakeholders have limited impact over the long term compared to stakeholders embedded inside the organization, what they have is legitimacy and expertise, which are invaluable for creating real and perceived accountability. Put another way, employees may not trust senior leaders, but they may trust reputable external experts. Third-party stakeholders can administer surveys and steward sensitive employee data, analyze the data from a nominally objective lens, develop recommendations, and act as a liaison between senior leaders and other employee stakeholders. They can serve as important sources of legitimacy and accountability so long as they are given the autonomy to work independently.

With these additional sources of accountability in place, your organization can "Assess the Present." And when the analysis has been conducted, accountability groups can play a large role in helping the organization "Tell a Story," as well.

Empower Non-leader Change-Makers

"Experiment Carefully" looks significantly different in medium-trust environments. In a high-trust environment, backers, strategists, builders, and reformers can cascade change from the top down, sometimes without the active participation of other movement roles. But doing the same in a medium-trust environment is likely to be met with doubt from stakeholders who worry that their exclusion will remove an important source of accountability and who suspect that leaders are more invested in perpetuating the status quo rather than changing it. And yet, it's backers, strategists, builders, and reformers that often have the formal power to get things done—the tension mentioned earlier. In a high-trust environment, backers, strategists, builders, and reformers take the lead, while advocates, educators, and organizers stay in reserve until needed. In a medium-trust environment, these roles must be equalized to strike a balance between those with the legitimacy to lead change and those with the power to authorize it. Change-making movements should be driven just as much by advocates, educators, and organizers, coordinated by accountability groups, as they are by backers, strategists, builders, and reformers coordinated by senior leaders.

This different model requires that the groups coordinating their respective movement halves—accountability groups and senior leaders—have a strong working relationship; if they do not trust each other, then the coordination of a collective movement breaks down. This is the point where DEI councils and working groups (not task forces, due to their impermanence) should be formalized as much as possible with decision-making authority, a clear scope of work, a mission and charter, and a process for membership and participation. Accountability groups and senior leaders should jointly create a set of clear expectations for the working relationship, including involvement in decision-making processes, the cadence of communication, and which sets of activities require coordination and which can be done independently without consultation. It must be said here that individuals in these groups, especially accountability groups, must take their own boundary- and expectation-setting seriously. Acting effectively as a non-leader change-maker requires some level of commitment and responsibility, and the people who may have the capacity for informal volunteer initiatives may not be the same people with the capacity for more accountable change-making. As intergroup expectations are being established, ensure that these conversations happen within groups as well, so people can protect their boundaries and adjust their participation, if needed. Setting good boundaries isn't easy, especially for those in marginalized communities who may feel that withdrawing from the work for their own well-being feels like abandoning an effort that "needs" them to succeed. For those who struggle with this, seek out resources and extend grace to yourselves as you make the decisions you need to.[6]

When this work is completed, with collaboration expectations set and responsibilities formalized, accountability groups and senior leaders can focus their efforts on building effective, "clever" coalitions[7] with as many stakeholder groups as possible and ensuring that the organization takes an approach to change-making that is pragmatic and effective.

Will reality be as straightforward as this? Absolutely not. In some organizations, stakeholders will coordinate without much resistance. In others, stakeholders will publicly and viscerally resist, doubt, and challenge these working relationships. So long as people are only skeptical and not cynical, conflict does not need to be anathema. Take it this way: if the conflict is at least nominally constructive, it's an indicator that stakeholders trust leaders enough to attempt to share feedback for the good of the organization.

An option worth mentioning is hiring an internal DEI professional to bridge employee-led movements and senior leaders formally. Though a role like a head of DEI may have any number of actual job responsibilities, the most important work they can do is formally occupy the tenuous space between formal leadership power and DEI legitimacy. If they are adequately resourced and supported, they can effectively empower non-leader change-making efforts while coordinating decision-making from senior leaders and important backers as needed. Why don't I recommend this as a universal best practice? Because that "if" is a very big "if." An ineffective formal DEI leader can be worse for trust than no formal DEI leader at all. Proceed carefully.

Small to Big Wins

Leaders in a high-trust environment have the ability to compel ambitious change-making initiatives like "create standardized metrics and rubrics for hiring decisions across the entire organization" by dint of their formal authority alone. This option isn't nearly as enticing in an organization with lower levels of trust because while leaders can technically make those decisions, they are likely to get substantial amounts of pushback and/or disengagement from a workforce without the patience or trust in an initiative that won't bear fruit for many months. Building and using stakeholder trust tactically is more important than simply experimenting without a plan, and an effective way to do so is through small wins. The small wins approach is straightforward: rather than large-scale efforts focused on compelling behavior at scale, focus instead on achieving relatively narrow and bite-sized goals, then communicating these achievements to the organization.[8] For example, making stakeholders aware of a previously unknown disparity like the gendered disparity in office housework can rapidly build support for new norms to equalize this outcome.[9]

Small wins don't create systemic change on their own, not by a long shot. But they buy trust and goodwill, valuable resources for change-making that are hard to come by through other means. Small wins can be created intentionally if accountability groups and senior leaders coordinate and line up the right challenges in front of movements. With each success, movements become more empowered, and stakeholders become more trusting. And eventually, with enough small wins achieved, organizations can secure the trust and buy-in needed to undertake the big initiatives needed to change systems. Think of it like this: if trust is the fuel of change, being strategic about how you deploy it is like a regenerative braking system. It makes your organization more efficient and extends the lifespan of its movements.

Move the Goalposts

Making change in a medium-trust organization starts with making a public commitment to change that puts something on the line. For that commitment to mean anything, it needs to have teeth: failure should have consequences. Success should, as well. If your organization has committed to cutting gender discrimination in half within two years and fails, then people should be held accountable. At the very least, executives should lose their bonuses.[10] But if the organization succeeds, then the original promise has been fulfilled. In exchange, stakeholders will become slightly more trusting…before looking expectantly to the next milestone. Senior leaders should have one waiting for them.

While the process is analogous to that of "Iterate, Celebrate, Reiterate," a slightly greater focus should be put on internal trust and accountability rather than external-facing celebration. To the extent that celebration happens, it must be done in such a way to indicate to stakeholders that appearances come second to the state of having measurably, genuinely, made a difference. The more trust the organization accrues by achieving successive goals, the more relaxed its stakeholders will become—and the easier it is to celebrate the wins.

Low Trust

The last and lowest tier of trust in an organization indicates perhaps *the* hardest environment to do effective DEI work within. In low-trust organizations, repeated breaches of trust have caused stakeholder skepticism to degrade into cynicism. They doubt organizational leadership, organizational processes, each other, and themselves. In these environments, trust is a sign of weakness, an opening to be exploited. And so, *any* DEI effort that requires that stakeholders trust each other is dead in the water almost as soon as it's proposed.

A workshop to bring junior and senior employees together to discuss their differences? Likely to be ignored and unattended by most stakeholders, erupt into unhelpful antagonism over past injustices, or devolve into insults. A new policy to compel compliance? Likely to be undermined or ignored in private once leaders aren't directly watching. An opportunity to comment on an important social issue? Leaders will shy away from it, their fear of open conflict from "saying the wrong thing" outweighing any value they can imagine coming from taking a stance, while stakeholders fume at the continued silence. Low-trust organizations have become that way because despite whatever tools and solutions well-meaning leaders have thrown at the problem, the status quo of structure, culture, and strategy in the organization is fundamentally inequitable. Any solution that even remotely resembles something that already exists, even if it's technically and theoretically sound, will be shunned on principle. Frankly, this is as hard as DEI gets—and if you're looking to solve this problem, you'd better be talking to more than just DEI experts to do so.

There is a silver lining. Low-trust environments have many more challenges than just DEI, but that means that making progress on any organizational challenge is likely to make DEI easier to achieve and vice versa. If the organization has a poor track record with accountability, then demonstrating accountability through a successful DEI initiative will have positive ripple effects throughout the organization. If a previously disengaged workforce is energized and engaged by a new policy change, that higher engagement will have positive ripple effects on DEI work.

Let Change Find You

Low-trust environments, unlike other ones, are inherently unsustainable so long as trust remains low. Because stakeholders have lost so much trust in senior leaders, senior leaders have functionally lost the means to command their workforce's respect. This isn't fixed by bringing in new leaders or creating new grievance procedures or any other top-down initiative. It's like offering a company-wide meditation hour at lunch to address the symptoms of overwork, only to realize that no one attends it because, at lunch, they're all busy overworking. Sometimes the symptoms of the problem itself prevent some solutions from being implemented. *This means that the goal of a low-trust environment isn't just to find its own unique way to make effective change but to as quickly as possible transition to a medium-trust environment.* How? Allow change to come from the bottom up instead of the top down.

As hard as it is for many to accept, initiating change in a low-trust environment means letting those with the least power make the first move. I don't typically recommend reactive leadership, but in this situation, it's a reliable way to increase stakeholder trust: by increasing the agency of disadvantaged employees to choose their own path forward, even at the expense of some of the control senior leaders hold over the workplace, employees will be more encouraged to speak up and share their experiences constructively.[11]

For those without formal power, the biggest hurdle to starting a movement will be trusting each other enough to share their experiences. That doesn't usually happen organically: it's often a precipitating external event that builds enough alignment in stakeholder reaction to create a (fragile) starting set of coalitions. For example, a high-profile act of hatred that makes the news or a well-publicized report documenting corporate sexism might galvanize communities around an issue, at least temporarily. These are situations in which advocates, educators, and organizers will rapidly emerge, and informal movements can quickly coalesce. It may take some time for these fledgling movements to build enough shared awareness to settle on a series of demands or asks (there is often bitter conflict, especially over what issues to prioritize, originating from low levels of trust all around). But eventually, a movement will make decisive contact with organizational leadership—perhaps by demanding a meeting, sending a strongly worded letter, or even going straight to social media with a list of demands.

Apologize and Cede Power

It can be enormously tempting for senior leaders to respond to these situations with intense threats and defensiveness and act decisively to shut these movements down. In these cases, progress resets to zero, and the whole painful cycle starts again. To actually make progress, senior leaders must react in the ways that the most skeptical stakeholders don't expect: with genuine apologies, recognition of failure, and decisions that change the balance of power within the organization.

Apology A: We are sorry to hear that some staff feel negatively about an organization that, in our experience, has been nothing but positive. We'll work hard to do better in the future.

Apology B: A recent letter has been circulating where employees have shared their experiences with racism, sexism, and inequity in the organization. We first would like to thank these employees for coming to us with these concerns; sharing feedback in this manner takes courage.

After reflection, we would like to issue a formal apology. This organization has not lived up to its ideals, and we, as a leadership team, are responsible. We are learning, more slowly than we would like, that many of our decisions have had profoundly harmful impacts on wide swaths of our workforce and that accountability measures have been inconsistent in the last five years. These are all unacceptable. Effective immediately, we will be allocating a budget for an employee-led DEI council that will have a role in our decision-making process and help us all hold each other accountable for following through on our intentions. We will also be speaking with our board about adding a rotating seat on it for current employees and have begun reaching out to vendors to help our organization conduct more extensive analysis on areas we can improve.

While we understand that these actions cannot make up for the ways in which we have come up short in the last few years, we hope that you see them as an earnest first effort to correct our mistakes. Over the following months and years, we will be continuously working to improve as an organization and regain your trust. You are all valuable members of this organization, and we as a leadership team thank you for your hard work and patience as we work to get this right.

How do these two apologies differ? Beyond the obvious—the second apology is far longer—these apologies differ profoundly in their validation of stakeholder concerns, their tone, and their real impact on the status quo.

Apology A is your typical "sorry, not sorry" apology. It actively minimizes and dismisses the concerns of employees, brushes over them with their own "positive" experiences, and makes an insincere-sounding promise with zero commitment and zero follow-throughs. As an apology, it is almost certain to inflame tensions and worsen the current situation when issued.

Apology B does a few things differently. First, it thanks employees for sharing their letter, even though doing so has initiated public conflict. This is an attempt to assure employees involved in the letter that their actions are at the very least legitimate and seen as important; by thanking employees for sharing tough feedback, this comment also aims to reinforce and increase the psychological safety of the organization.[12] Next, it explicitly validates the concerns of employees by acknowledging that not only is their perception of reality accurate but also that they as senior leaders are responsible for the experiences of their employees. It explicitly names two things as sources of harm: decision-making processes and accountability measures. By doing so, it also legitimates future efforts to improve these things. Apology B includes, most importantly, a formal commitment to make specific changes in the form of an employee-led DEI council, a potential rotating seat on a corporate board for employees,[13] and a third-party-led DEI assessment process. Finally, it includes an explicit recognition that employee sentiment will likely not be magically solved after one well-worded message, which leaves the door open to future feedback and further reinforces psychological safety.

A response like this is only possible if senior leaders are able to give up a little of what many hold sacred, especially those in low-trust environments: their power and control. In high-trust environments, trust flows freely and can be taken for granted. In medium-trust environments, trust is earned by sharing power and jointly achieving outcomes. In low-trust environments, trust is earned by ceding power and allowing stakeholders to take the lead.

Movements Lead the Way

In medium-trust environments, accountability groups like DEI councils coordinate movements' advocates, educators, and organizers, while senior leaders coordinate strategists, backers, builders, and reformers. In low-trust environments, it's the advocates, educators, and organizers that coordinate the direction of accountability groups and the accountability groups that coordinate senior leadership's deployment of strategists, backers, builders, and reformers.

Once movements and coalitions stabilize, their advocates, educators, and organizers are most likely to understand and identify the inequities and issues to prioritize when it comes to earning back their trust. It's up to all other roles to apply their expertise in the service of these movement goals for as long as needed until accountability groups and/or senior leaders gain enough trust for the organization to become a medium-trust environment.

"As long as needed" can obviously vary, but it's important to recognize that *what movements prioritize for themselves may not always immediately benefit the organization.* A senior leader, for example, may identify that the organization needs a DEI assessment to understand more about areas that it can improve in. But movements may take a drastically different direction—perhaps they don't feel enough trust even to want to participate in a DEI survey, for example—and request other things, like workshops to help prioritize their healing and well-being, changed policies around flexibility and remote work, or an employee resource group dedicated to providing community to employees of a particular identity only.[14] A valid critique of these requests may be that they may not be effective at scale for the organization or solve the right problems. And while correct, movements do not ask for these things because they're effective for the organization. *They ask for these things to regain enough trust to be working toward the benefit of the organization in the first place.* They will continue asking for these things until the organization has become a medium-trust environment.

Act Decisively in Windows of Opportunities

To a large extent, making change in a low-trust environment is about steadily shifting power down to those without it and enabling movements that represent stakeholders' needs better than existing leadership to rebuild trust in the organization. This work cannot be rushed or skipped, but it's important to understand that every so often, a window of opportunity comes up that, if handled appropriately, can dramatically improve the level of trust in an organization.

Windows of opportunity look different in every organization, but they all refer to situations involving a substantial organizational change or the possibility of it. Windows of opportunity occur when long-serving incumbents, whether senior leaders or other influential stakeholders, transition out of the organization. Windows of opportunity occur when an organization receives a large amount of public attention and is thrust, whether by choice, controversy, or coincidence, into the spotlight.

During these moments, stakeholders' cynicism will dictate their expectations. "The new CEO will be just as bad as the old one." "In front of the news cameras, it'll just be the same nice-sounding PR talk that ignores reality." "One settlement to shut up the unhappy employees behind an NDA, and things will go back to business as usual." If there is genuinely a desire to change, it must be in these high-stakes situations that desire becomes action, and stakeholders' expectations are explicitly subverted. Apologize. Redistribute power. Move beyond "self-regulation" by inviting other accountability groups in. Make some tough decisions regarding personnel or investment. Prove your skeptics wrong—and do so as definitively as you can.

For many organizations, the summer of 2020 was one such window of opportunity (granted, one that many squandered). One client I worked with during this period, which had long resisted calls from staff to address DEI issues beyond piecemeal volunteer initiatives, abruptly announced and then followed through on a major leadership change and structural reorganization, bringing on a full-time DEI role. Employees were distrustful but momentarily too stunned to challenge this enormous action after such a long period of inaction. It was far too much, too quickly, to simply be another performative effort. And when organizational leaders invited constructive feedback and ideas for how to follow up on these changes, some employees cautiously began sharing their experiences. This story is not a success story per se—as of writing this book, the organization had yet to materialize measurable DEI progress. But at least it's now regularly collecting metrics, when before that idea would have been a nonstarter. Because of the efforts taken by leadership, it was able to move from a low-trust to a medium-trust environment—giving folks more tools and more time to make a difference.

When stakeholders perceive that the organization has taken a genuine risk during a high-profile moment in time for the sake of DEI, their feelings of doubt or skepticism will suspend—if only briefly. This is the best possible time to turn over a new leaf and kick off change-making and trust-building efforts, to take advantage of the momentary lack of resistance to create and build upon the momentum needed to make change.

Over time, especially as the surprise and novelty of the action wear off, distrust may seep back in. But by that point, if leaders have done enough with the window of opportunity, stakeholders may trust them and the organization a little more—perhaps even enough to consider the organization a medium-trust environment.

Putting these strategies into practice is far from easy, and even the most thoughtful strategy gets warped by the difficulty of making change in real-world organizations. That's why it's not enough to simply have an academic or theoretical understanding of how to make change but build the experience that comes only from trying to put new interventions into action. If you've had some time to do this work yourself, it's helpful to check in and make sure you're covering your bases. That's the next chapter.

TAKEAWAYS

- **Trust is the currency of change.** Achieving DEI requires that your organization accurately understand how much trust it's able to work with, as trust is required to galvanize workforces, facilitate stakeholder sharing and vulnerability, and engage stakeholder participation in DEI initiatives and programs.

- **Effective DEI strategies differ dramatically depending on whether an environment is high, medium, or low trust.** Trust

can be measured formally by surveying stakeholders on their belief
that organizations will follow through and achieve the goals they
set, *or* informally by assessing the proportion of the workforce that
is openly skeptical or cynical and how their cynicism is received.
High-, medium-, and low-trust environments emerge over time
as a product of organizations' differing responses to controversy,
conflict, and harm.

- **Achieving DEI in high-trust environments can involve a relatively linear effort.** In high-trust environments, achieving DEI is a straightforward effort with discrete phases: priming organizations for change, assessing the present, telling a story, experimenting carefully, and iterating, celebrating, and reiterating.

- **Achieving DEI in medium-trust environments involves carefully maintaining enough trust to implement a nonlinear path to change.** Leaders must balance the relatively linear roadmap of a high-trust environment with ongoing efforts to build and maintain levels of stakeholder trust. They can do this by tying their own success to the success of DEI, creating additional accountability groups like DEI councils, empowering stakeholders without leadership titles to participate, and taking a small wins approach that scales to larger initiatives as stakeholder trust grows.

- **Achieving DEI in low-trust environments requires rebuilding enough trust to become medium-trust environments first.** Leaders must dedicate their efforts to becoming a medium-trust environment as quickly as possible—whether through achieving DEI or making other organizational changes. Allowing disadvantaged stakeholders to make the first move, ceding power, and taking advantage of windows of opportunity to make big moves can all accelerate this process.

EXERCISES AND REFLECTIONS

1. Think about the last few internal initiatives in your organization. Judging from the response to these initiatives from internal stakeholders, would you say your organization is more likely to be high trust, medium trust, or low trust? How do you know?

2. Name one action you've seen from a leader that effectively *increased* others' trust in them. Name one action you've seen from a leader that effectively *reduced* others' trust in them. What are some of the biggest differences between these two actions?

3. Think back on your potential movement role(s) as an advocate, educator, organizer, strategist, backer, builder, or reformer. How might the actual experience of these roles vary in practice if you were in a high-trust, medium-trust, or low-trust environment? What would change most about how you might think and act across these environments?

4. Imagine that you're advising a new leader on how they might move the needle on DEI in your organization. What advice would you give them on how to proceed? What are some pitfalls you want to make sure they avoid and some hidden opportunities you can bring to their attention?

PART 3
TOOLBOX

━ NINE ━

Expanding Your Repertoire

You may have come to this book with a specific DEI-related question that hasn't gotten answered yet. "Should I redact information from candidates' resumes or not?" "What are the pros and cons of funding my ERG leads?" By now, you have the foundation you need to start finding answers. You know how necessary it is to ground this work in outcomes rather than intentions, the importance of taking a nuanced approach to identity, and the process and practice of making systemic change no matter your organization. These fundamentals should help you process, analyze, and contextualize any new information you encounter as you research solutions.

With that established, I'll share my current understanding of the "what" of DEI work as of the early 2020s. This isn't uncontroversial—any effort to capture "best practices" is likely to capture the idiosyncrasies of a particular point in time. For this reason, I will avoid long oversimplified lists in favor of spending more time contextualizing the practices I include. Do not—and I repeat, *do not*—attempt to apply the practices listed here without first seriously considering the context you're using them in. Remember: DEI is about solving the right problems. Make sure you know your issues inside and out before you take to addressing them.

This chapter will be organized into three major sections, each covering a different swath of DEI work within organizations. The Foundational section covers practices regarding an organization's vision for DEI and its integration throughout, accountability for outcomes, and the structure through which DEI is implemented. The Internal section covers practices related to the most important internal processes in an organization, including recruitment and hiring, advancement and growth, and feedback and conflict resolution. It will also cover how to tackle challenges like compensation and employee well-being, and finally, how to engineer, maintain, and change organizational culture. Finally, the External section covers practices relating to an organization's engagement with external stakeholders, including community relations, services and products, marketing and communications, and social impact. This chapter will not have a Takeaways section, as the recommendations and practices are self-contained takeaways on their own.

Foundational

Vision and Integration

The vision that senior leaders of an organization have for DEI, as well as the extent to which that vision is embedded and integrated within the policies, processes, practices, structure, culture, and strategy of an organization, formalize an organization's commitment to DEI and its approach to achieving it. And, for it to be anything other than a toothless platitude, it has to articulate how DEI is integrated into the organization's mission and operations.

Think about the "usual" mission statement, something like the following:

Diversity, equity, and inclusion are a core part of our business and important to who we are as a company. DEI helps us be more profitable, innovative, creative, and representative to our stakeholders.

We care deeply about making a positive impact in [industry], and through our [core business activity], we hope to recognize and support the dignity of every person.

Some key ideas are the business case for diversity, the intention to integrate DEI into broader organizational functions, and corporate social responsibility. However, the purpose of a vision statement is to represent an organization's commitment to DEI and its approach to achieving it. There should be as many different kinds of vision statements as there are organizations, rather than the existing "one-size-fits-all" templates that have proliferated that lack the specificity necessary to make these statements powerful.

For organizations that do little in external communications, a DEI vision might not even live in a statement. For organizations that are highly process oriented but infrequently discuss nonwork topics, a DEI vision might ensure that DEI is contextualized as "work" and achieved procedurally like any other work outcome. For global organizations that must achieve DEI outcomes amid a plurality of different definitions and contexts, a DEI vision might be intentionally "glocal"—ensuring a common baseline that is universal enough to apply anywhere but flexible for regional variation as needed to frame local problems in local ways.[1] Whatever your vision, to formalize it in a way that will be most effective for your organization, consider the following:

- **Identify any outcome already known to be successfully integrated and achieved consistently across the organization.** For example, high levels of productivity.

- **Analyze how that outcome was achieved to identify as many factors that led to that outcome as possible.** For example, through charismatic leadership, a culture that rewards results, clear work processes, and shared expectations of collaboration and asking for help.

- **Create a vision for DEI that complements these existing successes and can be achieved in somewhat similar ways.** For example, "Diversity, equity, and inclusion will ensure that everyone's hard work will be rewarded and what makes our company such a great place to work, achieve, and collaborate is further strengthened."
- **Activate factors for success to integrate DEI based on what you know about the organization.** For example, through charismatic leadership, a culture that rewards results, clear work processes, and shared expectations of collaboration and asking for help.

Integrating DEI throughout an organization requires knowing how to create change and build trust, and be intentional and strategic about the vision you're trying to integrate. A vision for DEI should be less an external display of commitment and more an internal compass to guide effective implementation; in times of uncertainty, a vision or commitment should be strong enough to guide decision-making and make trade-offs confidently. Some questions to consider as you craft and integrate your DEI vision:

1. In situations where greater profit comes at the expense of people (e.g., workers' health, human rights abuses, legitimizing broader abuses committed by institutional or state actors) and/or the environment (e.g., emissions, deforestation, public health), where will your organization draw the line?

2. What do you want the DEI legacy of your organization to be? How do you want those who come after you to represent and remember your DEI impact?

3. What resources (time, money, expertise) are you willing to allocate across the organization to achieve DEI outcomes, and to what extent do your intended outcomes match your investment in them?

Accountability

"Accountability" refers to informal and formal mechanisms by which the organization and its leadership are held to task to achieve what they commit to. Accountability often requires consequences for both success and failure, and so is heavily reliant on *formal power* and *informal and formal reward* or *coercive power.* Best practices for achieving accountability in DEI can be reframed as answers to the question: "How can you align organizational incentives with achieving DEI goals?"

One method is to focus on key decision-makers. Organizations can tie a predefined percentage of executive pay or bonus to an organization's achievement of DEI-related goals, and make this relationship public, inviting accountability from stakeholders.[2] These goals can span areas of the organization like hiring, promotions, retention, supplier diversity, employee engagement, participation in training, and mentoring.[3] Similar efforts can tie certain DEI-related competencies to rise to a certain level of management[4] and incorporate an assessment of DEI competencies within multisource (also called "360") feedback processes.[5]

All organizations connecting the achievement of DEI goals to desired incentives should closely monitor whether the interventions they are using result in unintentional outcomes. For example, one study finds evidence that organizations seeking to achieve gender diversity goals prioritize certain "high-potential women," elevating them into higher roles while otherwise doing little to challenge the overall gender pay gap.[6] Without a clear focus on outcomes, these unintended consequences can proliferate when a diversity challenge in one area is "solved" by creating or exacerbating a diversity challenge elsewhere.

Other approaches to DEI accountability use legitimacy or trust as the incentive. Creating a DEI council that works with senior leaders in the organization to achieve change means that, to some extent, senior leaders must be accountable to that DEI council and what it represents to have their efforts taken seriously. If the DEI council shares with leadership that employees need to heal from negative incidents they've experienced before participating in an all-company initiative and senior leaders don't listen, they've weakened the trust the DEI council holds in them. In the worst-case scenario, if these breaches of trust occur repeatedly, the DEI council might refuse to work at all with senior leadership—an act that would significantly damage the legitimacy of senior leaders as actually willing to do the work and potentially downgrade a medium-trust organization into a low-trust one. And when an organization is transparent with data like its demographic representation or environmental, social, and governance (ESG) data, it is putting the general public and third-party watchdogs in the position of holding it accountable, with legitimacy and reputation on the line. Some questions to consider as you design your DEI accountability:

1. How can you build an efficient pipeline connecting accountability-related behaviors to important outcomes so that those engaging in these behaviors can receive frequent feedback on their effectiveness?

2. If accountability is achieved by everyone doing their part, how can you make it easy for each and every person to choose the behaviors you intend over potentially easier alternatives?

3. How can you make the actions required to ensure accountability proactive, normal, and positive, rather than reactive, unusual, or punitive?

Transparency

"Transparency" refers to the degree of information shared between different stakeholders inside and outside an organization. Within

DEI, it has largely been thought of as whether organizations choose to share specific demographic data of different levels. While increasing numbers of companies opt to share some data, the data is often too limited to be actionable or accountable to stakeholders. It is useful to know if Black representation inched up by 0.7% compared to the previous year.[7] But, without any more data than that, it's hard to see where an organization can take action—key for stakeholders interested in accountability. Greater transparency can come from collecting and sharing additional data beyond demographics, including data on pay transparency, pay equity, engagement, inclusion, promotion rates, employee retention, and discrimination by demographic.[8] This data can be collected internally or through third-party platforms that steward sensitive employee data.

Beyond data, transparency also includes information about learning, growth, success, and failure. Rather than only sharing positive stories of success, which stakeholders in low- or medium-trust environments may perceive as cherry-picking, organizations should also share stories of failure and learning to demonstrate humility and give other stakeholders a role in maintaining accountability.[9] Transparency is always a risk: opacity, its opposite, allows senior leaders to mask inequity, lower conflict, and preserve the status quo; embracing transparency invites some degree of conflict and empowers change. For example, while an opaque promotion process might draw little attention so long as it stays unknown, that opacity makes it especially vulnerable to critiques of favoritism, bias, and discrimination. While making the real processes transparent will guarantee some degree of critique, it also lays the foundation to make real change and shift processes for the better.

What should organizations consider being transparent about?

To external stakeholders:

- Environment, social, and governance (ESG) outcomes, including those related to climate change, natural resource usage, pollution and waste, product liability, labor management/safety/sourcing, corporate governance, and corporate behavior[10]

- DEI outcomes, including representation at all levels, people metrics including engagement, performance, and turnover, and other important outcomes like compensation, well-being, and discrimination cases, all disaggregated by stakeholder demographics

- Core organizational processes that bridge the internal and external sides of an organization, including hiring, product design, and customer/client-facing services

- Positions—including political positions—on topics important to your stakeholders, including climate change, economic inequity, social justice, and democracy

- Summary information about accountability groups and other elements of organizational structure dedicated to achieving important outcomes

To internal stakeholders:

- All information that external stakeholders see, and

- Core organizational processes that affect internal stakeholders like decision-making, promotion, firing, and conflict resolution

- High-level strategy, including but not limited to DEI strategy, naming all major stakeholders involved and their roles

- Stories of important successes and failures in the organization's past and present linked to what the organization learned as a result

It's not always optimal to pursue transparency in every situation, and too much transparency can undermine success if used for the wrong ends. When transparent facts lack causal attribution, they can create a culture of blame; when transparency becomes decoupled from accountability, it can become a tedious bureaucracy.[11] Yet, when transparency is part of a strong DEI foundation and contextualized within larger goals of learning and accountability as a means to an end, it becomes a powerful way to achieve DEI. Some questions to consider as you design your DEI transparency:

1. What role do disclosure and transparency play in helping your stakeholders hold you accountable? How might the information shared drive collaborative efforts to improve?

2. If transparency varies for different groups of stakeholders, what purpose does this serve? How can you communicate this variation in transparency effectively to stakeholders, especially leaders with formal authority across the organization?

3. Under what circumstances might you choose to share more or less information than usual to each stakeholder group, and what purpose does doing so serve?

Structure and Implementation

The structure of an organization's DEI efforts in many ways codifies its commitments and priorities for DEI. A structure must effectively achieve an organization's vision, integrate DEI, hold stakeholders accountable, and maintain transparency—and do so reliably and sustainably over time.

In an organization that's built a strong structure, a key leader could leave, and the accountability of the organization wouldn't change. Consistency is attained not just by passionate people doing their best but by a structure that normalizes and deploys a particular set of processes or practices to achieve diversity, equity, and inclusion at scale. While organizational structure varies enormously, there are a few consistent elements inherent in a structure that works:

- **DEI expertise is present and influential within the executive / senior leadership team.** This may take the form of a dedicated chief diversity officer but can look like a long-term consultant or advisor with influence in the group or even a non-DEI executive with DEI expertise (if this latter option, ensure that your standard for "expertise" is the same as that you would hold a separate advisor to). This expertise ensures that DEI-related topics are well represented and that decisions take DEI into account.

- **DEI outcomes on a given level are the remit of leaders with authority at that level.** This means that managers are responsible for creating diverse, equitable, and inclusive teams, and department heads are responsible for creating diverse, equitable, and inclusive departments, and so on and so forth.

- **Organizational functions and processes are influenced and ideally stewarded by employees with relevant DEI expertise.** DEI expertise is needed to ensure diverse, equitable, and inclusive outcomes. However, the forms of these outcomes will vary immensely. Each function might have its own DEI professional working alongside a senior leader. DEI might have an entire function to itself, acting cross-functionally in the same way that HR works cross-functionally to ensure hiring standards and consulting as needed.

- **Multiple accountability groups center on different levels of stakeholders.** Accountability centering different levels of an organization together informs a systemic approach to achieving DEI. Boards of directors provide top-down accountability. DEI councils and working groups, as well as advisory boards and organizational committees, provide accountability through trust. Labor unions[12] and institutional investors[13] provide formal accountability from the bottom up and top down, respectively. The more of these relationships exist, the more likely an organization's initiatives will be accountable and effective.

Some questions to consider as you design your DEI-related structure and implementation:

1. How might DEI-related structures resemble or differ from other structures in your organization? What purpose does this similarity or difference serve?

2. What infrastructure, resources, and support are needed to ensure your DEI-related structures are able to sustainably and reliably achieve their responsibilities?

3. What are the formal and informal mechanisms by which DEI-related structures engage with other structures in the organization, like existing units, departments, working groups, and the like? If DEI structures have a cross-functional remit, how can they be supported with cross-functional power, authority, and influence?

Internal

Recruitment and Hiring

Recruitment and hiring determine how employees enter an organization and their first impression of it. Recruitment is the ongoing process of identifying employee candidates and attracting them to the organization. Hiring is the process of evaluating and selecting interested candidates as needed to work for the organization as employees, part-time workers, or contractors. Recruitment and hiring processes need to take into account common pitfalls and work to proactively ensure diversity, equity, and inclusion, rather than hoping that these outcomes occur "organically." That said, the practices that can achieve this outcome are numerous—companies have sought to increase the diversity of their workforce for many decades now—and identifying the "best" among these is, by nature, highly subjective. Instead, I will share the overarching principles to keep in mind when achieving DEI through recruitment and hiring.

- **Attract candidates with transparency and honesty, not misleading and aspirational marketing.** Candidates are increasingly likely to be skeptical of highly sanitized or polished DEI recruiting campaigns and suspect that your organization is a far cry from the image it projects. While some campaigns may be intended to be aspirational and demonstrate commitment to a future that isn't yet realized, those intentions are likely to be perceived as performative and turn candidates away. The skepticism of candidates is well-rooted in research: a study found that paradoxically, a prominent commitment to achieving equity and inclusion in the hiring process led to *less diversity* in the pool of candidates hired. Non-White candidates voluntarily disclosed racial information about themselves after seeing the statement, faced a greater degree of discrimination as a result, and were hired far less often.[14]

- **Treat candidates like valued stakeholders rather than hot commodities.** A common recommendation is for recruiters to note the demographic representation their organization lacks and look for identity-based communities with that representation. For example, if an organization lacks Black employees, disabled employees, and LGBTQ+ employees, a recruiter might be advised to look for candidates at HBCUs (historically Black colleges and universities), disability-focused professional communities, and LGBTQ+ community centers. While this isn't necessarily bad advice, recruiters often wrongly assume that reaching communities alone will solve their problems when the more pressing challenge is that of trust. Building trust might look like engaging with prospective candidates where they gather, like colleges, professional communities, and community centers, but from a position of providing value *to them* rather than extracting talent *from them*. When trust has been achieved, any kind of outreach will readily result in interested candidates.

- **Have a handle on network effects.** Many people have personal networks of people similar to them and have conscious or unconscious preferences to prioritize these networks over others. Unmanaged network effects can lead to small organizations of men, White people, or prestigious university graduates becoming larger organizations of these same people, dramatically magnifying demographic skews or inequities.[15] Consider controlling or restricting network effects by incentivizing referrals not in employees' direct networks[16] or using network effects tactically by rewarding referrals of individuals with desired characteristics.[17]

- **Standardize processes to interrupt and safeguard against bias.** Ask ten different hiring managers to "find the best candidate," and you'll get ten different processes using ten different sets of criteria. While hiring processes and criteria can vary, it's important to target key moments or decisions in which bias can impact outcomes. If candidates react differently to job postings based on gendered words, standardize the usage of gender-neutral language.[18] If hiring managers lack alignment on how to evaluate candidates, develop standardized scoring rubrics and train all stakeholders involved in the hiring process (not just hiring managers but also any other employee that scores or interviews candidates) on how to use them and what each score means,[19] a step-by-step formalized process for all hires involving structured interviews,[20] skills or work sample tests,[21] and grading discussions to justify decisions before the final call is made. If candidates with certain identities are "falling off" early on in the hiring process, set expectations for the diversity of the candidate pool at each stage in the process,[22] benchmarking against the available talent pool.[23]

- **Handle identity with intentionality, not anonymization.** The "standard" best practice with resumes in the DEI space is to anonymize them, but I strongly advise caution. Proponents of resume anonymization argue that because the presence of gender and racial cues from names or hobbies can lead to hiring discrimination due to bias,[24] removing this information will interrupt it. They advocate for names, hobbies, profile pictures, and any other identifying information to be scrubbed from resumes and in the hiring process. However, research has documented unintended adverse consequences of resume anonymization: namely, that "neutral" characteristics that candidates from disadvantaged communities might face, like unemployment gaps, are perceived even more negatively when identifying information is removed. Additionally, companies that anonymize resumes tend to be more progressive and care more about supporting people's identities—increasing the damage done when identity is removed from the process. As a result, for the companies that deploy it, anonymization can backfire and result in even greater demographic disparity—opposite its intended effect.[25] For organizations that value any aspect of their employees beyond purely skills and competencies, anonymization may harm rather than help.[26] While it can be tempting to remove the human element from consideration (and many third-party firms have emerged to meet precisely this demand), consider taking the time to train hiring managers to handle identity with intentionality instead and collecting regular data on outcomes to maintain accountability.

- **Allocate the time and resources to achieve accountable diversity, equity, and inclusion.** If you gave me a week to fill a role, I would not use any of the recommendations above; I simply wouldn't have the time to. My hire would be directly exposed to any biases I have, and without any processes to moderate or mediate them, I would likely bring in the first friend of mine willing to be interviewed. Fine if you're looking for more of me, but not if you want diversity. Achieving DEI outcomes through structure and process is a trade-off between accountability and speed; there's no getting around that. If we want hiring managers to steward diversity outcomes for all candidates and new hires, they need the power, time, and resources to add rigor to their process and be thoughtful about their work. Without these, diversity hiring campaigns will universally end in failure.

Some questions to consider as you design your DEI-related recruitment and hiring efforts:

1. How might the formal and informal processes of recruitment and hiring accurately embody and reflect your organization's broader vision for DEI?

2. What groups of candidates does the current process underserve, where in the process do they slip through, and how might an improved process fill existing gaps?

3. In addition to evaluating candidates holistically and fairly, what means do you give candidates to evaluate your organization in the same ways? How does the organization learn from these "candidate evaluations"?

Advancement and Growth

"Advancement" and "growth" describe the personal and career betterment of an individual over the course of their tenure in an organization. It often refers specifically to the offering of harder, more complex, and more challenging opportunities to individuals as they become more skilled and experienced, and rewarding their success in these opportunities with higher pay, prestige, roles, and responsibilities.

To effectively achieve DEI in advancement, growth, and retention, organizations must address the often informal processes that prevent universal success and push some employees out of the organization faster than others.

· **Standardize the assignment of stretch assignments and housework.** High-value assignments, also called "glamor work," are challenging opportunities where employees can prove their ability to take on difficult work. Success in these opportunities is often seen as an informal indication that an employee is ready for promotion. Office housework, on the other end of the spectrum, describes routine tasks that are often invisible but still important to a functional workplace—think note-taking during meetings, sending reminders to attend an event, and ordering lunch. Individuals' biases, exacerbated by the lack of formal processes, cause large DEI-related disparities in who gets assigned each of these kinds of work.[27] To correct for this, establish standard procedures and expectations for how glamor work and office housework alike are assigned. For example, require that managers offer all of their direct reports at least one challenging assignment a year and include questions gauging this in feedback surveys or during review season. Create a rotating calendar—even making use of automated tools to do so—to determine whose responsibility it is on a given day to take on office housework.

· **Have the organization proactively enable every individual's career progression.** When within-organization career opportunities are only offered by word-of-mouth or given to employees able to invest time and energy into playing politics, wide disparities emerge between well-connected people able to advance rapidly and less-connected people left in the dark. If promotions only happen when employees lobby their managers, disparities emerge between

employees more empowered to self-advocate and those who feel
less safe or confident in doing so. Consider making career development a core responsibility of all managers and requiring managers
to regularly discuss their direct reports' careers at least once or
twice a year. Gauge this through surveys or reviews and expect
this for *all* managers of *all* employees to combat managerial biases
that may, for example, dissuade them from offering opportunities
and training to older employees,[28] pregnant people,[29] or mothers.[30]
In addition, or alternatively, consider an opt-out model where
employees are automatically considered for promotion after a set
number of years in a role. Encourage all functions or departments
to regularly post their openings to an internal page or location
that is easily accessed and seen by all employees, and celebrate
employees who move to a role they are satisfied with—even if the
move was made without their direct manager's blessing.

· **Demystify advancement through transparency.** In many
organizations, employees lack explicit knowledge as to the
requirements, skills, and competencies required to succeed at a
given level; typical career pathways for people like them; and the
process of getting promoted. Aspirational proxies ("improve your
own skills," "consistently deliver high-quality work") can fuel
discontent if people follow all the suggestions and yet find themselves waiting years for a promotion yet to come. Transparency
into formal processes—and of course, the accountable application
of those processes in practice—can address this. Consider creating
job leveling matrices, ensuring that these matrices and the expectations associated with them are understood by all employees, and
training all managers to use them in regular career discussions
with their direct reports to more easily discuss and set goals for
career progression.[31]

- **Set and follow standardized rules.** Like hiring, promotion processes can become easily hijacked by biased decision-making, even in the presence of standardized practices. Ensure that decisions are justified through regular reference to job leveling matrices, decision-makers receive training on practices for interrupting bias, and highly subjective metrics like "potential" are either quantified or removed entirely from decision-making.[32]

- **Accelerate change through sponsorship and mentorship.** In organizations that lack the above processes, simply establishing them will not immediately create desired outcomes. As an interim process, leaders in the organization can take a more proactive approach to rectify organizational disparities in advancement through sponsorship—active impression management and advocacy on behalf of a more junior employee, to other leaders—and through mentorship—help, guidance, and feedback directed at an employee.[33] Sponsorship, in particular, can dramatically interrupt organizational disparities on a person-by-person level.[34] While an effective sponsorship program that matches sponsors with proteges and involves many senior leaders[35] may not scale as easily as a universally applied promotion process, it is a valuable tool to accelerate change.

Some questions to consider as you design your DEI-related advancement and growth efforts:

1. How might you set an effective baseline where those who may not self-advocate in traditional ways aren't excluded while leaving room for individuals to shape their own career paths?

2. De facto advancement and growth processes may not always align with how the processes appear on paper. What are *all* the criteria in advancement and growth-related decisions, and how might the

structure, culture, and/or strategy shift to tighten the selection of and democratize access to these criteria?

3. When disparities in advancement emerge, they may indicate some degree of the organization needing to change to serve its employees and some degree of employees needing to change to serve their organization. Where does your organization find this balance, and how does it ensure that this is executed and communicated effectively to stakeholders?

Feedback and Conflict Resolution

Employees make mistakes. Human error can result in costly missteps, interpersonal harm, discriminatory behavior, and breakdowns in trust. Effective feedback and conflict resolution processes will not prevent mistakes from occurring, but they ensure that individuals involved learn from their mistakes and are able to resolve conflicts accordingly.

• **Create a regular cadence of proactive and actionable feedback.** Many people treat feedback as either a bureaucratic chore and obligation to be sped through once a year or a high-stakes revealing of the uncomfortable truth at the risk of retaliation. Organizations can achieve a healthy medium that routinizes feedback while keeping it actionable and useful for all involved. Normalize productive feedback[36] by offering feedback training during onboarding and as refreshers every few years to all employees. Regularly collect feedback using tools like regular pulse surveys[37] integrated into other standard processes (like weekly team meetings) or informal team-wide (anonymous) feedback boxes that have their submissions reviewed once every week or two. For formal feedback, like performance reviews, consider multisource or multirater feedback that integrates feedback from stakeholders beyond an individual's

direct manager or supervisor[38] and standardizes lightweight
feedback cycles on a shorter cadence than the usual annual review.
Note that any formal feedback processes, whether multisource or
not, can be compromised by organizational politics, inconsistent
training, and low trust and should be deployed mindfully. Research
suggests that even subtle differences in the kind of feedback
employees receive on the basis of their identities can exacerbate
inequities;[39] double-check to make sure this is not the case in your
organization.

- **Frame feedback and even conflict as constructive, not
  punitive.** By building an organizational culture that celebrates
  feedback as a source of learning, enables organizational trust,
  and normalizes authentic dialogue, organizations can improve
  individuals' perspectives on feedback.[40] Leaders can model the
  giving, and more importantly the receiving and soliciting,[41]
  of difficult feedback to increase the psychological safety of an
  environment and create a feedback-friendly culture.[42] Challenging
  conversations that result in increased vulnerability and trust, so
  long as they achieve these things, can contribute to a culture of
  effective feedback as well.[43] Finally, to maintain the trust of the
  workforce, ensure that individuals unwilling to learn and improve
  when given constructive feedback—even if they are senior leaders
  or high performers—are removed from the organization.[44]

- **Resolve conflict and harm by balancing safety with accountability.** When harm occurs, ensure that the proximal and
  root causes of that harm are addressed without putting those
  experiencing harm at risk. Employee assistance programs (EAPs)
  can help with dispute resolution and mediation.[45] Ombuds offices
  can informally resolve employee complaints and issues, especially
  for employees that are uncomfortable with formal processes.[46]

Anonymous formal reporting channels that are convenient, transparent, flexible, responsive, independent, and actionable, whether internal or offered through a third party, are likely to be utilized as well.[47] These interventions are effective, especially when organizational processes are distrusted.

Some questions to consider as you design DEI-related feedback and conflict resolution processes:

1. How might you ensure that anyone, anywhere in the organization, feels empowered to give and receive feedback effectively without fear of retaliation?

2. What formal and informal mechanisms ensure that feedback is accountable and that when challenges have been raised, this results in changed outcomes?

3. What kinds of behavior will you deploy a conflict resolution process for (e.g., persistent miscommunication problems) versus making use of a zero-tolerance policy with immediate consequences (e.g., embezzlement)?

Employee Well-Being

Finally, employee well-being covers every other aspect of a healthy workplace that enables its employees to thrive. This includes balance and flexibility, purpose and meaning, and a sense of community. To achieve DEI in these arenas, organizations must meet basic identity-related needs and empower employees to find the relationship between work and life that works best for their unique needs.

- **Meet the basic needs of a diverse workforce.** While employees are unlikely to complain about perks that meet their wants, prioritizing benefits that meet their needs is a high-impact best practice.

Offer community-specific resources to support employees' mental health,[48] paid floating holidays,[49] accessible[50] and inclusive[51] facilities and infrastructure, and inclusive healthcare benefits.[52]

- **Enable employee agency through flexibility and accountability.** So long as employees are able to meet the same expectations of productivity and work quality, increasing their control over when and how they work can increase their well-being. Offer employees flextime, or the ability to choose when their work begins and ends each day so long as they achieve a weekly or a monthly number of hours. Flextime includes arrangements like job sharing, a flexible schedule or workweek, and comp time.[53] Importantly, don't forget to double down on your genuine support for *all* employees making use of these expectations and accommodations, and highlight individuals and teams that thrive and succeed while taking advantage of flexible work arrangements—lest your words in support of flexibility policies are undermined by actions that punish employees who make use of it.[54]

- **Expect to expand and revise benefits to meet needs over time.** Case-by-case accommodations, even when not explicitly covered by benefits and policies, can increase trust and build goodwill. However, as well-being-related needs not covered by existing policies become more prevalent, expect to create new employee benefits guidelines, policies, and processes to standardize their usage and update existing offerings as the needs of a workforce evolve.

- **Use prestige to incentivize healthy working arrangements.** Flexible options are undermined if only a narrow set of working arrangements is formally or informally valued by the organization—in many organizations, taking time off is permitted by policy but widely seen as an employee putting their career second.[55] Prevent these outcomes by incentivizing and celebrating many different working arrangements, from the employee always physically present at the office and working a standard forty-hour nine-to-five workweek to the employee on reduced hours slowly easing back into work after having a child. Additionally, disincentivize overwork and burnout through policies that establish quiet hours or "unplugging" off hours, celebrate nonwork aspects of employees' lives, openly discuss mental health needs, offer mental health benefits, and reward workers who set good boundaries.[56] This can be framed using the substantial research demonstrating the paradoxical productivity dropoff associated with overwork.[57]

- **Model healthy boundary- and expectation-setting.** Rather than assuming that organizational leaders will be able to coerce behavior from employees or that employees will be able to get anything they ask for, engage respectfully to set healthy boundaries and expectations between stakeholders. For example, if junior employees want to work 100% remotely but senior leaders want employees to be physically present within the workforce, approach this dialogue as a respectful negotiation of what arrangement will best meet the needs of everyone involved and the organization, with no preconceived solutions in mind.[58] Senior leaders should take care to model the behavior they want to see from the rest of the organization, not just in dialogue and problem-solving, but in work schedules. When leaders or "star performers" are sending emails at two in the morning, responding to messages at all times of day, working on four committees, and never saying "no" to requests, any "well-being" initiative proposing that employees do differently is likely to be met with derision.

- **Support the autonomy of employee-organized communities.**
  Employees looking for greater connection and community may
  organize book clubs, exercise groups, employee resource groups,
  and other groups that foster a sense of community. For groups
  that are predominantly by and for the benefit of employees (rather
  than to benefit the organization explicitly), organizations can offer
  resources with no strings attached to support their activities on
  a trust-dependent basis ("on the honor code"). For groups that
  seek to benefit both employees and the organization, like some
  ERGs, senior leaders can involve them in organizational processes
  as accountability groups on an opt-in basis while simultaneously
  offering resources with no strings attached. That way, ERG
  members who wish to engage in "work" within the ERG for the
  organization's sake can feel valued, while ERG members who are
  only looking for a community can continue to engage without
  feeling obligated to benefit the organization.

Some questions to consider as you design DEI-related well-being
efforts:

1. What do employees say they "need" versus "want"? How might
   well-being initiatives and programs meet these needs outside of
   one-size-fits-all solutions?

2. In what ways should the organization directly support the well-
   being of its employees (e.g., healthcare benefits), and in what ways
   should it more indirectly support employees to do so themselves
   (e.g., employee resource groups)?

3. How might you ensure that well-being initiatives are used by all
   who stand to benefit from them, without specific groups or individuals avoiding them out of stigma or the perception that using them
   is "unconducive to career ambition"?

External

Environmental Impact

An organization's environmental impact refers to its environmental outputs—carbon emissions, water use, harmful pollutants, and the impacts of these outputs on the environment, life within it, and climate change. Note that environmental impact cannot be considered separately from DEI because organizations' impacts on their environments disproportionately affect marginalized communities. Thus, efforts to address an organization's environmental impact must be driven by both environmentalism—which centers on the nonhuman environment—and environmental justice—which centers on people and communities disproportionately harmed.[59] To effectively achieve DEI in environmental impact, organizations must seek to accurately understand, analyze, and capture their negative environmental externalities[60] and their disparate impacts on marginalized groups.[61] This requires moving from abstract efforts to "reduce emissions" to outcome-centered efforts to make better trade-offs with environmental impacts in mind, especially those that impact marginalized communities.

- **Track macro-level sustainability but center outcomes on the ground.** High-level sustainability standards and metrics like the TCFD Recommendations, CDSB Framework, Integrated Reporting Framework, SASB Standards, and WEF Stakeholder Capitalism Metrics—soon to be further standardized by the International Sustainability Standards Board[62]—are useful to track your performance from a bird's-eye view. However, an abstract ESG score means little when environmental damage and other harm regularly occur in practice;[63] stakeholder outcomes like health, well-being, and life expectancy should be centered instead[64] and shared with stakeholders to avoid accusations of greenwashing.[65]

- **Capture environmental externalities in decision-making.**
Every decision made by an organization has an environmental
impact on its stakeholders, and many of those impacts go unac-
counted for. The classic example is air pollution, which negatively
impacts many stakeholders beyond those within the organization
without a say in the decision to pollute. Facilities, supply chain
operations, manufacturing, consumption and usage of products
and services, and many other processes that organizations engage
in have environmental externalities in the form of air, water, soil,
noise, light, thermal, and radioactive pollution.[66] Work to understand and recapture your organization's environmental externalities with any planning process[67] using tools like impact-weighted
accounts.[68]

- **Reconsider trade-offs with disparate stakeholder impacts in
mind.** In addition to reducing its overall negative environmental
impact, every organization can make more informed trade-offs
that reduce stakeholder disparities. Extreme temperatures and
natural disasters exacerbated by climate change have disparate
outcomes on pregnant women and may increase rates of domestic
violence.[69] Hazardous waste is far more likely to be dumped near
low-income, predominantly Black and Latine neighborhoods[70] and
exported to low-income countries.[71] By explicitly analyzing the
environmental impacts of decisions by race, gender, class, nation,
and other socioeconomic factors, organizations can recontextual-
ize their decisions as explicit trade-offs with known human impacts
and modify their decision-making with these impacts in mind.

- **Design smarter, not harder.** Use tools to identify the issues most
relevant for your organization,[72] collect data, and set ambitious
goals, as these are more likely to result in success.[73] Look beyond
simply making processes more efficient and embrace novel ways to

operate. Consider redesigning and shortening your supply chains[74] while holding suppliers accountable for their own environmental impacts.[75] Consider adopting and innovating on circular business models,[76] moving toward carbon-free and renewable energy,[77] bringing the public and communities into decision-making,[78] and partnering with governments and stakeholders to regulate industries.[79]

Some questions to consider as you account for your organization's environmental impact:

1. What trade-offs is the current status quo making in terms of environmental externalities?

2. How might you recapture environmental externalities by operating differently, rather than simply "more efficiently"?

3. How do needs differ across the full range of stakeholder groups, and what is your process for integrating these needs into a strategy to address environmental impact?

Social Impact

An organization's social impact refers to its influence on the societies it is embedded within and encompasses community relations, social justice, and politics. Increasingly, organizations are evaluated not just by what happens in their workplaces but how they engage with their stakeholders and the general public, how they respond to larger societal issues and concerns, and the part they play—whether intentionally or not—in these issues. Like with environmental impact, to effectively achieve DEI in social impact, organizations must capture their negative social, cultural, and political externalities and understand their disparate impacts on marginalized groups. This will require that organizations understand that, given increasing awareness of their politicized impacts on an increasingly politicized world, they can no longer take "apolitical" positions or have their impacts on society overlooked.

- **Act decisively to align stakeholder behaviors.** The behaviors of one stakeholder group are increasingly being perceived as representative of all stakeholder groups in an organization.[80] When any group engages in controversial action that even remotely implicates or is associated with an organization, senior leaders must act swiftly to reiterate the organization's values and denounce the association. Over time, especially if these misalignments occur frequently, organizations should build trust and alignment between employees, senior leaders, board members, customers, and the general public regarding the organization's values and the issues it stands for—and what it will not tolerate.[81]

- **Leverage your position for long-term social equity.** The equitable future where people from all backgrounds thrive will not create itself. While goals like "increase the well-being of women customers" sound positive, they are so vague that leaders can convince themselves that a single marketing campaign or equally shallow intervention is enough to "achieve" them. Truly achieving these goals in practice requires accurately identifying systemic barriers that prop up inequity and decisively confronting them— even if these barriers are "corporate best practice," or unspoken norms in your industry, or even codified in law. A great many historical injustices were rationalized by laws until the changing tide of popular opinion was too much to ignore. Organizations can either proactively find their voice and take active stances on the political issues that affect their operations and stakeholders or be forced to catch up when social movements invariably catch them by surprise.[82]

- **Democratize decision-making by bringing external stake-holders into the process.** Senior leaders with even the best advisors will make poor decisions if they misunderstand the needs of their stakeholders. Consider shortening the distance between decision-makers and external stakeholders through stakeholder advisory boards[83] and increasing the cadence of proactive stakeholder engagement.[84] By bringing stakeholders into decision-making and engaging in two-way dialogue (rather than one-way advisory), organizations can better understand stakeholder needs, build trust, and make more equitable decisions.

- **Align external-facing positions with internal accountability.** These external actions mean little without internal accountability for creating equity. As organizations build relationships with external stakeholder communities, they should modify their internal policies, processes, and practices accordingly to align their operations with their aspirations. Adopt universal and inclusive design practices.[85] Detect and mitigate algorithmic bias in AI and machine learning systems.[86] Ensure that external and internal communications use the same standards for inclusive language,[87] and regularly update communication guides with these standards as they evolve. Make measurable progress on increasing your organization's diversity, achieving equity, building a culture of inclusion, and increasing the trust of your stakeholders.

Some questions to consider as you account for your organization's environmental impact:

1. What trade-offs is the current status quo making in terms of social externalities?

2. How might you recapture social externalities by operating differently, rather than simply "more efficiently"?

3. How do needs differ across the full range of stakeholder groups, and what is your process for integrating these needs into a strategy to address social impact?

The practices shared in this chapter are non-exhaustive. Many others exist at present and will exist in the future to achieve every aspect of DEI work if applied effectively. Some of these practices are easier than others. Some can be done with little preparation, while others require a more solid foundation.

Figure 7 might guide an initial DEI strategy in your organization. Practices are organized according to the level of difficulty it takes to initiate and execute them: Level 1 practices are "low hanging fruit" that any organization at any stage of DEI maturity can implement, while Level 4 practices often require substantial DEI data and the momentum of an effective change-making movement to deploy. Note that the practices and initiatives listed in this resource are just a sample of the many that exist. I encourage you to strategize with and expand on this document with practices of your own, putting everything you now know about power, trust, and movements into action.

The 4 Levels of Achieving DEI

Level 1	Level 1 actions can be done in any organization, with no prerequisites to their implementation. While the successful execution of these actions builds trust, Level 1 actions are unlikely to achieve DEI outcomes at scale on their own.
Level 2	Level 2 actions typically require greater resources and leadership commitment, but reliably benefit the organization and require few prerequisites. Level 2 actions build trust and create the infrastructure for future high-impact DEI work.
Level 3	Level 3 actions are highly valuable to organizations, but require significant amounts of information from surveys, focus groups, and employee feedback to solve the right challenges. This information requires trust to gather and obtain.
Level 4	Level 4 actions provide sustained impact and value over time, and thus require the most commitment, political will, trust, and momentum to execute. Change-making movements can be a reliable way to generate the trust and momentum required.

FIGURE 7. The Four Levels of Achieving DEI *(continued on next page)*

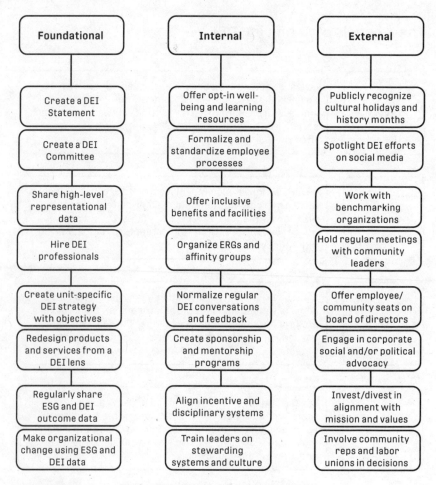

FIGURE 7 *(continued).* The Four Levels of Achieving DEI

1. Assess your organization's own practices by answering the questions in this chapter. A sample of questions from each section of this chapter is included below.

   a. What do you want the DEI legacy of your organization to be? How do you want those who come after you to represent and remember your DEI impact?

   b. How can you make the actions required to ensure accountability proactive, normal, and positive, rather than reactive, unusual, or punitive?

   c. What role do disclosure and transparency play in helping your stakeholders hold you accountable? How might the information shared drive collaborative efforts to improve?

   d. What infrastructure, resources, and support are needed to ensure your DEI-related structures are able to sustainably and reliably achieve their responsibilities?

   e. What groups of candidates does the current process underserve, where in the process do they slip through, and how might an improved process fill existing gaps?

   f. What are *all* the criteria in advancement and growth-related decisions, and how might the structure, culture, and/or strategy shift to tighten the selection of and democratize access to these criteria?

   g. How might you ensure that anyone, anywhere in the organization, feels empowered to give and receive feedback effectively without fear of retaliation?

   h. How might you ensure that well-being initiatives are used by all who stand to benefit from them, without specific groups or individuals avoiding them out of stigma or the perception that using them is "unconducive to career ambition"?

i. How might you recapture environmental externalities by operating differently, rather than simply "more efficiently"?

j. How might you recapture social externalities by operating differently, rather than simply "more efficiently"?

2. Each time you revisit this chapter, reflect on which of these high-level practices your organization implements, which it has yet to, and why. Where does your organization have the most room to grow?

3. Take one concrete DEI practice or intervention you have learned from a source other than this book. Where in this chapter might it fit? Why?

Conclusion

Despite the plethora of rhetoric critiquing everyone's favorite DEI punching bags (one-off unconscious bias trainings, performative diversity, and empty promises, oh my!), there have historically been few cohesive guides to the end-to-end achievement of DEI in an organizational setting that strike a balance between skepticism and idealism. And it's true—DEI is far from a fully known quantity. There's much we don't know about how to successfully make lasting organizational change in every setting; the full and long-term implications of the (as of early 2022) ongoing COVID-19 pandemic amid global social reckonings on race, gender, disability, sexuality, and social inequity in general; and the success rate of the many DEI initiatives that organizations hastily pursued post-2020. But what we do know now is the complex history of this work over the last half a century and beyond; the many challenges inherent to discussing identity, inequity, and organizational change; and the complexity of doing "the work" right. And with that knowledge, we can refocus our efforts on the present and the future to ensure that we solve the right problems and achieve the impact we want with DEI and more.

Revisiting the Challenges

I'll return to the five challenges that I referred to early on in this book and revisit my claim that solving them allows us to solve for DEI effectively. Given everything we've covered so far, to what extent do we know how to solve these problems?

1. "What are we trying to achieve through DEI work?"

DEI work builds on the legacy of social justice and Civil Rights Movements. It aims to create organizations and societies that populations perceive as trustworthy, safe, representative, respectful, and accountable, and it grounds itself in outcomes like success, stability, health, and general well-being. In a stable but inequitable status quo, DEI work inevitably requires making substantial changes to remake existing systems, rather than simply putting lipstick on a pig.

In the service of systemic change, DEI is trying to change not just the hearts and minds of individuals but also the structure, culture, strategy, policy, process, and practice of organizations. Achieving DEI requires that these elements of systems all work in concert and thus requires that change-makers engage in a high level of coordination rather than act naïvely with the assumption that isolated efforts will achieve desired outcomes.

2. "What ought we do for our workers, customers, and the world?"

Organizations of all kinds are increasingly expected to take on a greater level of responsibility for their stakeholders and the general public. Workers want workplaces free from discrimination that protect their dignity, pay them fairly for their labor, and support their well-being on and often off the job. Customers want organizations that recognize their concerns, help them thrive in spite of harmful systems, give them a voice to influence outcomes, and help them feel like responsible and conscious consumers. The world wants—or rather, *needs*—organizations that are able to own their externalities and contribute to solutions rather than problems. In the context of decreasing trust in institutions and communities, catastrophic climate change, and increasingly fascist, nationalistic, and authoritarian movements fueled by mis/disinformation, the world needs organizations willing to challenge and reverse these trends rather than capitalize on their acceleration.

3. "What is the role of power and the powerful in making change?"

Change is the responsibility of the powerful, and while everyone has power, that power varies depending on their role, identity, and position within organizations. By understanding where they have the ability to create the greatest impact using not only their formal power but also their informal power and ability to influence, individuals can specialize in those actions while working together within larger movements and coalitions to create change at scale.

Those with the most power have the most responsibility, but their pathways to create change depend on the trust other stakeholders place in them. With high levels of trust, they can use their power to make high-level decisions that directly change organizational systems. With lower levels of trust, however, they are more likely to succeed by ceding their power to other stakeholders to (re)build trust through collaborative decision-making.

4. "How should we approach identity and difference?"

Every individual has a complex and different relationship with identity, making simplified approaches like identity denial or identity dogmatism unsuitable for complex audiences and populations. In general, organizations should approach identity as a pragmatic lens to understand

and analyze the world, not an inherently taboo topic or simplistic hammer for every organizational nail. By framing all identities—including advantaged or privileged identities—as valuable sources of insight, organizations can defuse defensiveness and build familiarity and competence for all stakeholders in engaging with identity. And, by encouraging complex analyses of multiple identity dimensions at once (intersectionality), organizations can better understand the interconnectedness of stakeholder experiences.

Identity is also power. Accordingly, people with privileged or advantaged identities can build awareness of what power those identities accord them and use that power in the context of their role and position to make and accelerate change in their environment.

5. "What does the work look like?"

Creating systemic change through DEI requires that organizations build a strong foundation and integrate DEI across their organization's internal and external operations and relationships. It is spearheaded by a clear vision, kept accountable through transparency and widespread integration, and achieved by a structure that implements DEI at scale, a culture that supports and enables these outcomes, and choices on the individual level that collectively move toward equity and away from inequity. Within an organization, DEI targets policies that ensure a standard of success and well-being for employees from a wide range of backgrounds, identities, and circumstances; processes like recruitment, hiring, advancement, growth, feedback, and conflict resolution; and everyday practices in how people work, do, interact, collaborate, and engage. Outside of an organization, it spans the wide range of activities undertaken to recapture externalities and engage thoughtfully with environmental and sociocultural impacts.

All DEI work—every survey, training, workshop, talk, discussion, and analysis—is done in service of these larger goals to achieve desired outcomes in a larger context of organizational change. If these are the sites of change, DEI work collectively constitutes a toolbox of approaches and interventions to make change across these sites.

Ending the DEI-Industrial Complex

The current state of the diversity, equity, and inclusion industry is ineffective and untenable, despite its growing popularity. As senior leaders and organizations increasingly look for interventions that will appease their workforce, DEI practitioners willing to provide these services without thoughtful vetting or ensuring quality control will find themselves complicit in ineffective DEI efforts that at best perpetuate the status quo and at worst exacerbate the harm it causes disadvantaged communities. I say "will" here, but the reality of the matter is that this is already happening. Workers of all kinds, burned by ineffective DEI work from well-meaning but unaccountable practitioners, are already beginning to extend the skepticism and cynicism they hold toward their employers to the DEI practitioners their employers bring in. Unless this trend is reversed, DEI practitioners will further lose the trust of stakeholders until we are seen as little more than glorified "woke" PR. We cannot afford not to know what we're doing. It is unfortunate but understandable for organizations to be ignorant of DEI and effective change-making. It is absolutely unacceptable for DEI practitioners— the professionals brought in to fix organizations' problems—to be ignorant. Unless DEI practitioners or the organizations that seek them out demolish the DEI-Industrial Complex, they will both go down with the ship, their well-intentioned interventions remembered by history as expensive and flashy wastes of time—if they're even remembered at all.

Establish Expectations of Effectiveness

The process of finding a "good" DEI practitioner right now is inefficient and convoluted. Whether you search by industry ("DEI firms/

practitioners in finance"), service ("DEI firms/practitioners inclusive language training"), or identity ("LGBTQ+ DEI firms/practitioners"), it's increasingly easy to find practitioners and firms willing to do DEI work, but far more difficult to assess whether a given professional is the right one for an organization. To do that, organizations would need to be able to assess practitioners by effectiveness, approach, and style.

"Effectiveness" sums up the ability of the practitioner or firm to create the outcomes they say they will. If a practitioner offers a workshop series that promises to "increase participant understanding of race from an intersectional lens," then a more effective practitioner is able to increase participant understanding to a greater degree more consistently and with a lower rate of participant backlash than a less effective practitioner would. Effectiveness measures outcomes, not process; for this reason, it undergirds all else.

"Approach" refers to the methods a practitioner uses to achieve their desired outcomes, and it's here where variation is largest. Say several different practitioners all aim to "increase feelings of belonging for LGBTQ+ employees." One might create ERGs, affinity groups, or other employee-led communities. One might address homophobic and transphobic discrimination through new policies, while another might do the same by directly training all people managers. Where approach is most important is how it fits with a given organization's unique needs. An organization that has historically pursued affinity groups will likely be resistant to an identity-related organizing effort that excludes ERGs; for that reason, practitioners with ERG-centric approaches may be better set up for success.

Finally, "style" refers to the manner in which approaches are conducted and can vary enormously as well. Several practitioners running the exact same focus group to achieve the same goal might nevertheless have different styles in doing so. One might focus on active listening to reflect participants' thoughts back to them and encourage organic conversation. Another might nudge the conversation toward areas of divergence or disagreement. Yet another might use humor to defuse tension and take a lighthearted approach to gain participant insight.

It's no secret that I believe we spend too much time debating approach and style in the DEI space when we should be centering effectiveness. We should be asking, "Does it work?" "Why?" "How do we know?" And if we can't answer those questions, we should redesign our work to be more outcome oriented, track the data that matters, and enable experimentation until we can understand how and why we succeed. I cannot stress this point enough: if we don't know if the work we do definitively creates the outcomes we want it to, our work isn't up to par. Even if a workshop participant tearfully thanks us for the work we've done. Even if a corporate client closes out a project with a smile on their face. Unless we expect a basic standard of demonstrating effectiveness—whether with pre- and post-testing,[1] longitudinal impact tracking,[2] or careful deployment of evidence-based practices,[3] our work will fundamentally lack accountability.

Organizations and individuals not in the industry can do their part by holding DEI practitioners accountable to this basic expectation. Ask, "How did your work succeed, and how do you know that?" Ask, "How can we know that your work will succeed with us, and how will we know when it has?" Insist on these questions, no matter how large or small the DEI firm you're working with or how well-known the practitioner or expert.

All this should continue to accelerate the development of baseline standards in the DEI space. While imperfect, there are already useful resources attempting to outline these standards: notably, the Global DEI Benchmarks[4] and the International Organization for Standardization's ISO 30415:2021, Human Resource Management—Diversity & Inclusion.[5] These resources can supplement organizations' understanding of DEI prior to, during, and after the deployment of DEI practitioners and experts.

Formalize Industry Support and Learning

"Anyone with a socially disadvantaged identity can become a DEI practitioner now after reading a book or two," or so the cynical argument goes. It's not that far from reality. I've seen DEI practitioners enter the field after a lifetime in sales or marketing positions as a "passion project" before retirement. I've seen DEI practitioners quite literally read one or two bestselling books on race or gender and start (from what I can see, successful) businesses selling their personal workplace experiences as antiracism or antisexism advice. I genuinely appreciate that the relatively low barrier to entry in the DEI space has empowered many people to join it, especially post-2020. But the skyrocketing interest in DEI from new practitioners and organizations alike, coupled with the lack of standardization and quality control in the industry, in the context of plummeting trust from disadvantaged populations, make for an enormous risk that uninformed DEI work to come will do more harm than good. We can prevent this outcome if we work toward greater formalization and standardization of industry roles and their on-ramps and create easily accessed knowledge bases for practitioners and clients alike.

In Chapter 7, I listed a few examples of DEI professionals: trainers and facilitators, change management experts, and data analysts, in particular. But there are many more roles than just those, too many to name succinctly. I find it more useful to separate them into three (overlapping) groups: educators, integrators, and advisors. Educators increase clients' DEI-related knowledge and capacity and include workshop trainers, identity-related expert educators, discussion facilitators, and executive coaches. Integrators embed DEI within existing structures, cultures, policies, processes, and practices and include DEI specialists with change management, HR, product design, L&D, recruiting, and other organizational backgrounds. Advisors help clients make DEI-informed decisions and include strategists, consultants, and accountability partners. These different kinds of DEI work each require different skills to succeed.

Educators must be able to successfully change attitudes and behaviors in their clients and sustain that change over the long term, a difficult feat when their engagements with organizations tend to be short and discrete.

Building skill as an educator requires developing effective ways not just to communicate educational content but to rapidly build rapport with audiences that may not begin sessions feeling engaged, deploy interventions in real time that shift audiences' thoughts and behaviors, and respond to disruptions or changes in a plan without compromising effectiveness. This is *not* easy and cannot be learned from any book; even if an instructor's DEI-related knowledge is world class, it means nothing if that knowledge isn't retained by an audience three months after the session.

Becoming an effective educator requires first being an ineffective one and learning through experience. But while that learning is happening, ineffective educators run the risk of harming marginalized communities in the organizations they work with. This risk is exacerbated by the reputational nature of DEI education services: since no one wants to hire a rookie instructor, for an instructor to get hired they must market themselves as skilled and effective, regardless of their actual experience. The unfortunate tension embodied by this behavior frustrates organizations trying to bring in the right professional for the job, incentivizes junior practitioners to focus on exaggerating their skills rather than developing them, and leaves the intended audience of these educational interventions—rank-and-file employees of organizations—in a perilous position. Instructors-in-training looking to disrupt this toxic dynamic should aim to learn directly from established instructors who already do effective work, whether through direct training, shadowing, or mentoring. Established DEI firms and consultancies wishing that the quality of instructors was higher have responsibility for ensuring so by offering these opportunities.

Integrators must be subject matter experts in DEI and at least one other area of expertise and understand how the two (or more) subjects inform each other.

They are able to leverage their knowledge to make precise, insightful, and well-informed recommendations that only an insider deeply familiar with organizational processes would understand and follow through on their recommendations to make change. Building skill as an integrator requires developing effective methods to communicate expertise, build buy-in from decision-makers who may have significantly less understanding of a complex issue, and galvanize change-making efforts in messy, political organizational settings. Doing so consistently when organizational contexts—and thus their challenges—vary as much as they do is enormously difficult.

Becoming an effective integrator is not as simple as becoming a DEI expert "in addition" to your existing areas of expertise. Instead, the best integrators are able to understand how DEI expertise fundamentally transforms their existing expertise to make something new. Already an expert in machine learning? DEI expertise means understanding algorithmic justice and how to achieve it forward and backward.[6] Already an expert in financial services? DEI expertise means understanding everything there is to know about combatting redlining and discrimination in mortgage lending.[7] Aspiring integrators must be able to do more than simply possess DEI knowledge in the abstract. They must be able to stay on top of their chosen fields *and* new developments in DEI, and continually turn new information and experience into new expertise regarding how DEI should be deployed in practice. Communities of practice centered on areas of expertise ("DEI HR Specialists"; "DEI L&D Specialists"; "DEI Legal Specialists"), where members can share best practices, steward a knowledge base, and develop new ways of thinking and doing,[8] are a promising way to achieve this upskilling at scale. These communities of practice can help to create the mentorship and shared accountability needed to keep integrators effective at what they do.

Advisors must be able to ask the right questions, build an accurate understanding of complex problems, and know what recommendations to make and when.

Within a given area, advisors go broad rather than deep, focusing not on the minute execution of decisions but on the decisions themselves that are most likely to achieve intended outcomes. Effective advisors don't always give the same advice. Building skill as an advisor requires outgrowing limited toolkits of "pet solutions" or "universal best practices" in favor of more nuanced knowledge, including negative expertise (the knowledge of what *not* to do, when, and why). Like other kinds of DEI work, this requires not just book smarts but also the intuition borne from experience to identify the right problems to solve and match them with the right solutions—and the ability to collaborate with decision-makers that may not agree with them.

How does one become an effective advisor? A bit of everything. Communities of practice, while more difficult with advisors (there are few "best practices" that work in every setting), can nevertheless be valuable sources of support and mentorship. Shadowing other advisors, while more difficult for new or junior advisors (much of the "magic" happens inside people's heads and is unobservable), can still be valuable if more experienced advisors share their thought processes and knowledge base. And, of course, the tried-and-true way to gain skill as an advisor is simply with time and experience, starting in low-stakes situations and working up from there.

Active mentorship, learning by doing, and communities of practice must become staples of the DEI industry for new practitioners and longtime industry veterans alike. Industry leaders, whether practitioners with large networks and organizational infrastructure, institutional certification programs, or existing DEI-focused organizations, can take the first steps in making this infrastructure available to all.

Empowering Interdependence

I have never encountered an organization whose DEI challenges can be fully addressed by one practitioner or even one consulting firm, mine included. A given organization might need survey assessment and analysis, equity audits, network analysis, leadership training, coaching and development, consulting, manager training, policy guidance, job leveling guidance, hiring process and practice improvement, stakeholder mediation, and much more to fully achieve DEI. One firm providing all of this? Infeasible.

Achieving DEI requires that we recognize the importance of interdependence—the fact that different practitioners require each other to create the impact we all want, and that organizations should view the usage of multiple practitioners and DEI firms as the norm, not the exception. How?

- **Specialize.** Rather than racing to the bottom by promising the "most effective" off-the-shelf 90-minute training, practitioners can specialize in niches where they are most able to provide impact and value. This should encourage practitioners to differentiate themselves along lines that organizations will find valuable. If a mid-sized legal firm based in Europe at the beginning stages of its DEI journey is looking for a DEI practitioner with skill in facilitating a series of intra-staff conversations on challenging anti-Blackness in organizational culture, they deserve to find specialists with experiencing working in this background, rather than sifting through every DEI facilitator they come across online.

- **Refer problems to the right practitioners.** By building communities of specialized DEI practitioners, we are well-equipped to refer problems to the right practitioners with outcomes in mind. The more practitioners who do this, the less time is wasted for practitioners in searching for the right clients and for organizations in searching for the right practitioners. And the more practitioners understand and frame their services as discrete efforts to solve specific problems, the more easily practitioners can make referrals with confidence. We can't ignore as well the significant benefits better referral networks would bring to the current burnout crisis affecting DEI practitioners.[9] When practitioners are able to act knowing that organizations won't fall through the cracks if they say no, they are able to set better boundaries and better care for themselves.[10]

- **Build problem-solving teams right for the context.** Some DEI challenges are limited and separate enough that individual practitioners and firms can work serially or in parallel, without interaction, but most are not. In many situations, organizations can and should work with multiple unaffiliated firms and practitioners with different specializations at once to meet their needs. This might look like a larger DEI firm providing "end-to-end" services supplemented with a small number of additional specialists to fill in the gaps. This might look like many different DEI practitioners brought in to serve different roles on a well-scaffolded temporary team[11] that makes use of their skills and expertise. Flexibility with the deployment of the many different kinds of DEI practitioners that exist can allow organizations to solve complex, sprawling problems.

Equity, Maybe Even in Our Lifetime

Early on in this book, I made it clear that despite our best efforts, we as a society haven't gotten to where we need to be with DEI. Our organizations are nowhere close to achieving even a surface level of diversity. Our workplace environments are a far cry from inclusive. Equity, from just about every angle we can look at it, still eludes us. And perhaps as a result of this and other factors, we don't trust organizations to do the right thing anymore. Nor do we trust institutions, the media, each other, or of all industries, the DEI industry.

It makes sense to be a cynic, given everything. It does! I don't blame people for scoffing at DEI initiatives or turning their nose up at terms that sound academic because time and time again, they've been asked to have faith that new ways of thinking would result in new ways of doing and that new ways of doing would result in different experiences for women or Indigenous people or disabled people at work and so on, and that change never materialized. As my industry of choice became a multibillion-dollar behemoth, this change has still yet to materialize.

Where we are in the early 2020s is, in my opinion, one of the best shots any of us have to make real, substantive change. The reputation management CSR paradigm is being torn apart by newly empowered stakeholders. The training and conversation-focused DEI paradigm isn't far behind. If we can reconcile with our ineffective past so that we can create an outcome-oriented future, *we can work alongside our rightfully fed up stakeholders to get our collective act together.*

And if we don't, we can go down with the ship and throw our lot in with whatever new industry that springs up in our ashes. That would be a massive tragedy.

It is my hope that whatever your background, by the time you are reading this sentence, you are many things, but ignorant isn't one of them.

You know how and why DEI programs have historically failed. You know the importance of building and using trust to achieve real outcomes and systemic change, not empty intentions. You know how the structure, culture, and strategy of an organization affect the success of change-making initiatives. You know how to approach identity with the humility and respect it deserves. You know what interventions are most supported by evidence. You know the movement roles involved in making change and how regardless of your formal title, you can contribute to more diverse, equitable, and inclusive organizations. You know how to deploy a strategy dependent on your organization's trust and DEI maturity to create change-making movements that make real impacts and how to experiment with outcomes in mind. And we are *all*, as an industry and community of people who care, actively building an ever-expanding knowledge base of evidence-based interventions that, if deployed correctly, can help us get our act together.

All of this should give us a greater sense of efficacy than we had before knowing these things, and it's efficacy that turns otherwise useless naïve idealism into effective pragmatism. The question is not *whether* it's possible to achieve DEI but exactly which interventions, applied in what ways, will be most effective for a given organization.

Does having this knowledge mean our intentions will seamlessly translate into impact and that we'll never fail? Definitely not. We'll fail plenty—but hopefully, fail in new ways and not by making the same mistakes those before us have made for decades. Ignorance can no longer be an excuse for not being able to do the bare minimum of getting off the ground, whether we're practitioners or organization leaders.

Here's what I want to see your organization do:

I want leaders on every level, but especially executives and senior leaders, to recognize that DEI work is crucial not only to organizational success but also in maintaining the trust of stakeholders and fulfilling the moral and ethical responsibilities of organizations. DEI work is a long-term operational imperative requiring stamina and resilience, and with the right understanding and experience, it can all be achievable—it's possible to *succeed.*

I want organizations to recognize that they need to comprehensively understand themselves in as much detail as possible and engage in substantial assessment, need finding, discovery, and exploration endeavors to do so. By understanding and analyzing their systems, structures, cultures, policies, processes, and policies from a DEI lens, they can identify the foundations they can build on and the gaps they can work to fill. By understanding and analyzing the larger context they are situated in—and their impacts on the world—they can identify their role in the diverse, equitable, and inclusive future, and the path they must take in the present to get there.

Then, with this knowledge, I want organizations to fix their problems and embrace new opportunities using every tool at their disposal. I want leaders to strike a balance between decisiveness and overconfidence to make the decisions only they can make. I want every internal and external stakeholder to have an important role in the change-making process and feel valued for their contributions. I want organizations to be creative, proactive, and thoughtful in their use of expertise and labor from the DEI industry and beyond—and I want the DEI practitioners and every other stakeholder group that engages with these initiatives to hold organizations to high standards of accountability and transparency.

Then, periodically, I want organizations to assess with unfiltered honesty how these efforts have gone to determine if and to what extent they have achieved what they intended and why. I want those calling the shots to adjust their efforts accordingly, respond to whatever intended and unintended impacts have emerged thus far, and get back to it. When they succeed at achieving real impact, I want them to celebrate. When they fail and/or create harm, I want them to apologize and correct their errors. Rinse, repeat, grow, learn, and adapt. They should continue until diversity, equity, and inclusion have all been achieved within the organization and built on a strong foundation of trust, then focus on maintaining these outcomes as the organization evolves. They should continue until the organization's role in creating the future it and its stakeholders want is undeniably positive, then keep going to influence their industry and society at large in the right direction.

I've given you a roadmap and tools so that we can all get to a better future together. We'll have to face up to hard truths about the world and our organizations and recognize that sometimes we've been part of the problems we're trying to fix. We'll have to recognize that our positive intentions mean nothing if our work isn't creating the outcomes our stakeholders want. But if nothing else, know that on the other side of the hard work, analysis, and trust-, coalition-, and movement-building lies a better future. If we do DEI right, I truly believe that we can fix our problems and achieve equity within our lifetimes. That we can all *thrive*, truly and unapologetically, in the world that we've built together.

Do you?

RESOURCES

Reading List

This reading list is a non-exhaustive introduction to identity-related topics, focusing on breadth rather than depth by region. Topics covered primarily center on race/ethnicity, gender, sexuality, class, and disability, with a smaller number of resources on religion, age, neurodiversity, and other dimensions of difference. Many of these resources lean toward historical perspectives so that readers can understand how the themes explored in each book have evolved into our present-day status quo. I encourage you to use this resource as a starting point or milestone for your learning journey and explore additional ways you might augment your learning to fill gaps in knowledge or dive deeper into certain topics.

US and Canada

Bronski, Michael. 2014. *A Queer History of the United States*. Boston, MA: Beacon Press.

The Brookings Institution. 2020. "19A: The Brookings Gender Equality Series." Brookings.

Dunbar-Ortiz, Roxanne. 2015. *An Indigenous Peoples' History of the United States*. Boston, MA: Beacon Press.Lee, Erika. 2015. *The Making of Asian America: A History*. New York: Simon & Schuster.

Isenberg, Nancy. 2017. *White Trash: The 400-Year Untold History of Class in America*. London, England: Atlantic Books.

Murdocca, Carmela. 2014. *To Right Historical Wrongs: Race, Gender, and Sentencing in Canada*. Vancouver, BC, Canada: University of British Columbia Press.

Ortiz, Paul. 2018. *African American and Latinx History of the United States*. Boston, MA: Beacon Press.

Rose, Sarah F. 2017. *No Right to Be Idle: The Invention of Disability, 1840s–1930s*. Chapel Hill: University of North Carolina Press.

Ross, Loretta, and Rickie Solinger. 2019. *Reproductive Justice: An Introduction*. Oakland: University of California Press.

Latin America

Branche, Jerome, ed. 2019. *Race, Colonialism, and Social Transformation in Latin America and the Caribbean*. Gainesville: University Press of Florida.

French, William E., and Katherine Elaine Bliss, eds. 2006. *Gender, Sexuality, and Power in Latin America since Independence*. Lanham, MD: Rowman & Littlefield.

Galeano, Eduardo. 2009. *Open Veins of Latin America: Five Centuries of the Pillage of a Continent*. Brunswick, VIC, Australia: Scribe Publications.

Petras, James, and Henry Veltmeyer. 2017. *The Class Struggle in Latin America: Making History Today*. London, England: Routledge.

Europe

Azoulay, Ariella. 2019. *Potential History: Unlearning Imperialism*. London, England: Verso Books.

Barrett, James R. 2017. *History from the Bottom Up and the Inside Out: Ethnicity, Race, and Identity in Working-Class History*. Durham, NC: Duke University Press.

Bulmer, Martin, and John Solomos, eds. 2020. *Migration and Race in Europe*. London, England: Routledge.

Heng, Geraldine. 2019. *The Invention of Race in the European Middle Ages*. Cambridge, England: Cambridge University Press.

Herzog, Dagmar. 2020. *Unlearning Eugenics: Sexuality, Reproduction, and Disability in Post-Nazi Europe*. Madison: University of Wisconsin Press.

Timm, Annette F., and Joshua A. Sanborn. 2022. *Gender, Sex and the Shaping of*

Modern Europe: A History from the French Revolution to the Present Day. 3rd ed. London, England: Bloomsbury Academic.

West Asia and North Africa

Abdulhadi, Rabab, Evelyn Alsultany, and Nadine Christine Naber. 2015. *Arab and Arab American Feminisms: Gender, Violence, and Belonging.* Syracuse, NY: Syracuse University Press.

Betancourt, Roland. 2020. *Byzantine Intersectionality: Sexuality, Gender, and Race in the Middle Ages.* Princeton, NJ: Princeton University Press.

Gray, Doris H., and Nadia Sonneveld, eds. 2020. *Women and Social Change in North Africa: What Counts as Revolutionary?* Cambridge, England: Cambridge University Press.

Khalidi, Rashid. 2020. *The Hundred Years' War on Palestine: A History of Settler Colonialism and Resistance, 1917–2017.* Metropolitan Books.

Said Aly, Abdel Monem, Shai Feldman, and Khalil Shikaki. 2013. *Arabs and Israelis: Conflict and Peacemaking in the Middle East.* London, England: Red Globe Press.

Sub-Saharan Africa

Arnfred, Signe. 2011. *Sexuality and Gender Politics in Mozambique: Rethinking Gender in Africa.* Suffolk, England: Boydell & Brewer.

Falola, Toyin, and Nic Hamel, eds. 2021. *Disability in Africa: Inclusion, Care, and the Ethics of Humanity.* Rochester, NY: University of Rochester Press.

Murove, Munyaradzi Felix. 2019. *Greed in Post-Colonial Africa: The Demise of Colonial Capitalism and the Ascendancy of Political Capitalism.* Rochdale, England: Beacon Books.

Swarr, Amanda Lock. 2012. *Sex in Transition: Remaking Gender and Race in South Africa.* Albany: State University of New York Press.

Welz, Martin. 2021. *Africa since Decolonization: The History and Politics of a Diverse Continent.* Cambridge, England: Cambridge University Press.

East, South, and Southeast Asia

Bayly, Susan. 2001. *The New Cambridge History of India: Caste, Society, and Politics in India from the Eighteenth Century to the Modern Age.* Cambridge, England: Cambridge University Press.

Broadbent, Kaye, and Michele Ford, eds. 2010. *Women and Labour Organizing in Asia: Diversity, Autonomy, and Activism*. London, England: Routledge.

Ghai, Anita, ed. 2018. *Disability in South Asia: Knowledge and Experience*. New Delhi, India: SAGE Publications.

Reid, Anthony. 2015. *A History of Southeast Asia: Critical Crossroads*. Nashville, TN: John Wiley & Sons.

Scott, James C. 2009. *The Art of Not Being Governed: An Anarchist History of Upland Southeast Asia*. New Haven, CT: Yale University Press.

Tam, Siumi Maria, Wai Ching Angela Wong, and Danning Wang, eds. 2016. *Gender and Family in East Asia*. London, England: Routledge.

Additional/Global Resources

Bauer, Thomas. 2021. *A Culture of Ambiguity A Culture of Ambiguity: An Alternative History of Islam*. Translated by Hinrich Biesterfeldt and Tricia Tunstall. New York: Columbia University Press.

Chappell, Paul, and Marlene de Beer, eds. 2018. *Diverse Voices of Disabled Sexualities in the Global South*. Cham, Switzerland: Springer International Publishing.

Gendron, Tracey. 2022. *Ageism Unmasked: Exploring Age Bias and How to End It*. Lebanon, NH: Steerforth Press.

Nicol, Nancy, ed. 2018. *Envisioning Global LGBT Human Rights: (Neo)Colonialism, Neoliberalism, Resistance and Hope*. London, England: University of London Institute of Commonwealth Studies.

Parekh, Serena. 2020. *No Refuge: Ethics and the Global Refugee Crisis*. New York: Oxford University Press.

Price, Devon. 2022. *Unmasking Autism: Discovering the New Faces of Neurodiversity*. New York: Harmony Books.

Wiesner-Hanks, Merry E. 2021. *Gender in History: Global Perspectives*. Hoboken, NJ: Wiley-Blackwell.

Interactive Resources

Interactive resources included throughout the book are collected in the following pages. Use these to guide your thinking and turn your positive intentions into positive impact.

Organizational Structure and Culture

Aspect	Description	Low	Medium	High
Structure	The rules, roles, and responsibilities that coordinate people.			
Centralization	The degree to which decisions are made from the top down.	☐	☐	☐
Formalization	The degree to which organizational function is documented and follows strict rules.	☐	☐	☐
Complexity	The degree to which organizations divide work across jobs, divisions, and locations.	☐	☐	☐
Culture	Shared assumptions and expectations for behavior in an environment.			
Power Distance	The degree to which power differences are normalized and accepted.	☐	☐	☐
Interdependence	The degree to which people see themselves as connected to a broader group.	☐	☐	☐
Uncertainty Avoidance	The degree to which uncertainty or ambiguity is avoided or devalued.	☐	☐	☐
Failure Avoidance	The degree to which failure or imperfection is avoided or devalued.	☐	☐	☐

Each dimension of structure and culture can be low, medium, or high.

Stakeholder Power and Strategy

Stakeholder	Formal	Reward	Coercive	Expert	Info	Referent
You						
Objectives/Strategy						
Objectives/Strategy						
Objectives/Strategy						
Objectives/Strategy						
Objectives/Strategy						
Objectives/Strategy						
Objectives/Strategy						
Objectives/Strategy						

**Different aspects of power can be indicated for each
stakeholder with their objectives or strategy.**

Create a Power Map

Use this chart to map stakeholders related to your change effort.
The x-axis represents the stakeholder's position toward your goal.
The y-axis represents their amount of power relative to your goal.

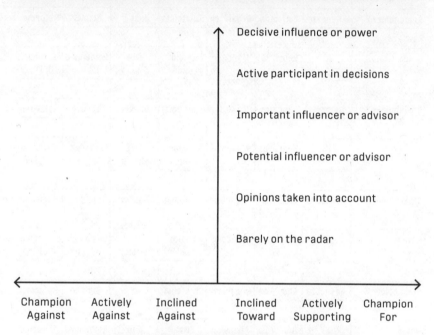

Decisive influence or power

Active participant in decisions

Important influencer or advisor

Potential influencer or advisor

Opinions taken into account

Barely on the radar

| Champion Against | Actively Against | Inclined Against | Inclined Toward | Actively Supporting | Champion For |

**A sample visual framework for mapping stakeholders
along two axes, by power and support/opposition to an agenda.**

Stakeholder Roles

Stakeholder 1	Advocate	Educator	Organizer	Strategist	Backer	Builder	Reformer
You							
Notes	IC	Senior IC	Manager	Senior Leader	DEI Group	Embedded DEI Pro	External DEI Pro
Stakeholder 2	**Advocate**	**Educator**	**Organizer**	**Strategist**	**Backer**	**Builder**	**Reformer**
Notes	IC	Senior IC	Manager	Senior Leader	DEI Group	Embedded DEI Pro	External DEI Pro
Stakeholder 3	**Advocate**	**Educator**	**Organizer**	**Strategist**	**Backer**	**Builder**	**Reformer**
Notes	IC	Senior IC	Manager	Senior Leader	DEI Group	Embedded DEI Pro	External DEI Pro
Stakeholder 4	**Advocate**	**Educator**	**Organizer**	**Strategist**	**Backer**	**Builder**	**Reformer**
Notes	IC	Senior IC	Manager	Senior Leader	DEI Group	Embedded DEI Pro	External DEI Pro
Stakeholder 5	**Advocate**	**Educator**	**Organizer**	**Strategist**	**Backer**	**Builder**	**Reformer**
Notes	IC	Senior IC	Manager	Senior Leader	DEI Group	Embedded DEI Pro	External DEI Pro

Stakeholders' movement and organizational roles can be indicated, along with a section to write notes for each stakeholder.

The 4 Levels of Achieving DEI

| **Level 1** | Level 1 actions can be done in any organization, with no prerequisites to their implementation. While the successful execution of these actions builds trust, Level 1 actions are unlikely to achieve DEI outcomes at scale on their own. |

| **Level 2** | Level 2 actions typically require greater resources and leadership commitment, but reliably benefit the organization and require few prerequisites. Level 2 actions build trust and create the infrastructure for future high-impact DEI work. |

| **Level 3** | Level 3 actions are highly valuable to organizations, but require significant amounts of information from surveys, focus groups, and employee feedback to solve the right challenges. This information requires trust to gather and obtain. |

| **Level 4** | Level 4 actions provide sustained impact and value over time, and thus require the most commitment, political will, trust, and momentum to execute. Change-making movements can be a reliable way to generate the trust and momentum required. |

[CONTINUED ON NEXT PAGE]

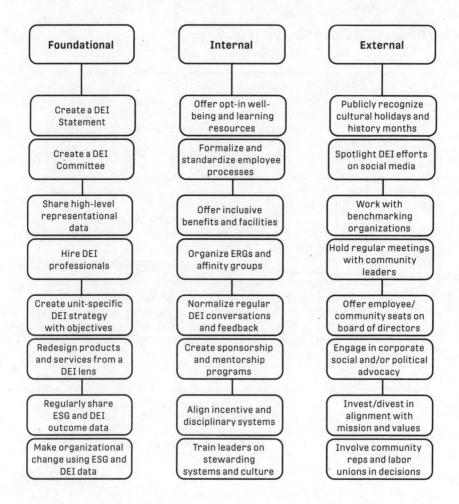

NOTES

Preface

1. Williams, Bärí A. 2021. "Did Tech Companies Keep Their Promises One Year after George Floyd's Death?" Fast Company. May 25, 2021.

2. Norwood, Candice. 2021. "Racial Bias Trainings Surged after George Floyd's Death. A Year Later, Experts Are Still Waiting for 'Bold' Change." PBS NewsHour. May 25, 2021.

3. McGregor, Jena. 2020. "Diversity Job Openings Fell Nearly 60% after the Coronavirus. Then Came the Black Lives Matter Protests." *Washington Post*, July 15, 2020.

4. Telusma, Blue. 2019. "Before You Share 'Trauma Porn' Videos on Social Media, Consider These Critical Things." TheGrio. April 4, 2019.

Introduction

1. Friedersdorf, Conor. 2020. "Purity Politics Makes Nothing Happen." *The Atlantic*. July 29, 2020.

2. "Against Politics of Disposability: Challenges to the Attacks on Andrea Smith, Challenges to a Politics of Disposability." 2015. Against a Politics of Disposability. July 7, 2015.

3. "tokenism." (2021, April 24). Merriam-Webster.Com.

4. In this book, I use the racial terms "Black," "Indigenous," "West / East / Southeast / South Asian," "Latine," "Mixed and Multiracial," and "White." To describe different genders, I use "men," "women," and "nonbinary people." To describe people with a different gender identity and/or gender expression than that assigned to them at birth I use the umbrella term "trans." To describe all gender and sexual minorities, I use the term "LGBTQ+." To refer to people

with hearing, vision, learning, psychological, and/or physical disabilities, I use the term "disabled people." To refer to people who differ from the norm in mental and cognitive function, I use the terms "autistic" (where relevant) and "neurodivergent."

Chapter 1. Intentions Aren't Enough

1. Dobbin, Frank, and Alexandra Kalev. 2016. "Why Diversity Programs Fail." *Harvard Business Review*, July 1, 2016.

2. "Diversity, Equity and Inclusion Policy." Resources and Tools: Sample Policies. Society for Human Resource Management (SHRM) by Atricore. 2021. Shrm.Org. April 9, 2021.

3. Lambouths, Danny III, William Scarborough, and Allyson Holbrook. 2019. "Who Supports Diversity Policies? It Depends on the Policy." *Harvard Business Review*, 2019.

4. Dover, Tessa L., Cheryl R. Kaiser, and Brenda Major. 2020. "Mixed Signals: The Unintended Effects of Diversity Initiatives." *Social Issues and Policy Review* 14 (1): 152–81.

5. "Bystander Intervention." 2019. Education & Training. December 10, 2019.

6. Coker, Ann L., Heather M. Bush, Candace J. Brancato, Emily R. Clear, and Eileen A. Recktenwald. 2019. "Bystander Program Effectiveness to Reduce Violence Acceptance: RCT in High Schools." *Journal of Family Violence* 34 (3): 153–64.

7. "HR Privacy—Protecting Privacy in Global Diversity and Inclusion Initiatives." 2018. Hldataprotection.Com. 2018.

8. Saunders, Benjamin, Jenny Kitzinger, and Celia Kitzinger. 2015. "Anonymising Interview Data: Challenges and Compromise in Practice." *Qualitative Research: QR* 15 (5): 616–32.

9. Andrade, Chittaranjan. 2021. "HARKing, Cherry-Picking, P-Hacking, Fishing Expeditions, and Data Dredging and Mining as Questionable Research Practices." *The Journal of Clinical Psychiatry* 82 (1).

10. Welbourne, Theresa M., Skylar Rolf, and Steven Schlachter. "Employee Resource Groups: An Introduction, Review and Research Agenda." *Academy of Management Proceedings* 1 (2015): 15661.

11. Levin, Sam. 2017. "Black and Latino Representation in Silicon Valley Has Declined, Study Shows." *The Guardian*, October 3, 2017.

12. Quillian, Lincoln, Devah Pager, Ole Hexel, and Arnfinn H. Midtbøen. 2017. "Meta-Analysis of Field Experiments Shows No Change in Racial Discrimination in Hiring over Time." *Proceedings of the National Academy of Sciences of the United States of America* 114 (41): 10870-75.

13. "Employment Discrimination Charges Filed under the Americans with Disabilities Act (ADA)." 2014. Disabilitystatistics.Org. April 19, 2014.

14. "70% of Physicians Unaware of How to Treat Someone with a Disability." 2022. Open Access Government. January 4, 2022.

15. "A Look at Gender Gains and Gaps in the U.S." 2018. Pew Research Center. March 15, 2018.

16. Findling, Mary G., Logan S. Casey, Stephanie A. Fryberg, Steven Hafner, Robert J. Blendon, John M. Benson, Justin M. Sayde, and Carolyn Miller. 2019. "Discrimination in the United States: Experiences of Native Americans." *Health Services Research* 54 Suppl 2 (S2): 1431–41.

17. Gruberg, Sharita, Lindsay Mahowald, and John Halpin. 2020. "The State of the LGBTQ Community in 2020." Center for American Progress. October 6, 2020.

18. McCann, Carly, and Donald Tomaskovic-Devey. 2021. "Pregnancy Discrimination in the Workplace." Umass.Edu. May 26, 2021.

19. "Discrimination and Poverty—Stanford Center on Poverty and Inequality." n.d. Stanford.Edu. Accessed January 29, 2022.

20. Quillian, Lincoln, Anthony Heath, Devah Pager, Arnfinn Midtbøen, Fenella Fleischmann, and Ole Hexel. 2019. "Do Some Countries Discriminate More Than Others? Evidence from 97 Field Experiments of Racial Discrimination in Hiring." *Sociological Science* 6: 467–96.

21. Rahim, Lily Zubaida. 2007. "Race, Discrimination and Citizenship in South East Asia (Draft)." Unrisd.Org. July 11, 2007.

22. "China: Gender Discrimination in Hiring Persists." 2020. Human Rights Watch. April 29, 2020.

23. Kim, Ji-Hye, Sarah Soyeon Oh, Suk Won Bae, Eun-Cheol Park, and Sung-In Jang. 2019. "Gender Discrimination in the Workplace: Effects on Pregnancy Planning and Childbirth among South Korean Women." *International Journal of Environmental Research and Public Health* 16 (15): 2672.

24. "Discrimination at Work in Asia." 2013. International Labor Organization September 9, 2013.

25. "Discrimination at Work in Africa." 2007. International Labor Organization, April 5, 2007.

26. "Discrimination at Work in the Middle East and North Africa." 2013. International Labor Organization. November 2, 2013.

27. "Get to Know Us." 2019. Me Too. November 22, 2019.

28. "#metoo Project Schlesinger Library—#metoo Digital Media Collection." 2018. #metoo Project Schlesinger Library. 2018.

29. Levy, Roee, and Martin Mattsson. 2019. "The Effects of Social Movements: Evidence from #MeToo." *SSRN Electronic Journal*.

30. "Four Years Later, Most Believe Women Have Benefited from the #MeToo Movement." 2021. AP-NORC. October 15, 2021.

31. "Not Harassing Women Is Not Enough—Working Relationships in the #MeToo Era, Key Findings." 2018. Lean In. February 7, 2018.

32. Johnson, Stefanie K., Ksenia Keplinger, Jessica F. Kirk, and Liza Barnes. 2019. "Has Sexual Harassment at Work Decreased since #MeToo?" *Harvard Business Review*, 2019.

33. Bower, T. 2019. "The #MeToo Backlash." *Harvard Business Review*, 2019.

34. "It's Not Just Peng. China Is Cracking down on #MeToo Movement." 2021. Taipeitimes.Com. November 25, 2021.

35. "It's Not Just Peng. China Is Cracking down on #MeToo Movement." 2021. Taipeitimes.Com. November 25, 2021.

36. Lopez, Oscar. 2020. "Factbox: Where Latin America Women Are Fighting the World's Highest Murder Rates." Reuters. March 7, 2020.

37. Hasunuma, Linda, and Ki-Young Shin. 2019. "#MeToo in Japan and South Korea: #WeToo, #WithYou." *Journal of Women, Politics & Policy* 40 (1): 97–111.

38. *Global Gender Gap Report 2021*. (n.d.). World Economic Forum. Retrieved April 1, 2022, from https://www.weforum.org/reports/global-gender-gap-report-2021

39. Tatum, Beverly Daniel. "Why Are All the Black Kids Sitting Together in the Cafeteria? and Other Conversations About Race." New York: Basic Books, 199.

40. "The Argument." 2021. Opinion. *The New York Times*, August 11, 2021.

41. Read, Bridget. 2021. "Inside the Booming Diversity-Equity-and-Inclusion Industrial Complex." The Cut. May 26, 2021.

42. Global Industry Analysts, *Global Diversity and Inclusion (D&I) Industry* San Jose, CA: Global Industry Analysts.

43. Newkirk, Pamela. 2019. *Diversity, Inc: The Failed Promise of a Billion-Dollar Business*. USA: Bold Type Books.

Chapter 2. DEI Building Blocks

1. University of Washington. 2019. "Diversity, Equity and Inclusion Glossary." College of the Environment—University of Washington. March 29, 2019.

2. "Eliminating the Black–White Wealth Gap Is a Generational Challenge." 2021. Center for American Progress. March 19, 2021.

3. Global Diversity Practice. 2019. "What Is Diversity & Inclusion?" Global Diversity Practice. September 24, 2019.

4. Substitute this word for the dominant group of men in your society, if not "White."

5. Apfelbaum, Evan. Interviewed by Martha E. Mangelsdorf. 2017. "The Trouble with Homogeneous Teams." MIT Sloan Management Review. December 13, 2017.

6. Schmidt, Anna. 2016. "Groupthink." *Encyclopedia Britannica.*

7. Lawson, M. Asher, Ashley E. Martin, Imrul Huda, and Sandra C. Matz. 2022. "Hiring Women into Senior Leadership Positions Is Associated with a Reduction in Gender Stereotypes in Organizational Language." *PNAS* 119 (9).

8. Sherrer, Kara. 2018. "What Is Tokenism, and Why Does It Matter in the Workplace?" Vanderbilt Business School. February 26, 2018.

9. Ware, Lawrence. 2016. "The Politics of Being Woke." The Root. July 14, 2016.

10. Lim, Jessica. 2020. "Do Diversity Hires Really Make Us More Diverse?" Ascent Publication. August 25, 2020.

11. "What Diversity, Equity, and Inclusion Really Mean." 2020. Ideal. December 10, 2020.

12. "Sense of Belonging." 2020. Cornell.Edu. June 18, 2020.

13. Romansky, Lauren, Mia Garrod, Katie Brown, and Kartik Deo. 2021. "How to Measure Inclusion in the Workplace." *Harvard Business Review,* 2021.

14. Thompson, Stephen. 2017. "Defining and Measuring 'Inclusion' within an Organisation." Ids.Ac.Uk. 2017.

15. "Rediscovering the Sense of Belonging in Social Research: A New Survey Measure." 2021. On Society. March 5, 2021.

16. Sweeney, Rose. 2020. "What the Heck Is a Proxy Metric and Why You Care." FactorLab. October 23, 2020.

17. Steinmetz, Katy. 2020. "She Coined the Term 'Intersectionality' Over 30 Years Ago. Here's What It Means to Her Today." Time.Com. February 20, 2020.

18. Jana, Tiffany. 2020. *Subtle Acts of Exclusion: How to Understand, Identify, and Stop Microaggressions.* Oakland, CA: Berrett-Koehler.

19. "What Is Psychological Safety at Work?" 2022. CCL. January 15, 2022.

20. Minsky, Marvin. 1994. "Published as 'Negative Expertise,' *International Journal of Expert Systems,* 1994, Vol. 7, No. 1, Pp. 13–19." Mit.Edu. January 4, 1994.

21. Parviainen, Jaana, and Marja Eriksson. 2006. "Negative Knowledge, Expertise and Organisations." *International Journal of Management Concepts and Philosophy* 2 (2): 140.

Chapter 3. To What End?

1. Kim, Michelle MiJung. 2018. "Compilation of Diversity & Inclusion 'Business Case' Research Data." Medium. *Awaken* (blog). April 2, 2018.

2. McKinsey & Company. (2020). "Diversity Wins—How Inclusion Matters."

3. Eidenmuller, M. E. n.d. "American Rhetoric: John F. Kennedy—Civil Rights Address." Americanrhetoric.Com. Retrieved April 1, 2022.

4. Banton, Caroline. 2022. "Path Dependency." Investopedia. January 21, 2022.

5. Mason, Wendy H. Revised by Joanie Sompayrac. 2006. "Sensitivity Training—Strategy, Organization, Examples, Model, Type, Company, Workplace, History." Referenceforbusiness.Com. May 5, 2006.

6. Anderson, Walter Truett. 2004. *The Upstart Spring: Esalen and the Human Potential Movement: The First Twenty Years*. iUniverse.

7. Blum, Beth. 2020. "The Radical History of Corporate Sensitivity Training." Newyorker.Com. September 24, 2020.

8. Lama, Rahul, and Sreejith Menon. 2020. "Robert P. Crosby, Memoirs of a Change Agent, T-Groups, Organization Development, and Social Justice." *NHRD Network Journal* 13 (3): 401-2.

9. Wolfe, Alan. 2001. "I'm O.K.—You're a Racist." *The New York Times*, December 9, 2001.

10. Hirsh, C. Elizabeth. 2009. "The Strength of Weak Enforcement: The Impact of Discrimination Charges, Legal Environments, and Organizational Conditions on Workplace Segregation." *American Sociological Review* 74 (2): 245-71.

11. *Handbook of Intercultural Training: Issues in Theory and Design v. 1*. 1982. London, England: Pergamon Press.

12. Hope, Richard O. 1979. *Racial Strife in the United States Military: Toward the Elimination of Discrimination*. Westport, CT: Praeger.

13. Alo House Recovery Centers. 2018. "An Outdated Treatment Model with Damaging Effects: The Case against Confrontation » Alo House Malibu." Medium. April 24, 2018.

14. Landis, Dan, and Richard W. Brislin. 2013. *Handbook of Intercultural Training: Issues in Training Methodology*. 1st ed. Pergamon.

15. "The History of Diversity Training & Its Pioneers." 2013. *Diversity Officer Magazine*. April 30, 2013.

16. Landis, Dan, Richard O. Hope, and Harry R. Day. 1983. "Training for Desegregation in the Military." Dtic.Mil. March 15, 1983.

17. Hiett, Robert L., Marcia Gilbert, and Dale K. Brown. 1978. "An Analysis of the Unit Race Relations Training Program in the U.S. Army." Dtic.Mil. July 1978.

18. Brown, Dale K., Peter G. Nordlie, and James A. Thomas. 1977. "Changes in Black and White Perceptions of the Army's Race Relations/Equal Opportunity Programs 1972-1974."

19. Luthra, Mohan, and Robin Oakley. 1991. "Combating Racism through Training: A Review of Approaches to Race Training in Organisations." Warwick. Ac.Uk. 1991.

20. Stafford, Kat. 2021. "Decades of DOD Efforts Fail to Stamp Out Bias, Extremism." Associated Press. December 29, 2021.

21. Anand, Rohini, and Mary-Frances Winters. 2008. "A Retrospective View of Corporate Diversity Training from 1964 to the Present." *Academy of Management Learning and Education* 7 (3): 356–72.

22. Tomaskovic-Devey, Donald, Catherine Zimmer, Kevin Stainback, Corre Robinson, Tiffany Taylor, and Tricia McTague. 2006. "Documenting Desegregation: Segregation in American Workplaces by Race, Ethnicity, and Sex, 1966–2003." *American Sociological Review* 71 (4): 565–88.

23. Harris, Adam. 2018. "The Supreme Court Justice Who Forever Changed Affirmative Action." The Atlantic. October 13, 2018.

24. Apfelbaum, Evan P., Michael I. Norton, and Samuel R. Sommers. 2012. "Racial Color Blindness: Emergence, Practice, and Implications." *Current Directions in Psychological Science* 21 (3): 205–9.

25. Gomer, Justin, and Christopher Petrella. 2017. "How the Reagan Administration Stoked Fears of Anti-White Racism." *Washington Post*. October 10, 2017.

26. Sandhu, Jay. 1988. "The EPA Abstracts—The Environmental Protection Agency in the 1980s." Nasa.Gov. 1988.

27. McCartin, Joseph A. 2011. "Opinion | The Strike That Busted Unions." *The New York Times*, August 3, 2011.

28. Welch, William M. 2021. "Thomas Presided over Shift in Policy at EEOC." Associated Press. May 2, 2021.

29. Dishman, Lydia. 2021. "Companies Have Been Trying (and Failing at) Diversity Training for 50 Years." Fast Company. February 15, 2021.

30. Ashkenas, Jeremy, Haeyoun Park, and Adam Pearce. 2017. "Even with Affirmative Action, Blacks and Hispanics Are More Underrepresented at Top Colleges than 35 Years Ago." *The New York Times*, August 24, 2017.

31. Brotherton, Phaedra. 2011. "R. Roosevelt Thomas, Jr." Main. May 19, 2011.

32. Bland, Karina. 2017. "Blue Eyes, Brown Eyes: What Jane Elliott's Famous Experiment Says about Race 50 Years On." *Arizona Republic*, November 17, 2017.

33. Bader, Hans. 2007. "Diversity Training Backfires." Competitive Enterprise Institute. December 26, 2007.

34. "Encounter Movement, a Fad Last Decade Finds New Shape." 1974. *The New York Times*, January 13, 1974.

35. Schofield, Janet Ward. 1986. "Causes and Consequences of the Colorblind Perspective." In *Prejudice, Discrimination, and Racism*, edited by John F. Dovidio, 337:231–53. San Diego, CA: Academic Press.

36. Apfelbaum, Evan P., Nicole M. Stephens, and Ray E. Reagans. 2016. "Beyond One-Size-Fits-All: Tailoring Diversity Approaches to the Representation of Social Groups." *Journal of Personality and Social Psychology* 111 (4): 547–66.

37. Kymlicka, Canada Will. 1995. *Multicultural Citizenship: A Liberal Theory of Minority Rights. Oxford Political Theory*. 2nd ed. Cary, NC: Oxford University Press.

38. Lai, Calvin K., Maddalena Marini, Steven A. Lehr, Carlo Cerruti, Jiyun-Elizabeth L. Shin, Jennifer A. Joy-Gaba, Arnold K. Ho et al. 2014. "Reducing Implicit Racial Preferences: I. A Comparative Investigation of 17 Interventions." *Journal of Experimental Psychology. General* 143 (4): 1765–85.

39. Plaut, Victoria C., Kecia M. Thomas, and Matt J. Goren. 2009. "Is Multiculturalism or Color Blindness Better for Minorities?" *Psychological Science* 20 (4): 444–46.

40. Meeussen, Loes, Sabine Otten, and Karen Phalet. 2014. "Managing Diversity: How Leaders' Multiculturalism and Colorblindness Affect Work Group Functioning." *Group Processes & Intergroup Relations: GPIR* 17 (5): 629–44.

41. Vorauer, Jacquie D., and Stacey J. Sasaki. 2011. "In the Worst Rather than the Best of Times: Effects of Salient Intergroup Ideology in Threatening Intergroup Interactions." *Journal of Personality and Social Psychology* 101 (2): 307–20.

42. Plaut, Victoria C., Flannery G. Garnett, Laura E. Buffardi, and Jeffrey Sanchez-Burks. 2011. "'What about Me?' Perceptions of Exclusion and Whites' Reactions to Multiculturalism." *Journal of Personality and Social Psychology* 101 (2): 337–53.

43. Wolsko, Christopher, Bernadette Park, Charles M. Judd, and Bernd Wittenbrink. 2000. "Framing Interethnic Ideology: Effects of Multicultural and Color-Blind Perspectives on Judgments of Groups and Individuals." *Journal of Personality and Social Psychology* 78 (4): 635–54.

44. Plaut, Victoria C., Kecia M. Thomas, Kyneshawau Hurd, and Celina A. Romano. 2018. "Do Color Blindness and Multiculturalism Remedy or Foster Discrimination and Racism?" *Current Directions in Psychological Science* 27 (3): 200–206.

45. Project Implicit. 2013. "About the IAT." Harvard.Edu. May 16, 2013.

46. Project Implicit. 2013b. "Select a Test." Harvard.Edu. May 16, 2013.

47. Nosek, Brian A., Mahzarin Banaji, and Anthony G. Greenwald. 2002. "Harvesting Implicit Group Attitudes and Beliefs from a Demonstration Web Site." *Group Dynamics: Theory, Research, and Practice: The Official Journal*

of Division 49, Group Psychology and Group Psychotherapy of the American Psychological Association 6 (1): 101–15.

48. Green, Alexander R., Dana R. Carney, Daniel J. Pallin, Long H. Ngo, Kristal L. Raymond, Lisa I. Iezzoni, and Mahzarin R. Banaji. 2007. "Implicit Bias among Physicians and Its Prediction of Thrombolysis Decisions for Black and White Patients." *Journal of General Internal Medicine* 22 (9): 1231–38.

49. Azar, Beth. 2008. "IAT: Fad or Fabulouss?" American Psychological Association. July/August 2008.

50. Dobbin, Frank, and Alexandra Kalev. 2018. "Why Doesn't Diversity Training Work? The Challenge for Industry and Academia." *Anthropology Now* 10 (2): 48–55.

51. Kalev, Alexandra, Frank Dobbin, and Erin Kelly. 2006. "Best Practices or Best Guesses? Assessing the Efficacy of Corporate Affirmative Action and Diversity Policies." *American Sociological Review* 71 (4): 589–617.

52. Paluck, Elizabeth Levy, and Donald P. Green. 2009. "Prejudice Reduction: What Works? A Review and Assessment of Research and Practice." *Annual Review of Psychology* 60 (1): 339–67.

53. Bowman Williams, Jamillah. 2017. "Breaking down Bias: Legal Mandates vs. Corporate Interests." *Georgetown Law Faculty Publications and Other Works. 1961.*

54. Unzueta, Miguel, Hannah Birnbaum, Robin Ely, Oriane Georgeac, and Sarah Kaplan. 2019. "Reevaluating the Business Case for Diversity: Consequences for Advocates, Women, Leaders, & Scholars." *Academy of Management Proceedings* 2019 (1): 13860.

55. Kaiser, Cheryl R., Brenda Major, Ines Jurcevic, Tessa L. Dover, Laura M. Brady, and Jenessa R. Shapiro. 2013. "Presumed Fair: Ironic Effects of Organizational Diversity Structures." *Journal of Personality and Social Psychology* 104 (3): 504–19.

56. Dobbin, Frank, and Alexan/dra Kalev. 2018. "Why Doesn't Diversity Training Work? The Challenge for Industry and Academia." *Anthropology Now* 10 (2): 48–55.

57. Captain, Sean. 2017. "Workers Win Only 1% of Federal Civil Rights Lawsuits at Trial." Fast Company. July 31, 2017.

58. *Global Gender Gap Report.* 2021. World Economic Forum. https://www3 .weforum.org/docs/WEF_GGGR_2021.pdf

Chapter 4. Real Change

1. Andrew, Scottie. 2021. "This Social Justice Buzzword Is Dictionary.Com's Word of the Year." Cnn.Com. December 6, 2021.

2. Attiah, Karen. 2020. "#BlackOutTuesday Was a Case Study in How Performative Solidarity Goes Awry." *The Washington Post*, June 3, 2020.

3. Abad-Santos, Alex. 2016. "The Backlash over Safety Pins and Allies, Explained." Vox. November 17, 2016.

4. Harrop, Mckinley. 2020. "Your Rainbow Logo Is Performative Activism." *Gays for Good*, July 26, 2020.

5. Caramanica, Jon. 2020. "This 'Imagine' Cover Is No Heaven." *The New York Times*, March 20, 2020.

6. Levine, Daniel S. 2020. "'COPS' Resumes Production after Cancellation, but Series Won't Air in the US." *Popculture*. October 3, 2020.

7. Mae, Kristen. 2018. "Here's the Problem with Performative Allyship." *Scary Mommy*. November 24, 2018.

8. Catalyst. 2021. "Beware Performative Allyship: 3 Signs to Look for." *Catalyst* (blog). January 25, 2021.

9. Edelman. 2018. "2018 Edelman Trust Barometer Reveals Record-Breaking Drop in Trust in the U.S." *Edelman*, January 22, 2018.

10. Aguilera, Jasmine. 2021. "An Epidemic of Misinformation. New Report Finds Trust in Social Institutions Diminished Further in 2020." *TIME*, January 13, 2021.

11. Turvill, William. 2021. "Most and Least Trusted US Media Outlets Revealed in Reuters Report." *Press Gazette*, June 23, 2021.

12. Barwick, Ryan. 2021. "Brand Trust Is at an All-Time Low, Study Says." *Morning Brew*, May 26, 2021.

13. Jameel, Maryam, and Joe Yerardi. 2019. "Workplace Discrimination Is Illegal. But Our Data Shows It's Still a Huge Problem." Vox, Co-Published in Partnership with the Center for Public Integrity. February 28, 2019.

14. Tomaskovic-Devey, Donald T., Carly McCann, and J. D. Swerzenski. 2021. "63% of Workers Who File an EEOC Discrimination Complaint Lose Their Jobs." *Government Executive*, July 19, 2021.

15. Jan, Tracy, Jena McGregor, and Meghan Hoyer. 2021. "After George Floyd's Death, Big Business Pledged Nearly $50 Billion for Racial Justice. This Is Where the Money Is Going." *Washington Post*, August 24, 2021.

16. O'Connell, Oliver. 2021. "How Much Does Jeff Bezos Make per Minute?" *Independent*, October 13, 2021.

17. Research and Policy Committee—Committee for Economic Development. 1971. "Social Responsibilities of Business Corporations."

18. Latapí Agudelo, M. A. Jóhannsdóttir, and B. Davídsdóttir. 2019. A Literature Review of the History and Evolution of Corporate Social Responsibility. *International Journal of Corporate Social Responsibility* 4(1).

19. Carroll, Archie B. 1979. "A Three-Dimensional Conceptual Model of Corporate Performance." *Academy of Management Review* 4 (4): 497.

20. Ben & Jerry. 2016. "Causes Ben & Jerry's Has Advocated for over the Years with Their Corporate Social Responsibility." www.benjerry.com. December 19, 2016.

21. "The Body Shop Marks 40th Year with Pledge to Be World's Most Ethical, Sustainable Global Company." 2016. Sustainable Brands. February 12, 2016.

22. Carroll, Archie B., and George W. Beiler. 1975. "Landmarks in the Evolution of the Social Audit." *Academy of Management Journal* 18 (3): 589–99.

23. Friedman, Milton. 1970. "A Friedman Doctrine—The Social Responsibility of Business Is to Increase Its Profits." *The New York Times*, September 13, 1970.

24. Cornwell, Rupert. 2006. "Milton Friedman, Free-Market Economist Who Inspired Reagan and Thatcher, Dies Aged 94." *Independent*, November 17, 2006.

25. Goodman, Peter S. 2008. "A Fresh Look at the Apostle of Free Markets." *The New York Times*, April 13, 2008.

26. Quillian, J. Patrick. 2016. "4 Accounting Fraud Cases That Defined the 1980s." *J. Patrick Quillian, P.C.* (blog). March 7, 2016.

27. Beck, Eckardt C. 1979. "The Love Canal Tragedy." *EPA Journal*, January 1979.

28. Warren, Tamara. 2015. "Ralph Nader Is Still Punching Companies Where It Hurts." The Verge. October 28, 2015.

29. Jones, William H., and John F. Berry. 1977. "Lockheed Paid $38 Million in Bribes Abroad." *The Washington Post*, May 27, 1977.

30. Noh, Jae-Eun. 2017. "The Role of NGOs in Building CSR Discourse around Human Rights in Developing Countries." *Cosmopolitan Civil Societies: An Interdisciplinary Journal* 9 (1): 1–19.

31. Meyer, Russ. 2010. "A History of Green Brands: 1980's—Green Shoots Appear." Fast Company. May 13, 2010.

32. Carroll, Archie B. 2009. *A History of Corporate Social Responsibility*. Edited by Andrew Crane, Dirk Matten, Abagail McWilliams, Jeremy Moon, and Donald S. Siegel. Oxford University Press.

33. Casey-Sawicki, Katherine. 2021. "Seattle WTO Protests of 1999." In *Encyclopedia Britannica*.

34. Mayer, Ann Elizabeth. 2009. "Human Rights as a Dimension of CSR: The Blurred Lines between Legal and Non-Legal Categories." *Journal of Business Ethics* 88 (S4): 561–77.

35. Swaen, Valérie, and Ruben C. Chumpitaz. 2008. "Impact of Corporate Social Responsibility on Consumer Trust." *Recherche et Applications En Marketing (English Edition)* 23 (4): 7–34.

36. Bögel, Paula Maria. 2019. "Company Reputation and Its Influence on Consumer Trust in Response to Ongoing CSR Communication." *Journal of Marketing Communications* 25 (2): 115–36.

37. Cai, Ye, Hoje Jo, and Carrie Pan. 2012. "Doing Well While Doing Bad? CSR in Controversial Industry Sectors." *Journal of Business Ethics* 108 (4): 467–80.

38. Stobierski, Tim. 2021. "15 Eye-Opening Corporate Social Responsibility Statistics." *Harvard Business School Online's Business Insights Blog*. June 2021.

39. Wazir, Burhan. 2001. "Nike Accused of Tolerating Sweatshops." *The Guardian*, May 19, 2001.

40. Cushman, John H., Jr. 1998. "International Business; Nike Pledges to End Child Labor and Apply US Rules Abroad." *The New York Times*, May 13, 1998.

41. "Nike: Behind the Swoosh: Just Don't Do It." 2001. *Nike: Behing the Swoosh* (blog). 2001.

42. Nike, Inc. 2001. "Nike Releases First Corporate Responsibility Report." *3BL CSRWire*, 2001.

43. Beder, Sharon. 2002. "Putting the Boot In." *The Ecologist* 32 (3): 24–28, 66–67.

44. Newell, Andrea. 2015. "How Nike Embraced CSR and Went from Villain to Hero." Triplepundit.Com. June 19, 2015.

45. Nike, Inc. 2006. "Nike Named Top 10 for Social Responsibility Reporting." *NIKE News*. November 9, 2006.

46. Zadek, Simon. 2004. "The Path to Corporate Responsibility." *Harvard Business Review* 82 (12): 125–32, 150.

47. Bernstein, Jill. 2018. "Why Nike Sees Social Responsibility as an Opportunity to Innovate." Fast Company. January 2018.

48. Greenhouse, Steven. 2010. "Pressured, Nike to Help Workers in Honduras." *The New York Times*, July 26, 2010.

49. Bain, Marc. 2017. "Nike Is Facing a New Wave of Anti-Sweatshop Protests." *Quartz*, August 1, 2017.

50. Waters, Cassandra. 2017. "Take the #NikeCoverUpChallenge and Demand Justice for Nike Workers." *AFL-CIO America's Unions* (blog). March 30, 2017.

51. Miedema, Christie. 2018. "Adidas and Nike Pay Record-Breaking Amounts to Footballers, but Deny Decent Wages to Women Stitching Their Shirts." *Clean Clothes Campaign*, June 11, 2018.

52. Bain, Marc. 2020. "Companies Still Can't Stop Labor Abuses at Chinese Factories." *Quartz*, March 3, 2020.

53. *Fashion Transparency Index 2021*. 2021. U.S.A.: Fashion Revolution.

54. Creswell, Julie, and Kevin Draper. 2019. "Black Superstars Pitch Adidas Shoes. Its Black Workers Say They're Sidelined." *The New York Times*, June 19, 2019.

55. Spence, Michael. 2017. "No More Excuses—Responsible Supply Chains in a Globalised World." Economist. 2017.

56. United Nations. 2016. "Explore Our Participants." Unglobalcompact.Org. December 21, 2016.

57. Sethi, S. Prakash, and Donald H. Schepers. 2014. "United Nations Global Compact: The Promise–Performance Gap." *Journal of Business Ethics* 122 (2): 193–208.

58. McCorquodale, Robert, Lise Smit, Stuart Neely, and Robin Brooks. 2017. "Human Rights Due Diligence in Law and Practice: Good Practices and Challenges for Business Enterprises." *Business and Human Rights Journal* 2 (2): 195–224.

59. LeBaron, Genevieve, Remi Edwards, Tom Hunt, Charline Sempéré, and Penelope Kyritsis. 2022. "The Ineffectiveness of CSR: Understanding Garment Company Commitments to Living Wages in Global Supply Chains." *New Political Economy* 27 (1): 99–115.

60. LeBaron, Genevieve, and Andreas Rühmkorf. 2017. "Steering CSR through Home State Regulation: A Comparison of the Impact of the UK Bribery Act and Modern Slavery Act on Global Supply Chain Governance." *Global Policy* 8: 15–28.

61. Fischer-Daly, Matthew. 2017. "Book Review: Achieving Workers' Rights in the Global Economy." *Industrial & Labor Relations Review* 70 (4): 1064–66.

62. Joint statement by ILO, FAO, IFAD and WHO. 2020. "Impact of COVID-19 on People's Livelihoods, Their Health and Our Food Systems." World Health Organization. October 13, 2020.

63. "The Disproportionate Impact of COVID-19 on Women of Color." 2020. SWHR. April 30, 2020.

64. National Council on Disability. 2021. "2021 Progress Report: The Impact of COVID-19 on People with Disabilities."

65. Dawson, Lindsey, Ashley Kirzinger, and Jennifer Kates. 2021. "The Impact of the COVID-19 Pandemic on LGBT People." KFF, March 11, 2021.

66. "Key Worker." 2022. Wikipedia, The Free Encyclopedia. January 9, 2022.

67. McElwee, Kevin. 2021. "The Fortune 100 and Black Lives Matter." Towards Data Science. January 29, 2021.

68. Nguyen, Terry. 2020. "Consumers Don't Care about Corporate Solidarity. They Want Donations." Vox. June 3, 2020.

69. BBC News. 2020. "Amy Cooper: Woman Sacked after Calling Police on Black Man." BBC News. May 28, 2020.

70. Rivera, Josh. 2020. "Here's What's Going on with 'Bon Appétit' and Why Editor in Chief Adam Rapoport Resigned." *USA Today*, June 8, 2020.

71. The William and Flora Hewlett Foundation's Effective Philanthropy Program. 2021. "How Funders Seek and Use Knowledge to Influence Philanthropic Practice." Hewlett.Org. June 2021.

72. Maurer, Roy. 2020. "New DE&I Roles Spike after Racial Justice Protests." SHRM. August 6, 2020.

73. Peakon. 2021. "Employee Expectations Report 2021."

74. Hardcastle, Kate. 2021. "Proud of Pride or Rainbow-Washing: How Do Retailers Step up to the Mark?" *Forbes*, June 22, 2021.

75. Kerr, Errol. 2020. "Autism and Performative Awareness." *Org.Uk* (blog). December 10, 2020.

76. Pulrang, Andrew. 2021. "3 Ways Disability Allyship Can Go off Track." *Forbes*, April 14, 2021.

77. Metzger, Logan. 2020. "The LGBTQIA+ Acronym and Its History." *Iowa State Daily*, January 26, 2020.

78. Doran, Kelly M., Elizabeth J. Misa, and Nirav R. Shah. 2013. "Housing as Health Care—New York's Boundary-Crossing Experiment." *The New England Journal of Medicine* 369 (25): 2374–77.

79. Casey, Logan, and Elizabeth Mann Levesque. 2018. "LGBTQ Students Face Discrimination While Education Department Walks Back Oversight." Brookings. April 18, 2018.

80. Mirza, Shabab Ahmed, and Caitlin Rooney. 2018. "Discrimination Prevents LGBTQ People from Accessing Health Care." Center for American Progress. January 18, 2018.

81. Jagannathan, Meera. 2021. "Almost Half of LGB Professionals Experience Discrimination at Work—and It's Even Worse for People of Color." MarketWatch. June 10, 2021.

82. The Inter-Agency Regional Analysts Network (IARAN). 2018. "A Global Outlook on LGBTI Social Exclusion through 2030."

83. Miller, Stephen. 2016. "For Same-Sex Couples, Benefit Issues Remain." *Society for Human Resource Management—HR Newsletter*, March 16, 2016.

84. National Center for Transgender Equality. 2021. "Housing & Homelessness." *National Center for Transgender Equality* (blog). August 22, 2021.

85. Movement Advancement Project and GLSEN—in partnership with the National Center for Transgender Equality and the National Education Association. 2017. "Transgender Students Face a Lot of Discrimination, and the Trump Administration Isn't Helping." *The Leadership Conference Education Fund*, April 13, 2017.

86. Rathjen, Reese. 2010. "New Report Reveals Rampant Discrimination against Transgender People by Health Providers, High HIV Rates and Widespread Lack of Access to Necessary Care." National LGBTQ Task Force. October 13, 2010.

87. Factora, James. 2021. "69% of Intersex People Have Experienced Discrimination in Past Year." *them.* (blog). October 27, 2021.

88. The Human Rights Campaign Foundation. 2020. "Discrimination against Transgender Workers." The Human Rights Campaign Foundation. October 30, 2020.

89. Privacy International. 2021. "My ID, My Identity? The Impact of ID Systems on Transgender People in Argentina, France and the Philippines." *Privacy International* (blog). January 15, 2021.

90. Ronan, Wyatt. 2021. "2021 Becomes Record Year for Anti-Transgender Legislation." *Equality Magazine*, March 13, 2021.

91. Cohut, Maria. 2020. "The Intersex Gap in Research and Healthcare." *Medical News Today*, July 1, 2020.

92. Krehely, Jeff. 2009. "How to Close the LGBT Health Disparities Gap." The Center for American Progress. December 21, 2009.

93. Palmer, Neal A., Emily A. Greytak, and Joseph G. Kosciw. 2016. "Educational Exclusion: Drop out, Push out, and School-to-Prison Pipeline among LGBTQ Youth." GLSEN.

94. Jones, Alexi. 2021. "Visualizing the Unequal Treatment of LGBTQ People in the Criminal Justice System." *Prisonpolicy.Org* (blog). March 2, 2021.

95. Ellsworth, Diana, Ana Mendy, and Gavin Sullivan. 2020. "How the LGBTQ+ Community Fares in the Workplace." Mckinsey.Com. McKinsey & Company. June 1, 2020.

96. European Union Agency for Fundamental Rights. 2014. *European Union Lesbian, Gay, Bisexual and Transgender Survey: Results at a Glance*. Publications Office of the European Union.

97. Müller, A., and K. Daskilewicz. 2018. "Mental Health among Lesbian, Gay, Bisexual, Transgender and Intersex People in East and Southern Africa." *European Journal of Public Health* 28 (suppl_4).

98. UNDP. 2020. "Being LGBTI in Asia and the Pacific." *United Nations Development Programme*, March 2020.

99. Caceres, Billy A., Kasey B. Jackman, Lilian Ferrer, Kenrick D. Cato, and Tonda L. Hughes. 2019. "A Scoping Review of Sexual Minority Women's Health in Latin America and the Caribbean." *International Journal of Nursing Studies* 94: 85-97.

Chapter 5. Knowing, Using, Ceding Power

1. Bass, Bernard M., and Ruth Bass. 2008. *The Bass Handbook of Leadership: Theory, Research, and Managerial Applications*. New York: Free Press.

2. Webster, Noah. 2019. *Merriam-Webster Dictionary*. Merriam-Webster, Incorporated.

3. Walter, Elizabeth. 1995. *Cambridge Advanced Learner's Dictionary*. Cambridge, England: University Press.

4. Foucault, Michel. 2018. *The Order of Things: An Archaeology of the Human Sciences*. London, England: Routledge.

5. Elias, Steven. 2008. "Fifty Years of Influence in the Workplace: The Evolution of the French and Raven Power Taxonomy." *Journal of Management History* 14 (3): 267–83.

6. Locklear, Lauren R., Shannon G. Taylor, and Maureen L. Ambrose. 2020. "How a Gratitude Intervention Influences Workplace Mistreatment: A Multiple Mediation Model." *The Journal of Applied Psychology* 106 (9): 1314–31.

7. Paul, Kari. 2021. "She Broke Her NDA to Speak out against Pinterest. Now She's Helping Others Come Forward." *The Guardian*, May 10, 2021.

8. Cialdini, Robert B. *Influence: The Psychology of Persuasion*. New York: Collins, 2007.

9. Child, John. 1972. "Organizational Structure, Environment and Performance: The Role of Strategic Choice." *Sociology* 6 (1): 1–22.

10. Eckhardt, George S. 2015. *Command and Control, 1950–1969*. North Charleston, SC: Createspace Independent Publishing Platform.

11. Morrison, Robbie, Natasha C. H. L. Mazey, and Stephen C. Wingreen. 2020. "The DAO Controversy: The Case for a New Species of Corporate Governance?" *Frontiers in Blockchain* 3.

12. Indeed Editorial Team. 2021. "Matrix Organizational Structure: Advantages and Disadvantages." *Indeed Career Guide* (blog). December 16, 2021.

13. Karki, Benjamin. 2016. "Organizational Structures for Small and Medium Sized Enterprises." Germany: Mönchengladbach.

14. Murphy, Keith. 2021. "Agile Organization Structure: Achieving an Agile Business Foundation." 2021. PLANERGY Software. May 25, 2021.

15. Corporate Finance Institute. 2000. "Centralization - Overview, Key Advantages and Disadvantages." Corporate Finance Institute. 2000.

16. Indeed Editorial Team. 2021. "7 Benefits of Centralized vs. Decentralized Structures." *Indeed Career Guide* (blog). June 10, 2021.

17. Assenova, Valentina A., and Olav Sorenson. 2017. "Legitimacy and the Benefits of Firm Formalization." *Organization Science* 28 (5): 804–18.

18. Mitchell, Wesley, and Michel Crozier. 2017. *The Bureaucratic Phenomenon*. London, England: Routledge.

19. Cohen, Michael D., James G. March, and Johan P. Olsen. 1972. "A Garbage Can Model of Organizational Choice." *Administrative Science Quarterly* 17 (1): 1.

20. Tolbert, P. S., and R. H. Hall. 2015. *Organizations: Structures, Processes and Outcomes*. London, England: Routledge.

21. Lawrence, Paul R., and Jay W. Lorsch. 1967. "Differentiation and Integration in Complex Organizations." *Administrative Science Quarterly* 12 (1): 1.

22. Klatzky, S. R. 1970. "Relationship of Organizational Size to Complexity and Coordination." *Administrative Science Quarterly* 15 (4): 428.

23. Kunda, G. 1992. *Engineering Culture Control and Commitment in a High-Tech Corporation*. Philadelphia, PA: Temple University Press.

24. Alvesson, Mats. 2013. *Understanding Organizational Culture*. 2nd ed. London, England: SAGE Publication

25. Hofstede, Geert. 2011. "Dimensionalizing Cultures: The Hofstede Model in Context." *Online Readings in Psychology and Culture* 2 (1).

26. Kafetsios, Konstantinos G., and Dritjon Gruda. 2018. "Interdependent Followers Prefer Avoidant Leaders: Followers' Cultural Orientation Moderates Leaders' Avoidance Relationships with Followers' Work Outcomes." *Frontiers in Communication* 3.

27. Effron, Daniel A., Hazel Rose Markus, Lauren M. Jackman, Yukiko Muramoto, and Hamdi Muluk. 2018. "Hypocrisy and Culture: Failing to Practice What You Preach Receives Harsher Interpersonal Reactions in Independent (vs. Interdependent) Cultures." *Journal of Experimental Social Psychology* 76: 371–84.

28. Shin, Lilian J., and Sonja Lyubomirsky. 2017. "Increasing Well-Being in Independent and Interdependent Cultures." In *Scientific Advances in Positive Psychology*. Edited by Meg A. Warren, 306:11–36. Santa Barbara, CA: Praeger.

29. Liang, Xingkun, and Yue Xu. 2020. "Independent or Interdependent Innovation: The Case of Huawei." In *Huawei Goes Global*, 265–89. Cham: Springer International Publishing.

30. Crossley, Alison Dahl. 2018. "Clash of Independence and Interdependence Creates Conflict, Fuels Gender Inequality." The Clayman Institute for Gender Research. March 20, 2018.

31. Snitker, Thomas Visby. 2010. "The Impact of Culture on User Research." In *Handbook of Global User Research*, 257–77. Elsevier.

32. Kirkpatrick, Andrew, Joshue O Connor, Alastair Campbell, Michael Cooper. 2018. "Web Content Accessibility Guidelines (WCAG) 2.1." W3.Org. June 5, 2018.

33. Ocampo, Anna Carmella G., Lu Wang, Kohyar Kiazad, Simon Lloyd D. Restubog, and Neal M. Ashkanasy. 2020. "The Relentless Pursuit of Perfectionism: A Review of Perfectionism in the Workplace and an Agenda for Future Research." *Journal of Organizational Behavior* 41 (2): 144–68.

34. Gino, Francesca, and Bradley Staats. 2015. "Why Organizations Don't Learn." *Harvard Business Review*, November 2015.

35. Cooper, Thomas, Alex Faseruk, and Shazli Khan. 2013. "Examining Practitioner Studies to Explore ERM and Organizational Culture." Na-Businesspress.Com. 2013.

36. Tang, Anita. 2019. "Power Mapping and Analysis." The Commons. February 20, 2019.

37. ASQ. 2020. "Force Field Analysis." Asq.Org. August 13, 2020.

38. Renton Technical College. 2016. "A Guide to Councils, Committees, Work Groups and Task Forces."

39. Cordivano, Sarah. 2019. "Understanding Employee Resource Groups: A Guide for Organizations." Sarah Cordivano. October 31, 2019.

Chapter 6. Identity and Difference

1. Northwestern University, Searle Center for Advancing Learning & Teaching. 2019. "Social Identities: Searle Center for Advancing Learning & Teaching." Northwestern.Edu. April 16, 2019.

2. McNamara, Brittney. 2019. "International Women's Day 2019: 17 Women Share What Womanhood Means to Them." *Teen Vogue.* March 8, 2019.

3. Vox First Person. 2021. "What Does It Mean to Be Asian American?" Vox. May 5, 2021.

4. Leadbitter, Kathy, Karen Leneh Buckle, Ceri Ellis, and Martijn Dekker. 2021. "Autistic Self-Advocacy and the Neurodiversity Movement: Implications for Autism Early Intervention Research and Practice." *Frontiers in Psychology* 12: 635690.

5. Metzger, Logan. 2020. "The LGBTQIA+ Acronym and Its History." *Iowa State Daily,* January 26, 2020.

6. Wade, Lisa. 2011. "Loretta Ross on the Phrase 'Women of Color'—Sociological Images." *Thesocietypages.Org* (blog). March 26, 2011.

7. Grady, Constance. 2020. "Why the Term 'BIPOC' Is so Complicated, Explained by Linguists." Vox. June 30, 2020.

8. Wood, Johnny. 2018. "104 Countries Have Laws That Prevent Women from Working in Some Jobs." *World Economic Forum,* August 13, 2018.

9. Rothstein, Richard. 2017. *The Color of Law: A Forgotten History of How Our Government Segregated America.* 1st ed. New York: Liveright Publishing Corporation.

10. Fisher, Allen. 2020. "Women's Rights and the Civil Rights Act of 1964." National Archives. August 7, 2020.

11. Rock, David. Reviewed by Ekua Hagan. 2017. "Is Your Company's Diversity Training Making You More Biased? Inclusion Programs Often Trigger an 'Us versus Them' Mindset." *Psychology Today* (blog). June 7, 2017.

12. Bleich, Erik. 2001. "Race Policy in France." Brookings. May 1, 2001.

13. Offermann, Lynn R., Tessa E. Basford, Raluca Graebner, Salman Jaffer, Sumona Basu De Graaf, and Samuel E. Kaminsky. 2014. "See No Evil: Color Blindness and Perceptions of Subtle Racial Discrimination in the Workplace." *Cultural Diversity & Ethnic Minority Psychology* 20 (4): 499–507.

14. Desmond-Harris, Jenée. 2017. "Why We Don't Have White History Month." Vox. February 7, 2017.

15. Eng, Joanna. 2021. "Why Isn't There a Men's History Month?" *ParentsTogether* (blog). March 19, 2021.

16. Lang, Nico. 2019. "The Distraction of Straight Pride, as Explained by LGBTQ Activists and Historians." Vox. July 1, 2019.

17. Guttmann, A. 2021. "Diversity and Inclusion in Advertising in the U.S.—Statistics & Facts." *Statista* (blog). March 24, 2021.

18. Okun, Tema. 2021. "(Divorcing) White Supremacy Culture: Coming Home to Who We Really Are." White Supremacy Culture. May 22, 2021.

19. Test, Lyssa, and Kelly Luc. 2021. "Company Holidays: 3 Models and How They Impact DEI." *Cultureamp.Com* (blog). 2021.

20. Wilson, Jason. 2020. "White Nationalist Hate Groups Have Grown 55% in Trump Era, Report Finds." *The Guardian*, March 18, 2020.

21. BBC News. 2019. "Europe and Right-Wing Nationalism: A Country-by-Country Guide." *BBC News*, November 13, 2019.

22. Musharbash, Yassin. 2021. "The Globalization of Far-Right Extremism: An Investigative Report." *Combating Terrorism Center at West Point* 14 (6).

23. Bejan, Raluca. 2020. "Robin DiAngelo's 'White Fragility' Ignores the Differences within Whiteness." The Conversation. 2020.

24. Stewart, Jeffrey C. 2019. "Fighting Racism Even, and Especially, Where We Don't Realize It Exists." *The New York Times*, August 20, 2019.

25. Deggans, Eric. 2020. "'Not Racist' Is Not Enough: Putting in the Work to Be Anti-Racist." *NPR*, August 25, 2020.

26. Harris, Elizabeth A. 2021. "Books on Race Filled Best-Seller Lists Last Year. Publishers Took Notice." *The New York Times*, September 15, 2021.

27. Cooper, R. 2020. The Limits of White Fragility's Anti-Racism. *The Week.* June 24, 2020.

28. re:Work, Google. 2016. "Guide: Understand Team Effectiveness."

29. Fuller, Ryan. 2014. "A Primer on Measuring Employee Engagement." *Harvard Business Review*, November 17, 2014.

30. Governors' Institute on Community Design. 2017. "The Why and How of Measuring Access to Opportunity—A Guide to Performance Management."

31. Nicholas, Joshua. 2020. "Measuring Employee Effectiveness: Engagement vs. Enablement." *Snap Surveys Blog* (blog). July 21, 2020.

32. Zheng, Lily. 2020. "Do Your Employees Feel Safe Reporting Abuse and Discrimination?" *Harvard Business Review*, October 8, 2020.

33. Williams, David R. 2011. "Everyday Discrimination Scale." Harvard University.

34. Office of Developmental Primary Care—UCSF Department of Family and Community Medicine. 2018. "Medical and Social Models of Disability."

35. The Planned Parenthood Action Fund. 2016. "State Attacks on Sexual and Reproductive Health." Plannedparenthoodaction.Org. March 21, 2016.

36. Villa, Virginia. 2020. "Women in Many Countries Face Harassment for Clothing Deemed Too Religious—or Too Secular." *Pew Research Center* (blog). December 16, 2020.

37. Francis, Ellen, Helier Cheung, and Miriam Berger. 2021. "How Does the U.S. Compare to Other Countries on Paid Parental Leave? Americans Get 0 Weeks. Estonians Get More than 80." *Washington Post.* November 11, 2021.

38. Universitat Pompeu Fabra-Barcelona. 2019. "Women Are 30 Percent Less Likely to Be Considered for a Hiring Process than Men." Phys.Org. March 26, 2019.

39. Claringbould, Inge, and Annelies Knoppers. 2007. "Finding a 'Normal' Woman: Selection Processes for Board Membership. *Sex Roles* 56, 495–507.

40. Dekkers, Tara. 2007. "The Relationship of Decision-Making and Division of Household Labor to Relationship Satisfaction." Iowa State University of Science and Technology - Digital Repository. January 2007.

41. Ellwood, Beth. 2021. "Men Who Catcall Claim It's a 'Normal Way of Flirting'—While at the Same Time Demonstrating Greater Hostile Sexism." PsyPost. September 16, 2021.

42. GoodTherapy. 2016. "Victim Blaming." *GoodTherapy* (blog). November 29, 2016.

43. Bennett, Jessica. 2016. "How to Fight Back against Sexism at Work." *Cosmopolitan.* August 16, 2016.

44. Perry, Elissa L., Alison Davis-Blake, and Carol T. Kulik. 1994. "Explaining Gender-Based Selection Decisions: A Synthesis of Contextual and Cognitive Approaches." *Academy of Management Review* 19 (4): 786–820.

45. Raggins, Bella Rose, and Eric Sundstrom. 1989. "Gender and Power in Organizations: A Longitudinal Perspective." *Psychological Bulletin* 105 (1): 51–88.

46. Takami, Tomohiro. 2018. "Gender Segregation at Work in Japanese Companies: Focusing on Gender Disparities in Desire for Promotion." *Japan Labor Issues* 2 (11): 1–12.

47. Taylor, Elizabeth A., Allison B. Smith, Natalie M. Welch, and Robin Hardin. 2018. "You Should Be Flattered! Female Sport Management Faculty Experiences of Sexual Harassment and Sexism." *Women in Sport and Physical Activity Journal* 26: 43–53.

48. Dietz, Gretchen A., Elliot P. Douglas, and Erica D. McCray. 2021. "Marginalization and the in/Authentic Workplace Experiences of Engineers." In *2021 CoNECD.*

49. Leskinen, Emily A., Verónica Caridad Rabelo, and Lilia M. Cortina. 2015. "Gender Stereotyping and Harassment: A 'Catch-22' for Women in the Workplace." *Psychology, Public Policy, and Law: An Official Law Review of the*

University of Arizona College of Law and the University of Miami School of Law 21 (2): 192–204.

50. Stamarski, Cailin S., and Leanne S. Son Hing. 2015. "Gender Inequalities in the Workplace: The Effects of Organizational Structures, Processes, Practices, and Decision Makers' Sexism." *Frontiers in Psychology* 6: 1400.

51. Bower, Tim. 2019. "The #MeToo Backlash." *Harvard Business Review*, 2019.

52. Brown, Lydia. 2011. "Identity-First Language (Originally Published as The Significance of Semantics: Person-First Language: Why It Matters)." Autistic Self Advocacy Network. August 2011.

53. Wong, Brittany. 2019. "It's Perfectly OK to Call A Disabled Person 'Disabled,' and Here's Why." *HuffPost*, June 14, 2019.

54. Ferrigon, Phillip, and Kevin Tucker. (2019). "Person-First Language vs. Identity-First Language: An Examination of the Gains and Drawbacks of Disability Language in Society." *JTDS—Journal of Teaching Disability Studies*.

55. Zheng, Lily. 2021. "To Dismantle Anti-Asian Racism, We Must Understand Its Roots." *Harvard Business Review*, May 27, 2021.

56. Barrett, Gena-Mour. 2018. "Why It's Time to Ditch the Term 'BAME.'" *Refinery29*, May 23, 2018.

57. Sales, Ben. 2020. "'Jew' Isn't a Slur. You Don't Have to Avoid Saying It. Call Me 'a Jew' Instead of 'a Jewish Person.' It's What I Call Myself." *The Washington Post*, October 5, 2020.

58. Burns, Katelyn. 2019. "TERFs: The Rise of 'Trans-Exclusionary Radical Feminists,' Explained." Vox. September 5, 2019.

59. Fisher-Borne, Marcie, Jessie Montana Cain, and Suzanne L. Martin. 2015. "From Mastery to Accountability: Cultural Humility as an Alternative to Cultural Competence." *Social Work Education* 34 (2): 165–81.

Chapter 7. Change-Maker: Everyone

1. Fowler, Katrina. 2021. "3 Inclusive Workplace Strategies to Defrost the Frozen Middle." *Ideal* (blog). June 16, 2021.

2. Chatterji, Aaron K., and Michael W. Toffel. 2018. "The New CEO Activists." *Harvard Business Review*, January 1, 2018.

3. This story has been edited to preserve confidentiality given the unique nature of the movement and program.

4. Childress, Boyd. Revised by Wendy H. Mason. 2006. "Coalition Building—Strategy, Organization, System, Examples, Manager, Definition, Type, Company, Business."

5. Rodgers, Chris. 2006. *Informal Coalitions: Mastering the Hidden Dynamics of Organizational Change*. Basingstoke, England: Palgrave Macmillan.

6. Carastathis, Anna. 2013. "Identity Categories as Potential Coalitions." *Signs* 38 (4): 941–65.

7. De Dreu, Carsten, and Laurie R. Weingart. "Task Versus Relationship Conflict, Team Performance, and Team Member Satisfaction: A Meta-Analysis." *Journal of applied Psychology* 88, no. 4 (2003): 741.

8. Derr, Alex. "Conflict Resolution in Coalitions: Causes and Solutions." Visible Network Labs. June 14, 2021.

Chapter 8. Achieving DEI

1. Lee, Stacy. 2021. "Promoting Diversity and Inclusion through Your Recruitment ATS." Business 2 Community. June 3, 2021.

2. Castaldo, Sandro, Katia Premazzi, and Fabrizio Zerbini. 2010. "The Meaning(s) of Trust. A Content Analysis on the Diverse Conceptualizations of Trust in Scholarly Research on Business Relationships." *Journal of Business Ethics* 96 (4): 657–68.

3. Pathak, Anjan. 2020. "10 Crucial Employee Engagement Metrics for Successful Surveys." *Nurture an Engaged and Satisfied Workforce | Vantage Circle HR* (blog). August 26, 2020.

4. Yamkovenko, Bogdan, and Stephen Tavares. 2017. "To Understand Whether Your Company Is Inclusive, Map How Your Employees Interact." *Harvard Business Review*, July 19, 2017.

5. Thomason, Bobbi, and Jennifer Franczak. 2022. "3 Tensions Leaders Need to Manage in the Hybrid Workplace." *Harvard Business Review*, 2022.

6. Hansen, I. L. Z. 2019. "Selling Out: The Diversity Issue We're Not Talking About." *Porchlight Books*. (blog). October 30, 2019.

7. Mortensen, Gemma. 2017. "10 Things You Need to Build Clever Coalitions." *Stanford Social Innovation Review*.

8. Wynn, Alison. 2018. "The Promise of 'Small Wins'—a Change Model to Achieve Gender Equality." Stanford University—The Clayman Institute for Gender Research. March 28, 2018.

9. Denend, Lyn, Paul Yock, and Dan Azagury. 2020. "Research: Small Wins Can Make a Big Impact on Gender Equality." *Harvard Business Review*, November 6, 2020.

10. Carlos, Iain. 2021. "DEI Is Now a Factor in Executive Pay. But There's One Big Disconnect." *Minneapolis / St. Paul Business Journal*, July 2021.

11. Madan, Shilpa, Kevin Nanakdewa, Krishna Savani, and Hazel Rose Markus. 2021. "Research: What Makes Employees Feel Empowered to Speak Up?" *Harvard Business Review*, October 13, 2021.

12. Edmonton, Amy, and Kathryn Roloff. 2009. "Leveraging Diversity Through Psychological Safety." *Rotman Magazine*.

13. Mertz, Jon. 2019. "Why You Should Consider Having Employees on Your Board." *The Startup*, December 9, 2019.

14. Logemann, Robert. 2022. "How to Incorporate Employee Resource Groups in Your Organization." *Forbes*, January 6, 2022.

Chapter 9. Expanding Your Repertoire

1. Patel, Fay, and Hayley Lynch. 2013. "Glocalization as an Alternative to Internationalization in Higher Education: Embedding Positive Glocal Learning Perspectives." *International Journal of Teaching and Learning in Higher Education* 25 (2): 223-30.

2. Glazer, Emily, and Theo Francis. 2021. "CEO Pay Increasingly Tied to Diversity Goals." *Wall Street Journal*, June 2, 2021.

3. Anand, Rohini. 2014. "Diversity and Inclusion, A Strategic Business Imperative: The Sodexo Story." October.

4. Alexander, Reed. 2021. "The Carlyle Group's D&I Chief Lays out Why She's Aiming to Tie Promotions to Inclusive Leadership, and Why Championing Diversity Is Every Employee's Responsibility." *Business Insider*, March 24, 2021.

5. "Inclusive Leadership 360 Degree Evaluation of Inclusive Leadership Behaviours." 2020. The Prince's Business Network.

6. Leslie, Lisa M., Colleen Flaherty Manchester, and Patricia C. Dahm. 2017. "Why and When Does the Gender Gap Reverse? Diversity Goals and the Pay Premium for High Potential Women." *Academy of Management Journal* 60 (2): 402-32.

7. Umoh, Ruth. 2020. "Google Diversity Report Shows Little Progress for Women and People of Color." *Forbes*, May 5, 2020.

8. Benjamin, Fran, and Monique Cadle. 2021. "Diversity Data Isn't Very Transparent: What's the Problem?" *TechCrunch* (blog). October 22, 2021.

9. Lukens, Mark. 2015. "How to Be More Transparent about Failure." Fast Company. December 16, 2015.

10. PricewaterhouseCoopers. 2021. "ESG Reporting—Boards Can Lead the Way on ESG. We Share the Why, What, and How of Effectively Overseeing ESG." PwC/Price Waterhouse Coopers. August 24, 2021.

11. De Cremer, David. 2016. "When Transparency Backfires, and How to Prevent It." *Harvard Business Review*, July 21, 2016.

12. Bivens, Josh, Lora Engdahl, Elise Gould, Teresa Kroeger, Celine McNicholas, Lawrence Mishel, Zane Mokhiber, et al. 2017. "How Today's Unions Help Working People Giving Workers the Power to Improve Their Jobs and Unrig the Economy." *Economic Policy Institute*, August 24, 2017.

13. Aguilar, Luis A. 2013. "Institutional Investors: Power and Responsibility." Harvard Law School Forum on Corporate Governance, April 2013.

14. Kang, Sonia, Katy DeCelles, András Tilcsik, and Sora Jun. 2016. "The Unintended Consequences of Diversity Statements." *Harvard Business Review*, March 29, 2016.

15. Takács, Károly, Giangiacomo Bravo, and Flaminio Squazzoni. 2018. "Referrals and Information Flow in Networks Increase Discrimination: A Laboratory Experiment." *Social Networks* 54: 254–65.

16. Harper, Everett. 2016. "Weak Ties Matter." *TechCrunch* (blog). April 26, 2016.

17. Zakrzewski, Cat. 2015. "Intel Doubles up on Hiring Women and Minorities." *Wall Street Journal*. August 3, 2015.

18. Gaucher, Danielle, Justin Friesen, and Aaron C. Kay. 2011. "Evidence That Gendered Wording in Job Advertisements Exists and Sustains Gender Inequality." *Journal of Personality and Social Psychology* 101 (1): 109–28.

19. Vallarta, Laudine. 2021. "Interview Rubrics: Hiring with Diversity in Mind." SmartRecruiters.

20. Bohnet, Iris. 2016. "How to Take the Bias out of Interviews." *Harvard Business Review*, April 18, 2016.

21. Bateson, John, Jochen Wirtz, Eugene Burke, and Carly Vaughan. 2013. "When Hiring, First Test, and Then Interview." *Harvard Business Review*, November 1, 2013.

22. Johnson, Stefanie K., David R. Hekman, and Elsa T. Chan. 2016. "If There's Only One Woman in Your Candidate Pool, There's Statistically No Chance She'll Be Hired." *Harvard Business Review*, April 26, 2016.

23. U.S. Bureau of Labor Statistics. 2022. "Labor Force Statistics from the Current Population Survey—Employed Persons by Detailed Occupation, Sex, Race, and Hispanic or Latino Ethnicity."

24. Bertrand, Marianne, and Sendhil Mullainathan. 2003. "Are Emily and Greg More Employable than Lakisha and Jamal? A Field Experiment on Labor Market Discrimination." *National Bureau of Economic Research*.

25. Behaghel, Luc, Bruno Crépon, and Thomas Le Barbanchon. 2015. "Unintended Effects of Anonymous Résumés." *American Economic Journal. Applied Economics* 7 (3): 1–27.

26. White, Maia Jasper. 2020. "Eyes Wide Shut—The Case against Blind Auditions." *NewMusicBox* (blog). September 10, 2020.

27. Williams, Joan C., and Marina Multhaup. 2018. "For Women and Minorities to Get Ahead, Managers Must Assign Work Fairly." *Harvard Business Review*, March 5, 2018.

28. Embroker Team. 2022. "Ageism in the Workplace and 7 Ways to Fight It." *Embroker* (blog). February 3, 2022.

29. Kitroeff, N., and J. Silver-Greenberg. 2020. "Pregnancy Discrimination Is Rampant Inside America's Biggest Companies." *The New York Times*, January 2, 2020.

30. Savat, Sara. 2021. "Mothers May Face Increased Workplace Discrimination Post-Pandemic, Research Warns." The Source—Washington University in St. Louis. July 23, 2021.

31. Przystanski, Andy. 2020. "What Is a Job Leveling Matrix?" *Lattice Magazine for HR Professionals*, July 10, 2020.

32. Player, Abigail, Georgina Randsley de Moura, Ana C. Leite, Dominic Abrams, and Fatima Tresh. 2019. "Overlooked Leadership Potential: The Preference for Leadership Potential in Job Candidates Who Are Men vs. Women." *Frontiers in Psychology* 10: 755.

33. Rohman, Jessica, Chinwe Onyeagoro, and Michael C. Bush. 2018. "How You Promote People Can Make or Break Company Culture." *Harvard Business Review*, January 2, 2018.

34. Chow, Rosalind. 2021. "Don't Just Mentor Women and People of Color. Sponsor Them." *Harvard Business Review*, June 30, 2021.

35. Culture@Work. 2022. "Building an Effective Sponsorship Program Resource Guide."

36. Barnard, Dom. 2017. "Essential Guide for Giving and Receiving Feedback." *VirtualSpeech* (blog). November 1, 2017.

37. Qualtrics EmployeeXM Team. 2019. "The Ultimate Guide to Employee Pulse Surveys—What Is an Employee Pulse Survey?" *Qualtrics* (blog). May 20, 2019.

38. Maier, Steffen. 2017. "Multi-Source Feedback Can Work If You Train It." *TLNT—Talent Management & HR* (blog). September 7, 2017.

39. Doldor, Elena, Madeleine Wyatt, and Jo Silvester. 2021. "Research: Men Get More Actionable Feedback Than Women." *Harvard Business Review*, 2021.

40. Baker, Amanda, Dominique Perreault, Alain Reid, and Céline M. Blanchard. 2013. "Feedback and Organizations: Feedback Is Good, Feedback-Friendly Culture Is Better." *Canadian Psychology / Psychologie Canadienne* 54 (4): 260–268.

41. Bregman, Peter. 2014. "How to Ask for Feedback That Will Actually Help You." *Harvard Business Review*, December 5, 2014.

42. Heather Hanselman, ed. 2021. "Psychological Safety and the Critical Role of Leadership Development." *Mckinsey.Com* (blog). February 11, 2021.

43. Garfinkle, Joel. 2017. "How to Have Difficult Conversations When You Don't Like Conflict." *Harvard Business Review*, May 24, 2017.

44. Steiman, Jonathan. 2018. "Do You Need to Fire a Top Performer? Here Are 4 Things to Do First. It Is Possible to Fire a High Performing Employee, but You Have to Do It Right." *Inc.* (blog). April 16, 2018.

45. MWI. 2016. "EAP Mediation." MWI. September 26, 2016.

46. Dobbin, Frank, and Alexandra Kalev. 2020. "Why Sexual Harassment Programs Backfire." *Harvard Business Review*, May 1, 2020.

47. Zheng, Lily. 2020. "Do Your Employees Feel Safe Reporting Abuse and Discrimination?" *Harvard Business Review*, October 8, 2020.

48. "Diversity, Equity, and Inclusion." n.d. Mindsharepartners.

49. "Guidelines for Developing Inclusive Holiday Policies." 2021. Kindred. September 2, 2021.

50. Lowenkron, Hadriana. 2021. "Creating More Accessible, Inclusive Buildings." Bloomberg.com. August 17, 2021.

51. Nagele-Piazza, Lisa. 2020. "Tips for Creating Multipurpose Accommodation Rooms for Employees." SHRM. February 12, 2020.

52. Woodridge, Scott. 2020. "Building a Benefits Plan That Supports DEI: Developing a Comprehensive Strategy." BenefitsPRO. December 1, 2020.

53. Pilipenko, Marina. 2021. "What Is Flex Time? A Beginner's Guide to Flexible Working." *ActiTIME* (blog). January 18, 2021.

54. Burkus, David. 2017. "Everyone Likes Flex Time, but We Punish Women Who Use It." *Harvard Business Review*, 2017.

55. Gaskell, Adi. 2022. "Masculine Norms Stop Men from Asking for Flexible Work." *Forbes*, January 4, 2022.

56. Forbes Business Council. 2021. "15 Tips For Combating Overwork Culture." *Forbes*, July 19, 2021.

57. Merle, Andrew. 2021. "This Is How Many Hours You Should Really Be Working." *Work Life by Atlassian* (blog). October 7, 2021.

58. Heathfield, Susan M. 2021. "How to Negotiate to Work from Home." *The Balance Careers* (blog). April 8, 2021.

59. Schlangen, Kaija. 2020. "Environmentalism vs. Environmental Justice." *University of Minnesota—Office of Sustainability* (blog). October 12, 2020.

60. Helbling, Thomas. 2020. "Externalities: Prices Do Not Capture All Costs." *International Monetary Fund* (blog). February 24, 2020.

61. Brown, Lynn, and Sam Laird. 2021. "A Guide to Intersectional Environmentalism." *Means and Matters—Bank of the West* (blog). April 23, 2021.

62. IFRS Foundation. 2021. "ISSB: Frequently Asked Questions." *IFRS Foundation* (blog). November 4, 2021.

63. Bassompierre, Leanne de, Saijel Kishan, and Antony Sguazzin. 2021. "Palm Oil Giant's Industry-Beating ESG Score Hides Razed Forests." *Bloomberg*, September 15, 2021.

64. Whitehead, Sarah J., and Shehzad Ali. 2010. "Health Outcomes in Economic Evaluation: The QALY and Utilities." *British Medical Bulletin* 96 (1): 5–21.

65. Love, Charmian, and Robert G. Eccles. 2022. "How Leaders Can Move Beyond Greenwashing Toward Real Change." *Harvard Business Review*, 2022.

66. Alpha Environmental. 2017. "The 7 Different Types of Pollution Explained." *Alpha Environmental* (blog). August 24, 2017.

67. Becker, Nir, David Soloveitchik, and Moshe Olshanskyc. 2011. "Incorporating Environmental Externalities into the Capacity Expansion Planning: An Israeli Case Study." *Energy Conversion and Management* 52 (7): 2489–94.

68. Cohen, Ronald, and George Serafeim. 2020. "How to Measure a Company's Real Impact." *Harvard Business Review*, September 3, 2020.

69. Ahmed, Osub. 2020. "Integrating a Reproductive Justice Framework in Climate Research." *Center for American Progress* (blog). March 6, 2020.

70. Bullard, Robert D., Paul Mohai, Robin Saha, and Beverly Wright. 2007. "Toxic Wastes and Race at Twenty 1987–2007." *United Church of Christ* 1 (1): 1–175.

71. Hamilton, James T. 2003. "Environmental Equity and the Siting of Hazardous Waste Facilities in OECD Countries: Evidence and Policies."

72. SASB Alliance. 2012. "Exploring Materiality—The Materiality Finder Is the New Way to Explore and Compare the SASB Standards Quickly." *Sustainability Accounting Standards Board* (blog). March 20, 2012.

73. Ioannou, Ioannis, Shelley Xin Li, and George Serafeim. 2016. "The Effect of Target Difficulty on Target Completion: The Case of Reducing Carbon Emissions." *The Accounting Review* 91 (5): 1467–92.

74. Bové, Anne-Titia, and Steven Swartz. 2016. "Starting at the Source: Sustainability in Supply Chains." *Mckinsey.Com* (blog). McKinsey & Company. November 9, 2016.

75. Walter, Gideon, Claudio Knizek, Elfrun von Koeller, Chrissy O'Brien, Elizabeth Millman Hardin, David Young, Miho Orimo, and Frank Cordes. 2020. "Your Supply Chain Needs a Sustainability Strategy." *BCG—Boston Consulting Group* (blog). July 14, 2020.

76. OECD. 2019. *Business Models for the Circular Economy Opportunities and Challenges for Policy*. Paris: OECD Publishing.

77. GAIN—Gateway for Accelerated Innovation in Nuclear. 2021. "Carbon Free Glossary." Inl.Gov. 2021.

78. Marasco Newton Group, Timothy Fields Jr., and Michael Steinberg. 2003. "Moving Towards Collaborative Problem-Solving: Business and Industry Perspectives and Practices on Environmental Justice."

79. Gittsham, Matthew. 2015. "More Big Businesses Push for Stricter Environmental Regulations." *The Guardian*, February 4, 2015.

80. Schonbrun, Zach. 2017. "Tarnished by Charlottesville, Tiki Torch Company Tries to Move On." *The New York Times*, August 20, 2017.

81. Emerson, Tricia. 2018. "What You're Willing to Tolerate Sets the Tone for Your Company Culture." *Forbes*, June 24, 2018.

82. Zheng, Lily. 2020. "We're Entering the Age of Corporate Social Justice." *Harvard Business Review*, June 15, 2020.

83. Murray, J. Haskell. 2017. "Adopting Stakeholder Advisory Boards: Stakeholder Advisory Boards." *American Business Law Journal* 54 (1): 61–106.

84. Global Corporate Governance Forum. 2009. "Stakeholder Engagement and the Board: Integrating Best Governance Practices."

85. May, Matt. 2018. "The Same, but Different: Breaking down Accessibility, Universality, and Inclusion in Design." *Adobe Blog* (blog). April 2, 2018.

86. Lee, Nicol Turner, Paul Resnick, and Genie Barton. 2019. "Algorithmic Bias Detection and Mitigation: Best Practices and Policies to Reduce Consumer Harms." Brookings Institution. May 22, 2019.

87. 18F Content Guide–U.S. General Services Administration. 2020. "Inclusive Language."

Conclusion

1. Harrison-Bernard, Lisa M., Allison C. Augustus-Wallace, Flavia M. Souza-Smith, Fern Tsien, Gregory P. Casey, and Tina P. Gunaldo. 2020. "Knowledge Gains in a Professional Development Workshop on Diversity, Equity, Inclusion, and Implicit Bias in Academia." *Advances in Physiology Education* 44 (3): 286–94.

2. Wingard, Deborah, Joann Trejo, Monica Gudea, Seneca Goodman, and Vivian Reznik. 2018. "Faculty Equity, Diversity, Culture and Climate Change in Academic Medicine: A Longitudinal Study." *Journal of the National Medical Association*, 1–9.

3. Radcliffe Institute for Advanced Study at Harvard University. 2008. "What Works?—Evidence-Based Ideas to Increase Diversity, Equity, and Inclusion in the Workplace."

4. The Centre for Global Inclusion. 2017. Centreforglobalinclusion.org. July 10, 2017.

5. ISO—The International Organization for Standardization. 2021. "Human Resource Management--Diversity and Inclusion." ISO 30415:2021, 42. ISO.Org. May 2021.

6. Algorithmic Justice League. 2021. "Algorithmic Justice League—Unmasking AI Harms and Biases." *Ajl.Org* (blog). March 1, 2021.

7. Healthy Rowhouse Project. 2020. "Redlining: How Systemic Racial Discrimination Has Impacted Access to Financial and Physical Well-Being." *Healthyrowhouse.Org* (blog). July 20, 2020.

8. McDonald, Jacquie, and Aileen Cater-Steel, eds. 2018. *Communities of Practice: Facilitating Social Learning in Higher Education*. Singapore: Springer.

9. Ward, Marguerite. 2021. "DEI Execs Are Burning out amid the Billion-Dollar Push to Diversify Corporate America: 'It's Hard to Be Both the Advocate and the Abused.'" *Insider*, April 9, 2021.

10. Zheng, Lily. 2020. "How Diversity, Equity, and Inclusion Changemakers Can Find Balance without Burnout." *Bkconnection.Com* (blog). March 18, 2020.

11. Holland, Roberta. 2015. "Build 'scaffolds' to Improve Performance of Temporary Teams." *HBS Working Knowledge* (blog). May 27, 2015.

ACKNOWLEDGMENTS

Thank you, first and foremost, to the people who this book couldn't have been written without. Thank you to Tracy Garrick for all you've done to fill in the blanks, keep me on task, and ensure I take breaks. Thank you to Richard DeVaul for the priceless wisdom and hard-hitting editorial advice and for helping me keep it real. Thank you to my incredible wife, Andrea Gaeta, for never failing to light up my world with your smile after a long day of writing and helping me celebrate the little things. Thank you to the team at Berrett-Koehler, especially Charlotte Ashlock, Lesley Iura, Valerie Caldwell, and Robert Fox, for having my back. Thank you to my parents; your encouragement means so much. Thank you to Shabnam Banerjee-McFarland for convincing me that this book deserved to be put out into the world.

Thank you to Andrea, Rich, Reena, Danger, Melissa, Crystal, Gayle, Amy, and Kristen for your boundless love and support; I love you all. I'm grateful for you.

Thank you to Meghan for making space for all of me.

Thank you to my friends, colleagues, and co-conspirators in the DEI space who have kept me inspired, held me accountable, and dreamt with me of a better future over the years. Thank you, Michelle Mi-jung Kim, Tiffany Jana, Mandy Bynum, Jennifer Brown, Lily Jampol,

Matthew Yazzie, Steven Huang, Aubrey Blanche, Rachel Etnire Parrott, Madison Butler, Dereca Blackmon, and so many others.

Thank you to Kimmy, Nghia, BJ, Sabrina, and Ruby for keeping me caffeinated.

Thank you to the many people who have shared their stories and trusted me to speak truth to power; you remind me who I do this work for. Thank you to the folks who've gotten their hands dirty alongside me and "done the work," even when it was messy or imperfect. Thank you to my LinkedIn community for reminding me of the impact thoughtful words can have and for keeping me on my toes and accountable every day. Thank you to the folks who came before me who made it so people like me could have a voice that matters. Thank you to the folks who will come after me and make things I can't even imagine.

And thank you to you, reader, for making this book a part of your journey, wherever you may be on it. I look forward to seeing what you do. I look forward to seeing what you'll build.

I look forward to striving alongside you and making a better world together.

INDEX

Individual contributors (ICs), 123, 133,
193f, 197
defined, 182
overview and nature of, 182–183
Industry support and learning,
formalizing, 278–282
Inequity, 24–28. *See also* Equity
diversity and, 43–44
LGBTQ+, 97, 101, 102f, 103
Information sharing. *See* Transparency
Informational power, 137, 139, 182
defined, 116, 136
nature of, 117
Informed intentions, from interested
ignorance to, 173
Integration, 238–240
Integrators, 278, 280–281
Intentional vs. unintentional acts, 160
Intentions, 29, 37, 60
aren't enough, 23, 27, 28, 32, 33. *See
also* Good intentions
informed, 173
organizational/corporate, 16, 103
Interdependence
defined, 136f, 144
empowering, 282–283
vs. independence, 126
Intersectionality, 54–55
Intersectionality and intersectional
identities, 54–55, 164–165

Kalev, Alexandra, 14–15
Kendi, Ibram X.
How to Be an Antiracist, 153–154, 157
Kennedy, John F., 63
King, Martin Luther, Jr., 66
Knowing what not to do. *See* Negative
expertise

Leonard, George, 65–66
LGBTQ+ inequity, 97, 101, 102f, 103
LGBTQ+ people, 85, 99, 103

poverty among, 97, 102f, 103
LGBTQ+ terminology, 18, 149, 335n4
Living wages, 96
Low trust, 223–224, 232. *See also under*
Medium trust
act decisively in windows of opportunities, 229–231
apologize and cede power, 225–228
let change find you, 224–225
movements lead the way, 228–229
Lucky Stores, 74

Majoritized populations. *See* Privileged/
overserved populations
Managers, 183–184. *See also specific
topics*
changes in representation among,
14, 15t
defined, 183
Managing diversity paradigm, 74, 82
Marginalized/disadvantaged/under-
served populations, 55
Marketing, 201, 202, 213, 248
Markus, Hazel, 126
Matrix organizations, 119
Maximizing your impact, 171–172
Medium trust, 215–216, 228, 232
empower non-leader change-makers,
219–221
get skin in the game, 216–217
vs. high trust, 216, 218, 219, 221, 228,
232
move the goalposts, 222–223
moving from low trust to, 224–225,
228–230, 232
prime or create additional accountability groups, 217–219
small to big wins, 221–222
Mentorship, accelerating change
through, 254
#MeToo movement, 25–26
Microaggression, 29, 55

ABOUT THE AUTHOR

Lily Zheng (they/them) is a Diversity, Equity & Inclusion strategist and consultant who works with organizational leaders to turn their positive intentions into positive impact. A dedicated change-maker and advocate named a Forbes D&I Trailblazer, 2021 DEI Influencer, and Top Voice on Racial Equity, Lily's writing and opinions have been featured in the *Harvard Business Review, New York Times,* and on NPR. They are the author of *Gender Ambiguity in the Workplace* (2017) and *The Ethical Sellout* (2019). Lily holds an MA in Sociology and BA in Psychology from Stanford University. They live with their wife in the San Francisco Bay Area and can frequently be found putting together yet another all-black outfit and enjoying good Chinese food.

Also by Lily Zheng
The companion workbook to *DEI Deconstructed*

RECONSTRUCTING DEI
A Practitioner's Workbook

The next step in your DEI journey starts here. Building on the knowledge base of *DEI Deconstructed*, Lily Zheng offers a workbook with 40 original exercises, worksheets, and other tools to help guide you and your organization toward more substantive and lasting DEI outcomes. Whether you're a new or veteran DEI practitioner looking to improve your practice, a leader looking to grow your leadership skills, or an advocate looking to play more powerful roles in movements, this book will give you the practical tools to do just that.

Paperback, ISBN 978-1-5230-0606-9
PDF ebook, ISBN 978-1-5230-0607-6
ePub ebook, ISBN 978-1-5230-0608-3

Berrett–Koehler Publishers, Inc.
www.bkconnection.com

Berrett–Koehler
Publishers

Berrett-Koehler is an independent publisher dedicated to an ambitious mission: *Connecting people and ideas to create a world that works for all.*

Our publications span many formats, including print, digital, audio, and video. We also offer online resources, training, and gatherings. And we will continue expanding our products and services to advance our mission.

We believe that the solutions to the world's problems will come from all of us, working at all levels: in our society, in our organizations, and in our own lives. Our publications and resources offer pathways to creating a more just, equitable, and sustainable society. They help people make their organizations more humane, democratic, diverse, and effective (and we don't think there's any contradiction there). And they guide people in creating positive change in their own lives and aligning their personal practices with their aspirations for a better world.

And we strive to practice what we preach through what we call "The BK Way." At the core of this approach is *stewardship,* a deep sense of responsibility to administer the company for the benefit of all of our stakeholder groups, including authors, customers, employees, investors, service providers, sales partners, and the communities and environment around us. Everything we do is built around stewardship and our other core values of *quality, partnership, inclusion,* and *sustainability.*

This is why Berrett-Koehler is the first book publishing company to be both a B Corporation (a rigorous certification) and a benefit corporation (a for-profit legal status), which together require us to adhere to the highest standards for corporate, social, and environmental performance. And it is why we have instituted many pioneering practices (which you can learn about at www.bkconnection.com), including the Berrett-Koehler Constitution, the Bill of Rights and Responsibilities for BK Authors, and our unique Author Days.

We are grateful to our readers, authors, and other friends who are supporting our mission. We ask you to share with us examples of how BK publications and resources are making a difference in your lives, organizations, and communities at www.bkconnection.com/impact.

Dear reader,

Thank you for picking up this book and welcome to the worldwide BK community! You're joining a special group of people who have come together to create positive change in their lives, organizations, and communities.

What's BK all about?

Our mission is to connect people and ideas to create a world that works for all.

Why? Our communities, organizations, and lives get bogged down by old paradigms of self-interest, exclusion, hierarchy, and privilege. But we believe that can change. That's why we seek the leading experts on these challenges—and share their actionable ideas with you.

A welcome gift

To help you get started, we'd like to offer you a **free copy** of one of our bestselling ebooks:

www.bkconnection.com/welcome

When you claim your **free ebook**, you'll also be subscribed to our blog.

Our freshest insights

Access the best new tools and ideas for leaders at all levels on our blog at ideas.bkconnection.com.

Sincerely,

Your friends at Berrett-Koehler